THE NORWEGIAN ECONOMY 1920-1980

The Norwegian Economy 1920-1980

Fritz Hodne

CROOM HELM
London & Canberra

ST. MARTIN'S PRESS
New York

© 1983 F. Hodne
Croom Helm Ltd, Provident House, Burrell Row,
Beckenham, Kent BR3 1AT
Croom Helm Australia, PO Box 391,
Manuka, ACT 2603, Australia

British Library Cataloguing in Publication Data

Hodne, Fritz
    The Norwegian economy 1920-1980.
    1. Norway — Economic conditions — History
    I. Title
    330.9481'004   HC365
    ISBN 0-7099-0021-X

© 1983 F. Hodne

Library of Congress Cataloging in Publication Data

Hodne, Fritz.
    The Norwegian economy, 1920—1980.

    Bibliography: p.
    Includes indexes.
    1. Norway—Economic conditions—1918-
I. Title.
HC365.H553   1983   330.9481'04   83-13690

ISBN 0-312-57938-1

CONTENTS

LIST OF TABLES

LIST OF FIGURES

PREFACE

When at the 8th International Economic History Congress in Edinburgh professor Lennart Jørberg, of Lund in Sweden, raised the question of my writing a volume on Norway for the present Croom Helm series on the contemporary economic history of Europe, I thought at first that it would be an easy enough task. In 1975 I had published a volume on the economic history of Norway, and an enlarged version in Norwegian was published in 1981. In both the main emphasis was on the developments of the nineteenth century. To the editor of the series, Professor Derek H. Aldcroft, I wrote optimistically that I expected to have the volume ready by the end of 1981. As it turned out, the delivery date could not be honoured.

There were two reasons for this. One was that very little had been done on the economic aspects of the war years, and what had been done was specific, some of it biased, with some outstanding exceptions, including the volume by a British historian Alan Milward, titled *The Fascist Economy in Norway 1940-1945*. The result was that I found I had to read much more than anticipated. The other reason was not so much lack of sources, as the task of making a balanced selection among them. The recent economic past invites any number of topics relevant to the historian. The difficulty was establishing some guide posts that would justify a reasonable selection of themes.

My guide posts have been found in the modern theory of economic growth, which, I take it, involves three elements; namely, a theory of causation, a theory of values, and a theory of means. Thus the reader interested in the details of retail trade will no doubt find himself disappointed, as I believe its causal role to have been slight in the formation of the postwar economy. By the same token, readers looking for economic planning will find a good deal here, and for the opposite reason. Next, as value judgements necessarily are open to objections, I have tried to keep mostly to reporting the facts. When venturing comments, as I have done in the concluding chapter, Chapter 14, the reader will have no difficulty in recognising the change of role. Again, when a country has had a social democratic government for 29 out of 36 years, and those governments have maintained a strong element of economic planning as an instrument for building a welfare state for its voters, it is inevitable that the present volume should reflect more of planning experiments than of traditional market allocation theory. The examples will suggest how I have gone about solving the problem of selection in constructing the story.

Special thanks are due to Dr. oecon. Ole Gjølberg who read chapters One to Seven. My debts are great to Mrs Lajla Johannessen and her colleagues, Mrs Laila Kyrkjebø, Mrs Anne Marie Carlson, Mrs Kristin Pedersen and Mrs Karin Berge, who managed to give the manuscript a readable form. To the editor I am grateful for discovering many inconsistencies and errors. Those remaining are the sole responsibility of the author.

Fritz Hodne
The Norwegian School of Economics
and Business Administration
Bergen

EDITOR'S INTRODUCTION

By comparison with the nineteenth century, the twentieth has been very much more turbulent, both economically and politically. Two world wars and a great depression are sufficient to substantiate this claim without invoking the problems of more recent times. Yet despite these setbacks Europe's economic performance in the present century has been very much better than anything recorded in the historical past, thanks largely to the super-boom conditions following the post-Second World War reconstruction period. Thus in the period 1946-75, or 1950-73, the annual increase in total European GNP *per capita* was 4.8 and 4.5 per cent respectively, as against a compound rate of just under one per cent in the nineteenth century (1800-1913) and the same during the troubled years between 1913-50. As Bairoch points out, within a generation or so European *per capita* income rose slightly more than in the previous 150 years (1947-75 by 250 per cent, 1800-1948 by 225 per cent) and, on rough estimates for the half century before 1800, by about as much as in the preceding two centuries.[1]

The dynamic growth and relative stability of the 1950s and 1960s may however belie the natural order of things as the events of the later 1970s and early 1980s demonstrate. Certainly it would seem unlikely that the European economy, or the world economy for that matter, will see a lasting return to the relatively stable conditions of the nineteenth century. No doubt the experience of the present century can easily lead to an exaggerated idea about the stability of the previous one. Nevertheless, one may justifiably claim that for much of the nineteenth century there was a degree of harmony in the economic development of the major powers and between the metropolitan economies and the periphery which has been noticeably absent since 1914. Indeed, one of the reasons for the apparent success of the gold standard post 1870, despite the aura of stability it allegedly shed, was the absence of serious external disturbances and imbalance in development among the major participating powers. As Triffin writes, 'the residual harmonization of national monetary and credit policies depended far less on *ex post* corrective action, requiring an extreme flexibility, downward as well as upward, of national price and wage levels, than on an *ex ante* avoidance of substantial disparities in cost competitiveness and the monetary policies that would allow them to develop'.[2]

Whatever the reasons for the absence of serious economic and political conflict, the fact remains that through to 1914 international development and political relations, though subject to strains of a minor nature from time to time, were never exposed to internal and external shocks of the magnitude experienced in the twentieth century. Not surprisingly therefore, the First World War rudely shattered the liberal tranquillity of the later nineteenth and early twentieth centuries. At the time few people realised that it was going to be a lengthy war and, even more important, fewer still had any conception of the enormous impact it would have on economic and social relationships. Moreover, there was a general feeling, readily accepted in establishment circles, that following the period of hostilities it would be possible to resume where one had left off — in short, to recreate the conditions of the prewar era.

For obvious reasons this was clearly an impossible task, though for nearly a decade statesmen strove to get back to what they regarded as 'normalcy', or the natural order of things. In itself this was one of the profound mistakes of the first postwar decade since it should have been clear, even at that time, that the war and postwar clearing-up operations had undermined Europe's former equipoise and sapped her strength to a point where the economic system had become very sensitive to external shocks. The map of Europe had been rewritten under the political settlements following the war and this further weakened the economic viability of the continent and left a dangerous political vacuum in its wake. Moreover, it was not only in the economic sphere that Europe's strength had been reduced; in political and social terms the European continent was seriously weakened and many countries in the early postwar years were in a state of social ferment and upheaval.[3]

Generally speaking, Europe's economic and political fragility was ignored in the 1920s, probably more out of ignorance than intent. In their efforts to resurrect the prewar system statesmen believed they were providing a viable solution to the problems of the day, and the fact that Europe shared in the prosperity of the later 1920s seemed to vindicate their judgement. But the postwar problems — war debts, external imbalances, currency issues, structural distortions and the like — defied solutions along traditional lines. The most notable of these was the attempt to restore a semblance of the gold standard in the belief that it had been responsible for the former stability. The upshot was a set of haphazard and inconsistent currency stabilisation policies which took no account of the changes in relative costs and prices among countries since 1914. Consequently, despite the apparent prosperity of the latter half of the decade, Europe remained in a state of unstable equilibrium, and therefore vulnerable to any external shocks. The collapse of US foreign lending from the middle of 1928 and the subsequent downturn of the American economy a year later exposed the weaknesses of the European economy. The structural supports were too weak to withstand violent shocks and so the edifice disintegrated.

That the years 1929-32/3 experienced one of the worst depressions and financial crises in history is not altogether surprising given the convergence of many unfavourable forces at that point in time. Moreover, the fact that a cyclical downturn occurred against the backdrop of structural disequilibrium only served to exacerbate the problem, while the inherent weakness of certain financial institutions in Europe and the United States led to extreme instability. The intensity of the crisis varied a great deal but few countries, apart from the USSR, were unaffected. The action of governments tended to aggravate rather than ease the situation. Such policies included expenditure cuts, monetary contraction, the abandonment of the gold standard and protective measures designed to insulate domestic economies from external events. In effect these policies, while sometimes affording temporary relief to hard-pressed countries, in the end led to income destruction rather than income creation. When recovery finally set in in the winter of 1932/3 it owed little to policy contributions, though subsequently some western governments did attempt more ambitious programmes of stimulation, while many of the poorer eastern European countries adopted autarchic policies in an effort to push forward industrialisation. Apart from some notable exceptions, Germany and Sweden in particular, recovery from the slump, especially in terms of employment generation, was slow and patchy and even at the peak of the upswing in 1937 many countries were still operating below their resource capacity. A combination of weak real growth forces and structural imbalances in development would no doubt have ensured a continuation of resource under-utilisation had not rearmament and the outbreak of war served to close the gap.

Thus, by the eve of the Second World War Europe as a whole was in a much weaker state economically than it had been in 1914, with her shares of world income and trade notably reduced. Worse still, she emerged from the second war in 1945 in a more prostrate condition than in 1918, with output levels well down on those of prewar. In terms of the loss of life, physical destruction and decline in living standards Europe's position was also much worse than after the First World War. On the other hand, recovery from wartime destruction was stronger and more secure than in the previous case. In part this can be attributed to the fact that in the reconstruction phase of the later 1940s some of the mistakes and blunders of the earlier experience were avoided. Inflation, for example, was contained more readily between 1939 and 1945 and the violent inflations of the early 1920s were not for the most part perpetuated after the Second World War. With the exception of Berlin, the map of Eurpe was divided much more cleanly and neatly than after 1918. Though it resulted in two ideological power blocks, the East and the West, it did nevertheless dispose of the power vacuum in Central/ East Europe which had been a source of friction and contention in the interwar years. Moreover, the fact that each block was dominated or backed by a wealthy and rival super-power meant that support was forthcoming for the satellite countries. The vanquished powers were not, with the exception of East Germany, burdened by unreasonable exactions which had been the cause of so much bitterness and squabbling during the 1920s. Finally, governments no longer hankered after the 'halcyon' prewar days, not surprisingly given the rugged conditions of the 1930s. This time it was to be planning for the future which occupied their attention, and which found expression in the commitment to maintain full employment and all that entailed in terms of growth and stability, together with a conscious desire to build upon the earlier social welfare foundations. In wider perspective, the new initiatives found positive expression in terms of a readiness to co-operate internationally, particularly in trade and monetary matters. The liberal American aid programme for the West in the later 1940s was a concrete manifestation of this new approach.

Thus despite the enormity of the reconstruction task facing Europe at the end of the war, the recovery effort, after some initial difficulties, was both strong and sustained, and by the early 1950s Europe had reached a point where she could look to the future with some confidence. During the next two decades or so virtually every European country, in keeping with the buoyant conditions in the world economy as a whole, expanded very much more rapidly than in the past. This was the super-growth phase during which Europe regained a large part of the relative losses incurred between 1914 and 1945. The eastern block countries forged ahead the most rapidly under their planned regimes, while the western democracies achieved their success under mixed enterprise systems with varying degrees of market freedom. In both cases the state played a far more important role than hitherto, and neither system could be said to be without its problems. The planning mechanism in eastern Europe never functioned as smoothly as originally anticipated by its proponents, and in due course most of the socialist countries were forced to make modifications to their systems of control. Similarly, the semi-market systems of the West did not always produce the right results so that governments were obliged to intervene to an increasing extent. One of the major problems encountered by the demand-managed economies of the West was that of trying to achieve a series of basically incompatible objectives simultaneously — namely full employment, price stability, growth, stability and external equilibrium. Given the limited policy weapons available to governments this proved an impossible task to accomplish in most cases, though West Germany managed to achieve the seemingly impossible for much of the period.

Although these incompatible objectives proved elusive *in toto*, there was, throughout most of the period to the early 1970s, little cause for serious alarm. It is true that there were minor lapses from full employment; fluctuations still occurred but they were moderate and took the form of growth cycles; some countries experienced periodic balance of payments problems; while prices generally rose continuously though at fairly modest annual rates. But such lapses could readily be accommodated, even with the limited policy choices, within an economic system that was growing rapidly. And there was some consolation from the fact that the planned socialist economies were not immune to some of these problems, especially later in the period. By the later 1960s, despite some warning signs that conditions might be deteriorating, it seemed that Europe had entered a phase of perpetual prosperity not dissimilar to the one the Americans had conceived in the 1920s. Unfortunately, as in the earlier case, this illusion was to be rudely shattered in the first half of the 1970s. The super-growth phase of the postwar period culminated in the somewhat feverish and speculative boom of 1972-3. By the following year the growth trend had been reversed, the old business cycle had reappeared and most countries were experiencing inflation at higher rates than at any time in the past half century. From that time onwards, according to Samuel Brittan, 'everything seems to have gone sour and we have had slower growth, rising unemployment, faster inflation, creeping trade restrictions and all the symptoms of stagflation'.[4] In fact, compared with the relatively placid and successful decades of the 1950s and 1960s, the later 1970s and early 1980s have been extremely turbulent, reminiscent in some respects of the interwar years.

It should of course be stressed that by comparison with the interwar years or even with the nineteenth century, economic growth has been quite respectable since the sharp boom and contraction in the first half of the 1970s. It only appears poor in relation to the rapid growth between 1950 and 1973 and the question arises as to whether this period should be regarded as somewhat abnormal, with the shift to a lower growth profile in the 1970s being the inevitable consequence of long-term forces involving some reversal of the special growth-promoting factors of the previous decades. In effect this would imply some weakening of real growth forces in the 1970s which was aggravated by specific factors, for example energy crises and policy variables.

The most disturbing feature of this later period was not simply that growth slowed down but that it became more erratic, with longer recessionary periods involving absolute contractions in output, and that it was accompanied by mounting unemployment and high inflation. Traditional Keynesian demand management policies were unable to cope with these problems and, in an effort to deal with them, particularly inflation, governments resorted to ultradefensive policies and monetary control. These were not very successful either, since the need for social and political compromise in policy-making meant that they were not applied rigorously enough to eradicate inflation, yet at the same time their influence was sufficiently strong to dampen the rate of growth, thereby exacerbating unemployment. In other words, economic management is faced with an awkward policy dilemma in the prevailing situation of high unemployment and rapid inflation. Policy action to deal with either one tends to make the other worse, while the constraint of the political consensus produces an uneasy compromise in an effort to 'minimise macroeconomic misery'.[5] Rostow has neatly summarised the constraints involved in this context: 'Taxes, public expenditure, interest rates, and the supply of money are not determined antiseptically by men free to move economies along a Phillips curve to an optimum trade-off between the rate of unemployment and the rate of inflation. Fiscal and monetary policy are, inevitably, living parts of the democratic political process.'[6]

Whether the current problems of contemporary western capitalism or the difficulties associated with the planning mechanisms of the socialist countries of eastern Europe are amenable to solutions remains to be seen. It is not, for the most part, the purpose of the volumes in this series to speculate about the future. The series is designed to provide clear and balanced surveys of the economic development and problems of individual European countries from the end of the first world war through to the present, against the background of the general economic and political trends of the time. Though most European countries have shared a common experience for much of the period, it is nonetheless true that there has been considerable variation among countries in their rates of development and the manner in which they have sought to regulate and control their economies. The problems encountered have also varied widely, in part reflecting disparities in levels of development. While most European countries had, by the end of the First World War, achieved some industrialisation and made the initial breakthrough into modern economic growth, nevertheless there existed a wide gulf between the richer and poorer nations. At the beginning of the period the most advanced region was north-west Europe, including Scandinavia, and as one moved east and south so the level of *per capita* income relative to the European average declined. In some cases, notably Bulgaria, Yugoslavia and Portugal, income levels were barely half the European average. The gap has narrowed over time but the general pattern remains basically the same. Between 1913 and 1973 most of the poorer countries in the east and south (apart from Spain) raised their real *per capita* income levels relative to the European average, with most of the improvement taking place after 1950. Even so, by 1973 most of them, with the exception of Czechoslovakia, still fell below the European average, ranging from 9-15 per cent in the case of the USSR, Hungary, Greece, Bulgaria and Poland, to as much as 35-45 per cent for Spain, Portugal, Romania and Yugoslavia. Italy and Ireland also recorded *per capita* income levels some way below the European average.[7]

The third volume in the Contemporary Economic History of Europe Series shifts the focus of attention to Scandinavia. Norway, a cold, dark country with a small population and a relatively large land mass, was one of the poorer countries in Europe at the beginning of the twentieth century. Though not without natural resources, the country has a for-bidding geographical structure, and for centuries the population had depended upon agriculture, trade and maritime activities for its liveli-hood. Industrially Norway was still backward at the turn of the century and in terms of the level of manufacturing *per capita* she was destined to remain so through to the present.[8] Such observations however belie the latent potential of this small northern country. Economic progress had been steady if unspectacular in the latter half of the nineteenth century, and though this inevitably created an economic structure skewed towards her natural advantages, based on primary and maritime activities, it nevertheless demonstrated that vitality and enterprise were not lacking. Thus while Norway by the eve of the First World War may not have been among the leading industrial nations, her *per capita* income was considerably above that of the poorer countries of eastern and southern Europe,[9] and she had already reached the stage of devel-opment where, given favourable conditions and indigenous enterprise, the prospects for sustained compound growth were quite promising.

It is important therefore not to underplay Norway's potential at this time since it provided a firm launching pad for her response to the vicissitudes of the twentieth century, a response which, half a century or so later (early 1970s), produced one of the highest *per capita* incomes in Europe.[10] It is scarcely conceivable that such an achievement could have been realised had her economic base not been reasonably sound. Much of Norway's relative gain was in fact secured in the traumatic period between 1913 and 1950, embracing as it did two world wars, a great depression and the attendant problems of reconstruction. Norway did not of course emerge unscathed from these events, but judging by the macre-economic indicators she undoubtedly fared much better than the majority of European countries.

In this volume Professor Hodne demonstrates the way in which Norway adapted to the changes of the first half of the twentieth century, not only by continuing to specialise in areas in which she retained a comparative advantage, but also by embarking on new developments which involved a transformation of her economic structure. This transformation was not achieved without friction and costs but it nevertheless ensured that Norway was prepared to participate and share fully in the supergrowth phase after the Second World War through to the oil and gas bonanza of the 1970s and beyond. However, whether Norway's comparatively better economic performance – in terms of employment, inflation, exports and output growth – in the turbulent conditions of the last decade rests on secure foundations[11] is a point on which Professor Hodne would wish to reserve judgement.

Notes

1 P. Bairoch, 'Europe's Gross National Product: 1800-1975', *The Journal of Economic History*, 5 (Fall 1976), pp. 298-9.

2 R. Triffin, *Our International Monetary System: Yesterday, Today and Tomorrow* (1968, New York), p. 14; see also D. H. Aldcroft, *From Versailles to Wall Street, 1919-1929* (1977), pp. 162-4. Some of the cost of the gold standard system may however have been borne by the countries of the periphery, for example the Latin American.

3 See P.N. Stearns, *European Society in Upheaval* (1967).

4 *Financial Times*, 14 February 1980.

5 J.O.N. Perkins, *The Macroeconomic Mix to Stop Stagflation* (1980).

6 W.W. Rostow, *Getting From Here to There* (1979).

7 See Bairoch, 'Europe's Gross National Product', pp.297, 307.

8 P. Bairoch, 'International Industrialization Levels from 1750 to 1980', *Journal of European Economic History*, 11 (1982), p. 286.

9 See Bairoch, 'Europe's Gross National Product', p. 307.

10 *Ibid.*, p. 307; though compare Maddison's comparative GDP levels per head which suggest a less favourable showing. A. Maddison, *Phases of Capitalist Development* (1982), p. 8.

11 See D.H. Aldcroft, *The European Economy 1914-1980* (1980), pp. 234-7; Maddison, *Phases of Capitalist Development* pp. 44-5, 60, 208.

1 INTRODUCTION

The Economic Background

Around the turn of the century Norway was one of the poorer countries in Europe. With 1870 as base year (1870=100), its *per capita* income in 1910 was a mere 161 as against 214 for Denmark and 231 for Sweden.[1] These figures yield a modest rate of growth of 1.2 per cent per year for Norway between 1870 and 1910. This was far behind the performance of Sweden, whose growth rate in the period was 2.1 per cent, and even behind Denmark's 1.9 per cent. In the forty-year period Norway had thus fallen 30 per cent behind Sweden and 25 per cent behind Denmark in terms of economic development and *per capita* income growth. With a population mainly of fishermen, sailors and farmers, Norway was the Sicily of the north, picturesque, with beautiful fiord lanscapes, but industrially a rather backward nation. Seventy years later *The Economist* ranked Norway among the three richest industrial countries of the world, ahead of both Sweden and Denmark. How this came about is the theme of this book. The focus is mainly, though not exclusively, on economic growth and structural change from 1920 to the present. In the intervening period the national accounts data indicate that Norwegian *per capita* income rose from 12 000 to 69 000 Norwegian kroner (1980-kroner), corresponding to an average yearly rate of 3.0 per cent over a period of sixty years. In a European context this is a respectable record, indeed.

We turn first to some basic facts of geography and population. With four million inhabitants in 1980 Norway has the smallest population of any mainland West European country, except for Luxembourg and Andorra. Its population was one million in 1830, two million in 1890 and three million in 1943, which yields a long term growth rate of about one per cent per year. This demographic record would seem to be less starkly Malthusian than that of some developing countries in our own time. In certain low-income countries today population growth rates may exceed two and three per cent annually. Yet for limited periods in the early nineteenth century Norway experienced combinations of baby booms and reduced mortality rates that in all likelihood would have caused social strain except for the fortuitous opening-up of the North American continent. Land-hungry Norwegians contri-

1

buted quite actively to the colonisation of the American prairies: indeed, in the hundred years after 1830 about 800,000 Norwegians emigrated to the USA. This was a massive haemorrhage, considering the small population of the country. Only Ireland sent a larger percentage share. The extent of the emigration together with the *per capita* income evidence cited above, indicates that the economic prospects at home looked bleak for successive generations of young Norwegians.

Not that they lacked space. Though the population is small, its territory is considerable. In terms of land area Norway together with Finland ranks fourth among the West European countries, trailing France, Spain and Sweden. Svalbard excepted, Norway's mainland territory is 324,000 km.[2] This places it in front of Britain, Italy and even West Germany. But its geography is forbidding: its aerial length of 2,000 km corresponds to the distance Oslo-Rome, but the coastline is indented by so many fiords and inlets that its total coastline, including islands, is about 55,000 km long. About one fourth is located north of the 67th parallel, the Arctic Circle. A mere 3 per cent is arable land, 60 per cent is mountainous and barren, and a good deal of the central plateau is a mountain massif 3,000 feet above sea level. A further 21 per cent is forested, and another 7 per cent consists of islands, of which about 2,000 out of a total of 50,000 are inhabited. Relating land area to population, we find 13 inhabitants per sq. km. Apart from Iceland, Norway is the most thinly populated country in Europe. By comparison Britain has 229 inhabitants per sq. km, France 98, West Germany 247, and the Netherlands 344.

The above suggests that the sea and seaborne communication were destined to be vital in the life of the people inhabiting those shores. indeed, boats, boat building, navigation and seafaring skills have been preconditions for survival until our own time. Equally, shipping ranks as an important factor in the modern era of economic development from the 1850s onwards.

Though located in a cold, dark climate, the country is not poor in natural resources. It has large spruce forests, the off-shore waters teem with fish, the mountains contain iron, silver, pyrites, and smaller amounts of a number of other metals, all of which provide exports to supplement the country's meagre agricultural harvests. For centuries the Norwegians have sold their fish and timber in return for foodstuffs from abroad, including grain, salt, hemp, cloth, wine and brandy. By 1800 exports amounted to one fourth, possibly one third of total national output according to recent estimates; it dropped to about 20 per cent in the 1830s, but the share climbed to 26 per cent by the mid 1860s.[2] Even in pre-industrial times Norway maintained a relatively large foreign trade. For that reason trade can only have been a permissive, not a decisive factor in the rise of the modern industrial civilisation. Trade reminds us, however, of the fortunate location of Norway, its proximity to Great Britain and the Continent, which constituted the richest nations and the best markets for fish, timber and ores.

In the context of economic history the modern era, essentially, originated in Norway as everywhere else with the introduction of new machinery and new forms of energy; in other words, with new forms of vastly more efficient production technology. In respect of key indicators such as investment, output *per capita*, consumption and structural change, the modern epoch, as just defined, may be traced back to the 1840s. From then on till the present total output has tended to grow almost every year. No major reversals in either production or population have occurred since then. This alone distinguishes the modern from the pre-industrial era. Sporadically, surpluses were known also in the pre-industrial era, but they were usually consumed directly. Similarly, reinvestment in new equipment was episodic rather than systematic. As a result no sustained and cumulative growth in total or *per capita* product could be expected. Ownership of land was also pre-modern till the mid-1850s, when enclosure legislation paved the way for full, individual ownership in agriculture, releasing at the same time the incentives to save and invest. In other words, it would seem likely that *per capita* consumption even as late as 1830 was no higher on the average than say 1530, three hundred years earlier. In the following decade the evidence is unmistakeable: regarding investment, output and *per capita* consumption the trends depart from the old cyclical pattern; henceforth they show an uninterrupted, long-term, upward tendency.

In an attempt to trace the provenance of and the pathway to the modern industrial economy, we shall assume that the economic development since the 1840s may best be described in terms of a sequence of growth sectors.[4] The cultural values that secured acceptance of economic and societal change had gained ascendancy in the previous centuries. Progress from the 1840s had become the keyword both of public debate and government policies, implying above all a positive evaluation of change. That is, over time the most dynamic sectors have tended to change: from fisheries in the 1830s to shipping in the period 1850-75, from forest-product industries 1880-1910 to the canned goods industry 1900-20, followed by electro-metal and electro-chemical industries, based on hydro electricity, around the turn of the century. In the present century industry, and in some periods shipping, have been the most dynamic sectors, notably the engineering industries. Quite recently North Sea oil has added to the list of growth industries in the country's economic development.

Not only industrialisation, but also the rise of the modern towns and urban mode of living may be traced back to the 1840s. In the seventy five years 1845-1920 a total of 21 new towns were incorporated and 40 town borders were extended. Coming in addition to the existing 40 towns and urban agglomerations, the new towns increased the urban share of the population from 15 to 46 per cent by 1920, while the rural population dropped from 85 to 54 per cent. Four out of every ten Norwegians lived in an urban setting already by 1910.

Towns go back to the middle ages, as centres for trade, crafts and administration. Around 1840 the majority of them still based their existence on traditional functions, among them the timber towns along the banks of inner Oslofjord, the shipping towns along the south coast, and the fishing towns from Stavanger northward. One could even talk of garrison towns (Kongsvinger), mining towns (Kongsberg, Røros), and even administrative towns (Hamar). Industrialisation gave a massive boost to existing towns, while creating new towns and urban clusters. Thus, the rise of the modern saw mills, based on steam engines and circular saws from 1806, paved the way for the rapid expansion of towns like Fredrikstad, Sarpsborg, Moss and inland Hønefoss. The canning industry stimulated the continued growth of Stavanger, Haugesund and Ålesund from 1900 onwards. The electro-chemical industry from about the same time likewise led to the rapid growth of townships like Skien, Notodden, Rjukan, Odda, Sauda and Høyanger. Oslo, the capital, was also the manufacturing centre. One out of every four manufacturing workers lived there, both in 1870 and in 1920. Combining traditional and new activities, Bergen and Trondheim maintained their position as second and third largest towns. Oslo had 100,000 inhabitants in 1875, 228,000 by 1900, and 375,000 ten years later. Between 1875 and 1930 Bergen increased its population from 42,000 to 113,000, Trondheim from 24,000 to 66,000 and Stavanger from 24,000 to 51,000 inhabitants. It should be added that in a European setting the Norwegian towns remained small scale.

The waves of industrialisation upset the traditional occupational pattern. In 1850 there were 12,000 manufacturing workers against 80,000 fifty years later. Secondary occupations represented 14 per cent of the working population in 1865 and 26 per cent by 1910. Tertiary occupations increased in the same period from 21 to 32 per cent. By contrast the primary occupations declined from 59 to 39 per cent in those years. Not only the occupational structure, but also the old class structure was altered. The political and social elite in the pre-industrial period included civil servants, many of Danish lineage, forest families, town merchants in the import-export trade, and in the north, fishing houses, controlling fishing grounds and the local fishing trade. Against a European background, the social structure, while presenting clear, horizontal layers, was neither aristocratic nor estate bound in any formal sense. Indeed, the present Constitution of 1814 expressly forbade future granting of any nobility patents. Industrialisation paved the way for the urban industrial capitalist class and the industrial proletariat. Henceforth the bottom strata included workers in towns and the agricultural labourers in the villages. The middle strata included, besides the farmers, the rapidly growing group of government servants, the professional classes, lawyers, physicians, and their recent additions like architects, engineers and economists. To the middle classes belonged also all those engaged in trade and transport services.

Essentially also middle class was the old social elite, the civil servants, whose economic position was gradually undermined by virtue of the fact that their salaries were voted in Parliament, the Storting, which was dominated by rural farmers and their spokesmen. When this is said, one could select criteria in such a way as to make a case for a social elite also in the modern industrial society that gradually replaced the old social pyramid. The new elite included new and traditional wealth and talent, as demonstrated by the rising shipowners and the industrial entrepreneurs, whose education, name or family connections enabled them to go into the promising new avenues. But in so far as they succeeded in maintaining their positions, they did so by virtue of competence rather than unearned influence. Henceforth society was an open, porous fabric in which social position was determined by skill, competence and education. In no way was this confined to Norway, of course; the social transformation attending industrialisation has its counterpart in the other industrial societies. Perhaps Norway stands out from the others in the sense of the more even distribution of incomes and property.

The demographic, social and locational shifts indicated above were accompanied by a good deal of social strain, as seen in the surprising rise of political and interest organisations, among them the political parties, trade unions, professional societies, consumer organisations and the host of religious, cultural and teetotallers' societies in the period to 1920. These voluntary organisations counted 86 societies in 1890, against 145 in 1900 and 412 in 1920. Again, the rise of this organisational infrastructure may be observed in neighbouring countries. But while creating hardships, the industrial society offered rewards. Between 1851 and 1907 the real wages for men in the textile industry improved by a yearly 2.0 per cent, a pace that may be taken as representative for industry in the period. The mortality rate came down from 35 to 20 per thousand between 1854 and 1910. The corresponding increase in life expectation was also impressive, up from 48 to 61 years for men between 1870 and 1920. Already by 1860 typhoid fever, smallpox and cholera were things of the past.

The economic progress inaugurated in the 1840s was borne on a sustained wave of free trade in the international economy. Free trade offered the country an historic opportunity for economic growth through specialisation. This view fits the rythm of economic development, its discontinuous, if not its cyclical character. Between 1820 and 1850 fish products were the biggest export articles, followed by timber and shipping incomes. Next came the astonishing expansion (1850-75) of shipping, when the country, utilising the combined assets of low wages and home-built sailing vessels, elbowed itself up from seventh to third place among the leading shipping nations of the world. A third growth impulse stemmed from the rise of the modern forest product industry 1870-1900, with mechanical pulp in the 1870s, chemical pulp in the 1880s, and newsprint paper in the following decade. Though modest by later standards, the new export products raised significantly the value-adding element of the country's exports. Moreover, the raw material from the forests provided at the same time a stepping stone to successively higher stages of industrial competence: chemical pulp required bleaching, which ushered in the modern chemical industry; newsprint faced elastic demand in respect of increases in incomes, hence a growing market; and finally, as the machinery was constructed locally, the pulp industry ushered in the modern engineering industry, which is strategic for continued industrialisation and economic progress. In other words, the forest resources, in contrast to say grapes or cotton, permitted Norway to industrialise in step with the rise in incomes and shifts in demand in the most advanced nations, which were also the markets for the country's exports.

Since the concept of growth sector or growth industry crops up later in this book, a few words on its nature and role in the process of economic development would seem in order. A growth industry, in contrast to Rostow's 'leading sectors', may be defined as an industry or sector, coming in addition to existing industries of the economy and having for a certain period rates of growth of output, sales, employment, productivity and profits higher than the average for the economy. Because its productivity level and growth exceeds the average, the growth sector for a time is able to offer returns to both labour and capital higher than the average. By attracting labour from other sectors of the economy, the growth industry raises the average overall productivity level directly, and indirectly by reducing employment in the low-productive sectors. The effect is thus double with respect to growth.

The period of expansion lasts till imitators by their entry have reduced returns to factors down to the average, or even below, at which point the motive for continued investment subsides, and saturation or stagnation sets in. The idea suggested corresponds to the one that inspires the legislation regarding patents: the inventor is granted a limited period of monopoly, usually ten or fifteen years, after which the legal protection is recalled. At that point any one is free to avail himself of the patented idea. Rushing in, the imitators quickly erode the original motive for investing in the new patent.

To identify the mechanisms of growth, in other words, we should move down from the macro-level, to the level of individual branches or sectors. As followers of Joseph Schumpeter would argue, economic development on this level of disaggregation presents itself as a series of discontinuous innovations that periodically give rise to new growth industries.[3] These provide successive opportunities for new investments, jobs and products, how many, depending on the originality and impact of the innovation. At the same time they upset the basis for established firms, products and markets. The innovations, creators and destructors at the same time, range from new technology, new goods, new markets, to new forms of organisation. The growth-sector concept is also reconcilable with the concept of the product life cycle. Not only products, but industries as well should be conceived as following the law of the life cycle.

Summarising, we will expect Norwegian economic development in the twentieth century to proceed, not in terms of balanced or uninterrupted expansion. Rather we shall be concerned to examine how far the process of growth can be described and explained as a sequence of the rise, gradual deceleration and final disappearance of a train of growth sectors. From the point of view of the producers the process offers an illustration of the law of diminishing marginal returns; from the point of view of the consumers, a picture of the law of declining marginal utility. Each sector for a time imparts its growth dynamism to the whole system; how long being a matter that, given the nature of innovations, can only be settled *ex post*.

Our story begins around 1920. At that time the country had just come away from World War I as 'a neutral ally' of Britain, with some scars, and a solid surplus in its foreign balance as a result of record-high shipping incomes and exports of commodities, among which were some rather new ones. The new exports stemmed from the recent expansion in hydro-electricity and the start-up of new power-intensive industries in electro-metallurgy and electro-chemistry. In regard to the country's previous experience and standards, the new industrial undertakings were large-scale, capital intensive and export-oriented. For that reason the political authorities had been forced to grapple with the issue of the role and implications of foreign capital in the nation's economic development. Since the nation had achieved full sovereignty as late as 1905, when Norway broke away from its union with Sweden, sovereignty was a hot issue. Prior to the union with Sweden, Norway had been under Danish hegemony for four hundred years. The size and speed of foreign investments in mining, water-power stations and power intensive industries, such as aluminium, carbide, cyanamide and other fertilizers, were felt as a new threat: foreign capital in 1909 owned 38.8 per cent of total share capital in Norwegian industrial companies, up from a fraction ten year earlier. Political pressure arose to the effect that Parliament, the Storting, in 1906, 1909 and again in 1917 enacted an elaborate concession legislation that sought to regulate the conditions under which foreign ownership of Norwegian natural resources, including the ownership and exploitation of real estate, forests, mines and waterfalls, should be permitted.[5]

In an international context the Norwegian concession laws broke new ground in the sense that private capital interests were brought under obligation also to further the common interest, on the rather novel assumption that conflict rather than harmony dominated their relations. The Norwegian authorites were later to put to good use their experience of the hydro-electric bonanza in their dealings with foreign concessionaires in the North Sea oil bonanza in the 1970s. The main points should be stated.

According to the concession act of 1917 Norwegian registered companies, in which the capital stock is more than 20 per cent in foreign hands, or in which not all the members of the local board of directors are Norwegians domiciled in Norway, are obliged to seek a concession if they wish to rent or own real estate. The concession, usually for 60 years, is to be considered as an *ad hoc* agreement between the investor and the Norwegian government. Individual foreigners may own property of all kinds, generally under the same provisions of the concession laws as apply to foreign corporations. Rental of real estate, which does not pertain to mines, waterfalls or to an industrial enterprise, does not require concession. A trading company is required to register only; it does not need a concession agreement. Granted a concession agreement is obtained, the foreign consessionaire is placed under some mandatory requirements, that stipulate' for instance that:

— the right of ownership of natural assets reverts to the state on the termination of the lease, usually after 60 years.
— the corporation's seat be located in Norway.
— a majority of the board of directors be Norwegian citizens.
— a certain part of the capital stock be held by Norwegians.
— a production fee be paid to the Norwegian government.
— the property must not be sold or transferred without permission.
— preference be given to Norwegian labour and materials.

The regulations correspond in principle to the present standard conditions for oil exploration, drilling and oil production on the continental shelf in the North Sea. The subject of intense debate at the time, the concession laws today scarcely cause the winking of an eye; moreover, there is a new awareness of the fragility of the physical environment which induces industry to accept tougher government regulations intended to prevent possible damage to the ecological balance, whether at sea or on land. In this context the concession laws appear justified.

There is another reason why they seem to loom large. They have been the focal point for a good many long standing cleavages in the nation's life. These run deeper than elsewhere and give Norway a character of a dualistic society in respect of language, religion, political conversions and economic interests. They tend to fuse into a double cleavage, between traditionalists and modernists on the one hand and between radical socialism and conservatism on the other. These cleavages were dominant between 1906-9 in the controversy preceding the concession laws; they were also decisive in the battle concerning Norway's membership of the EEC in 1970-2. The continuity deserves our attention.

It is of interest to note that the concession laws of 1909 were formulated by the dominant Liberal Party, not by the socialist Labour Party, though the latter warmly supported the idea of controlling and regulating capital. The laws were opposed by the Conservative Party, representing the modern sectors, on the grounds that the conditions were so strict as to remove the incentive for foreign capital to utilise the nation's resources. In fact, the warning proved premature but so did the fear of foreign capital infringing national sovereignty. Foreign capital apparently did not halt industrialisation, nor did it pose a threat to native social values or political institutions. In view of the experience elsewhere, though, the happy outcome may have been due to the prior existence of the concession legislation. Its mere existence may have served to remove possible causes for conflict over sovereignty.

Experience in the sixties suggests that this view may be correct. In 1962 Norway, in line with Britain and Denmark, applied for membership of the EEC. The Socialist People's Party on Labour's left flank, founded in 1961 in opposition to NATO, immediately launched a campaign against the idea of EEC-membership. The main argument was that Norwegian sovereignty would be curtailed and the continuance of socialist regulations and institutions to control foreign capital would be threatened. For slightly different reasons party spokesmen for rural and traditionalist interests joined hands with the SPP in opposing the idea of resigning sovereignty to supra-national organisations.

There is an economic dimension to the cleavages sketched here that will concern us throughout our story. The inward looking ideology that inspires the traditionalists and their socialist allies ignores the real dependence of a small country on the international economy. One sign of the dependence is the fact that exports averaged 44 per cent of GNP in the 1946-80 period. With imports of corresponding magnitude, Norway thus has a trade-income ratio surpassed only by the Netherlands. One standing complaint among the modernists is that the foreign sector is not given sufficient weight in debates on national economic welfare. One version of that complaint is that at a time when the traditional industries, fishing and agriculture, live off subsidies, the least one would expect is that their spokesmen should accept the conditions under which the modern sectors of the economy alone may be able to continue to provide those subsidies. The conditions, in the opinion of the modernists, include a commitment to continued free trade in goods, transport and capital services. For a small country, continued economic growth cannot even begin to be conceived unless in a context of free exchange in the international economy. Openness has its dangers; isolation takes a higher price. Our story offers illustrations of both.

Notes

1 Lennart Jörberg, 'The Nordic Countries 1850-1914', in *The Fontana Economic History of Europe*, ed. Carlo M. Cipolla, 1973, vol. 4.2, p. 386.

2 Fritz Hodne, 'Growth in a Dual Economy. The Norwegian Experience 1814-1914', *Economy and History*, vol. XVI, 1973, pp. 81-110.

3 Joseph Schumpeter, *The Theory of Economic Development*, Cambridge, Mass. 1934, (Orig. 1911. New edition 1951.); Joseph Schumpeter. *Business Cycles*, 2 vols., New York & London, 1939; Francis Sejersted, ed., *Vekst gjennom krise. Studier i norsk teknologihistorie*, Oslo, 1982. An anthology. (Growth through crisis. Studies in Norwegian technological history.)

4 Refer, as an initial step in this direction, to my article 'Omstillinger i historisk perspektiv: Er oljesektoren spesiell?', *Sosialøkonomen* 1981, nr. 10, pp. 11-18. (Structural changes in an historical perspective. Is the oil sector special?)

5 Arthur Stonehill, *Foreign Ownership in Norwegian Enterprises*, Oslo, 1965, pp. 28-30.

2 A DECADE OF LABOUR CONFLICTS

Collapse of the War Time Boom 1920-1921

Located on the northern fringe, with a large mercantile fleet, neutral Norway, like Sweden and Denmark, had profited from World War I. On the one hand the shipping earnings had been extraordinary. While Norway in 1914 had a net debt abroad of 860 million gold kroner, it now had a net claim against the external world of 1,360 million kroner. Inflation had reduced the value of the krone by about two thirds, but the situation was auspicious. During the war the foreign debt, public and private, had in effect been repaid, and most of the assets repatriated. Foreign-held assets in industrial companies were a mere 6.7 per cent in 1919, down from 38.8 per cent in 1909. The war, moreover, had created a boom for the nation's goods, including the traditional ones, fish, timber and pulp, as well as the new commodities based on hydro electricity: aluminium, copper, zinc, iron pellets, cynamide and other chemical fertilizers. The level of activity remained high, unemployment dropped out of sight: between 1914 and 1919 the percentage of unemployed trade unionists fluctuated between 0.8 per cent and 2.4 per cent.

On the other hand, the wartime inflation was worse than elsewhere. The consumer index climbed from 36 in July 1914 to 110 in 1920, the peak year. The currency depreciation was of similar magnitude: the internal buying power of the krone dropped by 67 per cent between 1914 and 1920. Food shortages increased as the war went on; bitterness spread among townspeople, notably the working population, whose wages tended to lag behind during the first two years of the war. Rationing with coupons was introduced in January 1918. Sentiments were shocked at the news of 2,000 seamen killed in attacks by German submarines on Norwegian neutral ships. The fleet was reduced by 27 per cent, down from 2.6 million gross registered tons in1914, to 1.9 million by mid-1918. According to an estimate by the Norwegian Shipowners' Association in 1919, the restoration of the fleet to earlier levels would require £33 million.[1] At traditional exchange rates this amounted to something like 660 million kroner, which, as it turned out, was only slightly in excess of the real rebuilding costs.

Worse, in retrospect, for the economy were the wartime controls adopted, and put into effect by the Liberal government. The intentions were all very sensible but the means ill-advised. At best the extensive controls, including 92 diverse government agencies, were improvisations hit upon to deal with events as they appeared. They were unco-ordinated, costly, and on the whole ineffective. They were abolished too late, and when abolished, released a foreseeable import spree through 1919 that wiped out in one stroke all the gains of the war, including the entire foreign currency holdings. As an example of reck-less imports of consumer goods, consider the importation of 5,130 tons

Figure 2.1: Exports, Imports and Terms of Trade 1918-1924

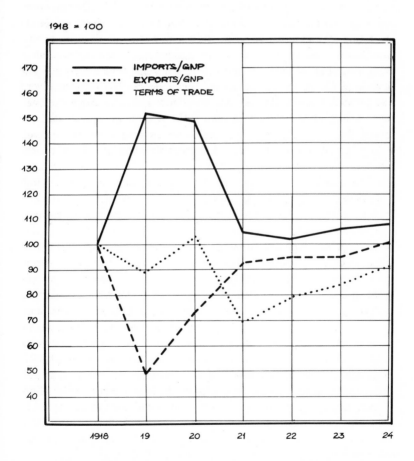

Source: National Accounts 1865-1960, Nos XII, 163, Oslo 1965, Tables 50, 51.

of tobacco leaf in 1919, against 1,000-1,400 tons in a normal year. The wealth of the country virtually went up in smoke. Figure 2.1 shows how the country's terms of trade deteriorated after 1918.

Fiscal mismanagement during the war cast shadows over government finances for almost a decade afterwards. The ordinary state budgets and budget accounts during the war years showed a net government surplus, but this was due to the fact that the new central government agencies had operated separate accounts. When their activities were summed up provisionally in a financial review after the war, the public learnt that the short term government debt had quadrupled, from 357 million kroner in 1914 to 1,130 million in 1920. When all the short-term borrowing transactions had surfaced, they were converted to a long-term government debt, which by 1925 amounted to 1,731 million kroner. At that time the external value of the krone was nearly back to prewar level. Local government debt tells a similar story. It was 254 million kroner in 1915 but 1,501 million in 1925 when it culminated. The legacy of Gunnar Knudsen, Liberal premier 1912-20, was thus one of moral and economic decline. A host of government controls had been introduced, all backed by legislation and funds, all providing careers for bureaucrats, and though some of the offices were closed afterwards, much of the legislation was never formally abolished. Notably, the government's controls of prices, dividends, wages and rents remained on the statute book. The export bans, including the ban on fish products, were lifted too late. The foodstuffs then proved unsaleable. Similarly, a good deal of the provisioning done by the government turned out to have been ill-advised.

The public debt was of such crushing proportions after the war, that both local and central governments were made virtually powerless. The local debt especially stemmed from costs incurred on electrification projects. Since the Liberal premier Gunnar Knudsen and his colleague, Johan Castberg, had rammed through the world's strictest concession laws then in existence for water power utilisation, we are also entitled to say that the municipal debt burden was an effect of hasty government intervention. When private capital was barred, local governments, generally less versed in evaluating risks and market outlooks, were lured into electrification projects in a period of inflation, which in the end proved financially disastrous for a number of municipalities. A third of the country's 600 municipalities were said to be bankrupt in 1930. In several cases local self-government was suspended. And when the bubble burst in the summer of 1920, the class divisions were perhaps more ominous than in 1917. The entire liberal society came under attack from organized labour. According to the new slogans, bourgeois society had a lot to account for.

Militant Labour and Unemployment

Lenin's Soviet revolution in Petersburg in 1917 whipped up radical fervour among workers and labour parties everywhere in Europe. Finland apart, the revolutionary fever seems to have struck harder in Norway than in any other West European country. Little in its history foreshadowed revolution. True, the Norwegian Labour Party from its start in 1887 was a socialist rather than a reformist party, basing its programme on appeals to class conflict, revolution and socialisation of the means of production. In practice, however, the party, like its counterparts in Denmark and Sweden, took its programme from the German mother party, Sozialistisches Partei Deutschlands, dating back to 1869. Under August Bebel the German SPD had turned into a gradualist party; it worked for practical gains for industrial workers within the existing social and political structure, in close harmony with the trade unions. The early reformist attitude of the Norwegian Labour Party was due in part to the influence of the German SPD. The occupational figures offer another clue to the party's initial moderation. After-all, the number of manufacturing workers was a mere 100,000 in 1900 as against a workforce totalling 883,000 employees in that year. Agriculture, fishing and forestry employed 360,000, while 232,000 were engaged in secondary activities, manufacturing, building, construction, and the crafts. The rest, 291,000 employees, found a living in the service sector: shipping, trade, banking, transport, teaching and the other professions.[2] Hence, 100,000 manufacturing workers out of 883,000, though concentrated in urban centers, were as yet hardly in a position to threaten the social order. Then followed a quick burst of hydroelectric construction projects and the birth of the modern electro-chemical and electrometal industries. The workforce in industry, including construction and the building trades but excluding the crafts, shot up from about 154,000 in 1900 to 161,000 men in 1910 and 207,000 by 1920.[3] Industrial workers became a substantial social class. Recent events also speeded up the development of class consciousness, including the agitation from trade union leaders like Martin Tranmael, the war itself and, of course, the Soviet revolution. The new mood surfaced both in trade union militancy and in the radical turn of the Norwegian Labour Party.

Trade unions date back to the 1870s. The Norwegián Federation of Labour (LO), was set up in 1899, but as late as 1902 membership was a mere 7,500.[4] However, during the ensuing period of industrialisation, recruitment from unskilled workers picked up, with 25,000 paid-up members in 1906, 68,000 in 1914 and an astonishing 144,000 at the end of 1919. The unions in Norway had an elected Secretariat, with a mandate over the national strike fund that gave it effective central control. Martin Tranmael (1879-1967) won control of the centre in 1912. His entry marked the beginning of a new aggressive line. In one address against strike breakers Tranmael suggested that union workers, to fend off the strike breakers, should leave behind 'dynamite in the bore holes'. This branded him as a syndicalist troublemaker, bent on the idea of 'direct action'. The war nourished grievances rather than patriotism. In the unions' eyes patriotism was merely a cloak for militarism.

The Norwegian Labour Party won its way to the Storting, the country's elected national parliament, in 1903. The first representatives, four in all, came from the northern fishing districts and the industrial towns of the south. The party was in fact a coalition of the two strata. By 1912, despite gerrymandering, the party had 23 candidates. A new electoral law, based on the principle of proportional representation, was passed in 1919. It gave Labour 29 members in the ensuing election of 1921, out of a total of 150 representatives. Too late, for at the party's annual congress in 1918, the party's radical opposition conquered the party. As a result the programme was revolutionised. Revolution, workers' soviets, and the dictatorship of the proletariat were the new catchwords. When Lenin set up the Third International Comintern on 4 March 1919 in Moscow to act as general staff for the coming world revolution, the Norwegian Labour Party took up membership. Curiously, it was the only social democratic party in Western Europe to do so. The apocalyptic enthusiasm for revolution culminated in 1920 when the party also accepted the notorious Moscow theses that outlined the Soviet centralist principles for the Comintern's leadership in the worldwide revolution ahead.[5]

The Rhetoric of Revolution

All this apparent revolutionary fervour raises a question. Had the Norwegian workers experienced untoward repression to an extent that made revolution at all an understandable reaction? Naturally, no precise answer can be given, but consider some of the evidence relevant to its evaluation.

Socialist revolution was voiced in 1848 in the Communist Manifesto drawn up by Marx and Engels. Two of the demands set forth do suggest an alternative road to working class power. They were the demand for progressive taxation and the franchise. By virtue of their superiority in numbers the workers, once in power legally, would be able to set up socialist government by parliamentary means, without revolution. Now the full franchise for men in Norway had been enacted in 1898, direct income tax came in 1892, and the rates were made progressive three years later. Hence, two of the cardinal demands of labour had been conceded in Norway even before there was a labour movement.

Workingmen's compensation for industrial injuries came in 1894, the premiums being paid by the employers. The first factory act passed the Storting in 1892, with special provisions protecting children and women. Next, consider the right of unionisation. The right was implicit in the 1814-Constitution. What about co-operation? Workers' cooperatives were set up in the 1890s and a national organisation was established in 1906. The co-operatives handled production, wholesale and retail business. Annual coupons returned some of the profits back to customers. Legislation offered special tax concessions to help their growth. The trade unions ran their own news service, they owned and operated 29 newspapers already by 1914, with a daily production of 80,000 at a time when membership in the unions as yet did not exceed 70,000.[6]

Nor did the employers seriously question the workers' right to organise or the right to conclude collective agreements. The first local agreements were signed in the 1870s and the first national contracts reached in 1907 between the employers and the iron and metal workers. The agreement contained elements that set the standard for other national contracts, among them provisions for a minimum wage, a ceiling for working hours, and recognition of the national union's right to bargain for workers. The employers' union, the Norwegian Employers' Federation, including the dominant firms in Norway, accepted its principles. The unions in return accepted the employers' right to maintain control over labour standards and to hire unorganised as well as organised workers. The eight-hour day was won in 1919. In the same year followed an agreement on the right to twelve days annual paid holiday for industrial workers. True, unlike the farmers and the cottars, the industrial workers had as yet no special government loan or housing bank, offering long term mortgage loans at reduced rates of interest. For the unpropertied wage earners in towns there was recourse instead to the local pawnshop, the first dating back to 1847.

Weighing the above together, it would seem that the workers in Norway had gained entry before knocking, and lacked in fact the pretext for breaking the door. The events also confirmed this view. Revolution, mouthed by the Tranmael opposition, was very much rhetoric and little else. So why revolution? Historians, notably English-speaking scholars, have recently revamped an explanation, originally put forward by a Norwegian marxist historian Edvard Bull Sr in 1922.[7] According to this, the social disruption of traditional values in a way came too fast, and the workers, now unskilled workers rather than craftsmen, were so alienated that they fell for the idea of a violent overthrow of the existing order. Uprootedness is measured by such variables as the number of illegitimate births, migration to towns, and votes cast for leftwing parties. In its strong versions the theory has not succeeded in reconciling the relevant evidence with its predictions and implications. In a weaker version the theory remains at least a useful point of view, in that it directs attention to the relation between the tempo of industrialisation and the amount of social strain accompanying rapid change.[8] Admittedly, the pace of industrialisation was rapid up to 1920, but the war was probably an equally disrupting force, with the Soviet revolution its point of culmination. The unskilled workers felt not only dissatisfaction; the militarism around them also provided extra justification for pressing their demands. In general they believed there was more to collect — an idea that survived the war. The idea gained a boost in 1920 when the Labour Court in that year's tariff negotiations awarded the workers an average pay rise of 23.5 per cent, up from 1.70 to 2.10 kroner per hour. With fringe benefits and overtime work the wage increase would be even higher. The court's chairman, Chief Justice Kristoffer Thinn, was a jurist, not an economist.

Then followed the collapse of the postwar boom in late summer 1920. With the bonanza over, the labour leaders now faced the task of reconciling the union workers with the facts of an altered situation. In the ensuing strain the labour movement split into warring ideological factions, which paralyzed for seven years the labour parties and to some extent the trade unions. Worse, in the scramble to avoid the stigma of reformism and retreat labour struck a revolutionary and militant posture that scared the settled strata of society and poisoned political debate for more than a decade. Nor should one forget that tensions existed within the trade unions themselves. Communist-dominated unions fought those affiliated with the Labour Party. Old craft unions rivalled with the more recent unions of unskilled labour. And the highly-paid union members saw the value of solidarity differently from those at the bottom of the pay scale. All these cleavages provided material for conflicts. Not least, from these internal rivalries stemmed the truculence shown the common enemy, bourgeois society. From here the effects can be traced in many directions, notably the retrenchment observed in figures for aggregate investment.

Summing up, the evidence suggests that the rank and file of labour was not revolutionary. This lack of revolutionary fervour reflects the absence in the country's earlier history of any organised movement to hinder the emancipation of the working class. However, among the leaders undoubtedly revolution was a matter of faith that justified their bid for power. In the event the issue was reduced to a tactical element in their attempts to hold on to disheartened union workers when economic hardship set in after 1920. Hence, revolution as a rhetorical device, both in the 1920s and later, was a convenient pretext for pressing their claims and a vicarious motive for justifying their own leadership.

As for the political disintegration, division began when the moderates of the Norwegian Labour Party (DNA) organised a reformist party early in 1921 in opposition to the new revolutionary programme of the mother party. The new party called itself the Social Democratic Party, and it polled 9.3 per cent of the votes in that year's Storting election; against 21.3 per cent for the Labour Party. Next, the mother party in 1923 rebelled against Comintern, when it became clear that Norwegian Labour was to be directed from Moscow. The party seceded from Comintern, but retained its revolutionary marxist programme. It did not return to the Social Democratic fold. The party's irascible left wing thereupon separated, and organised Norway's Communist Party late in 1923. This Moscow-oriented party captured an insignficant 6.1 per cent in the elections of 1924. As for trade unionism, the 1920s became the decade of strikes, legal and illegal, and some violence.

Industrial Strikes

The first serious strike of the decade occurred in December 1920. Responsible were the railway workers, whose employer was the government, since the railways were operated as a state monopoly. The government, fearing that wage demands by one group would unleash landslide demands from other public servants, refused to negotiate.

Mediation, introduced by the Labour Disputes Act of 1915, was tried, but again the government proved adamant. The workers went on strike on the first of December, but returned to their jobs after 16 days, without having achieved anything worthwhile. The ordinary trade union member was disconcerted to read in the socialist newspapers that he was a revolutionary participant in the final struggle for control over the state; he merely wanted compensation for war time price rises.[9]

The political overtones of trade union activity became more pronounced in the following spring. In line with the new trend of falling prices, management now demanded tariff revisions and wage cuts, matching the drop in living costs. The era of the price index was at hand. The trade union leaders, however, saw the matter differently, at least publicly. Tariff agreements for nearly 50,000 men were cancelled by the employers in the spring of 1921 together with demands for an immediate 33 per cent wage reduction.

The seamen's union was the first to negotiate. The union, as noted above, refused the pay reductions out of hand, declaring instead that its members would go on strike by 8 May. To show sympathy with the group that had taken the hardest beating during the war, the trade union leaders declared a nationwide sympathetic strike. The strike was partly meant as a 'general strike' to pave the wave for revolution; for the majority of the trade union secretariat it was a 'major strike' to demonstrate protest against wage cuts.[10] The strike, comprising at one time 154,000 workers, represented a record loss of 3.5 million work days. It lasted from 26 May till 10 June that year, and was on the face of it a major setback for the trade unions. Membership dropped from a high point of 144,000 in 1919 to 96,000 by the end of 1921 and 84,000 the following year. The government called out military personnel to maintain communications, besides providing protection for strike breakers at work in harbours and elsewhere. Local middle class committees, calling themselves the Community Help, were organised in the major towns to maintain essential functions, among them the baking of bread, and the supply of gas, water, and electricity.

Chaos was prevented, though urban society from now on was divided in two antagonistic groups. In the countryside and in the smaller towns sentiments on existing class divisions remained unchanged. It was thus urban Norway, rather than the nation as a whole, that was at war with itself. The strike funds emptied, the union leaders beat a retreat. Negotiations were resumed, and when the sailors went on board again, their wages were down an average 16 per cent rather than 33 per cent.

The cuts, however, were largely nominal, for prices had dropped in the meantime. By 1921 membership in the stokers' union dropped from 4,254 to 1,258, down by 70 per cent. The strike had been a failure, at least in contemporary opinion, but it had perhaps demonstrated that strong unions are the best defenders of the workers' wages in periods of increasing unemployment. Indeed, in the depressed situation that message was important to get across, for the slump tended to call in question the usefulness of unions and the weekly union fee. After all, the percentage of jobless union workers climbed from 1.8 per cent in August 1920 to a temporary 25 per cent in March 1922. Trade union membership dropped by one third, as noted, down from 144,000 at the peak in 1919 to 84,000 in 1922. It took a decade to recoup the loss. Unemployment also stayed at a consistently high level throughout the entire interwar period [See figure 2.2.] Another lesson of the 'general strike' in 1921 was unmistakeable: wage rates could also go down, a point not lost on the employers. They could use the outcome of the great strike as a model for future rounds of wage bargaining. Later that year paper and saw mill workers suffered wage cuts of up to 23 per cent while the average reductions were 20 per cent.

The next serious labour conflict, in the fall 1923, was triggered by the meaning of an index clause, inserted in a tariff contract for the iron workers the previous year. This clause gave both the workers and the employers the right to demand a revision of wage rates if the index for living costs at a certain date exceeded or dropped below an agreed figure. This was the principle of semi-automatic index regulation. Now, as living costs continued to fall, the employers in 1923, without much bargaining, put into effect a 5 per cent wage reduction for the iron industry workers. The workers claimed that the fall was not a fall in living costs, but merely reflected tax reductions, whereupon they went on strike. The walkout obviously was illegal, (see next section) and a Labour Court verdict confirmed this; the workers, mostly in Oslo, still refused to go back. Tension increased, and when negotiations for harbour workers got bogged down, they too went on strike. Escalation now set in on both sides. The employers answered by lockout for the entire transport industry, whereupon the trade union leaders marched the paper workers out in a countrywide stoppage to show sympathy. The conflict, involving 63,000 workers, dragged on for more than 7 months. It was the more pointless as the cost-of-living index meanwhile had jumped 15 points. In the end the conflict was settled, and when the workers returned to work on 30 May 1924, they did so with a 5 per cent increase in wages, rather than a 5 per cent reduction. Clearly,

Figure 2.2: Unemployed Trade Union Members Registered at the Unemployment Office, in % 1905-1955

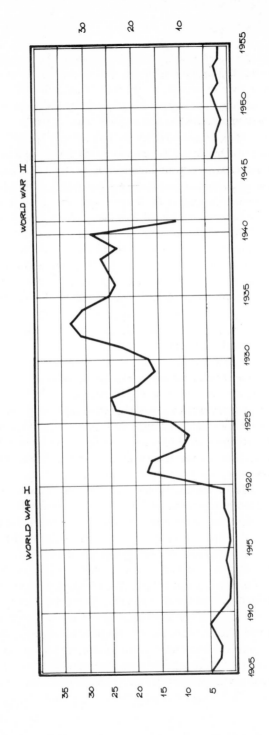

Source: *Historical Statistics 1968*, Nos XII, 245, Oslo 1968. Table 57.

index regulation worked both ways.

When the recession and the deflation deepened, as reflected in a higher external value of the krone, the cost of living fell again. The employers demanded wage cuts, and again the unions protested. As a result the years 1926 and 1927 saw another series of industrial strikes, against wage cuts and strike-breakers, though not as widespread as in 1921 and 1924. In June 1928 the building workers staged a six week 'illegal' strike, which was supported morally and financially by many trade unionists and the national leaders of labour. Increasingly the conflicts were thus settled, not by the partners directly, but through mediation by the State Mediator, operating under the clauses of the Labour Disputes Act of 1915, or by way of compulsory arbitration, reintroduced in 1922, substantially in the same form as the earlier legislation of 1916.[11] The latter legislation was *ad hoc*, usually valid for one year, after which renewals had to be passed. In this way both sides tried to keep the government on the side lines.

Undermining of the Labour Market Legislation

Since the principles for conflict resolution in the labour market crop up time and again in our story, a word about its salient points is perhaps in order. The legislation of 1915 distinguished between disputes of right and disputes of interest. To settle disputes of right, regarding meaning of an existing agreement, the act provided for a Labour Court, which was to hear cases and produce verdicts, binding for both parties. Stoppage in these cases was not to be tolerated. The idea was to avoid unnecessary tension. Disputes of interest, arising over, say, wage claims in a new contract, were to be submitted to a national mediator (riksmeklingsmann) before a stoppage could be called. Neither side was compelled to bow to the mediation proposal. The test here was the opinion of the majority. When the negotiating parties agreed to a proposal, the proposal was voted upon by the members of the unions affected, whose yes or no decided the issue. The machinery of mediation, by providing a 'cooling-off-period', built a fence against wild-cat strikes, and was the more effective in that both parties were made equally responsible.

Third, a difficult question was how to prevent stoppage, in cases when mediation failed. The answer was compulsory state arbitration. As noted, provisional legislation for this passed the Storting in 1916, only to lapse in 1920. The law empowered the government, if it considered that a labour dispute threatened 'important public interests', to forbid stoppage, and order the parties to abide by existing conditions until a verdict could be had from a tripartite arbitration board. The board's decision, if accepted beforehand by the parties, was to be valid for a period not to exceed three years, and had the same effect as collective agreements.

Fourth, there was the matter of damages to be collected in case of breach of contract. Since in practice the individual worker could not be held liable for illegal action, the issue was in Norway, as elsewhere, how far trade union funds should be tapped in cases of unlawful stoppages. The law of 1915 held a trade union liable for breach of a collective agreement, but the burden of proof lay with the injured party. Extenuating circumstances were, however, provided for, when the court decided on a complaint. The employers, faced with an increase of illegal actions, demanded stiffer liability provisions. This was achieved by new legislation in 1927, which shifted the burden of proof in cases of illegal stoppages to the trade union side. This was the principle of guilty until proven innocent. In 1933 the provisions for liability were tightened again, in that trade unions were made automatically liable for contract breaches committed by their members. Practice was lenient, however, for the Court normally waived damages entirely in extenuating circumstances; hence, repeal of the provision was never demanded by the union leaders.[12]

Arbitration by legal fiat was unpopular. It brought in the government, a third party, whose decisions were bound to be biased. Compulsory arbitration also broke down in the disruptive twenties. The illegal strike staged by the building workers in 1928 was thus a direct response to an arbitration decision handed down by the arbitration court. It proved the end of arbitration for the interwar period. Its legality was called into question, and this tended to undermine the entire labour market legislation. Notably, new legislation in 1927 to protect strike breakers against molestation was such that trade union leaders felt they were being criminalised, when fighting strike breakers. On the other hand, they failed too often to stop illegal strikes. The spirit of confrontation flared up one last time, in the 'Menstad battle' of 1931, the climax of the most devastating labour conflict in this century. At one time the 1931-conflict involved lock-out for more than 60,000 workers and lasted about 5 months, at a cost of 7.5 million lost work days. See Table 2.1.

The background for the confrontation in 1931 was much the same as earlier. With an eye on the fall in the living cost index, the

Table 2.1: Industrial Labour and the Labour Market 1919-1939

	Membership of trade unions (000s)	Percentage of trade union members unemployed	Number of work stoppages	Workers on strike (000s)	Days lost (000s)	Hourly earnings for industrial workers (current kroner)	Real wage (1900 =100)
	1	2	3	4	5	6	7
1919	144	1.6	—	—	—	1.87	166
1920	143	2.3	—	—	—	2.34	194
1921	96	17.6	89	154	3584	2.20	217
1922	84	17.1	26	2	91	1.77	210
1923	86	10.6	57	25	796	1.68	194
1924	93	8.5	61	63	5152	1.81	191
1925	96	13.2	84	14	667	1.93	202
1926	94	24.3	113	51	2204	1.76	211
1927	94	25.4	96	22	1374	1.62	205
1928	106	19.1	63	8	304	1.48	207
1929	127	15.4	73	5	197	1.47	213
1930	140	16.6	94	5	240	1.47	227
1931	145	22.3	82	60	7586	1.44	228
1932	153	30.8	91	6	394	1.43	238
1933	158	33.4	93	6	364	1.41	237
1934	173	30.7	85	6	235	1.42	237
1935	224	25.3	103	4	168	1.43	232
1936	217	18.8	175	15	396	1.47	232
1937	323	20.0	195	29	1014	1.56	233
1938	345	22.0	248	24	567	1.72	249
1939	357	18.3	81	16	860	1.76	250

Sources: Columns 1-5, *Historical Statistics 1968*, Tables 57, 60.
            "   6-7, Erling Petersen, *Norsk Arbeidsgiverforening 1900-1950*, p. 671.
                       Gerhard Stoltz, *Økonomisk utsyn 1900-1950*, p. 177.

employers' federation NAF called for reductions of wages in April, adding the threat of lock-out. The unions, with more self confidence, countered that reductions could be achieved by cutting working hours rather than reducing the pay rates. Mediation failed and by May 1931 about 60,000 men were in conflict. In June demonstrating workers at one of Hydro's plants at Menstad, Skien, led by local Communist trade unionists, clashed with a para-military police force, called out by the Minister of Defence, Vidkun Quisling, to protect strike breakers. Molestations occurred, three policemen were injured – they were said to have been provocative – but no shots were fired. Despite contributions from their sister organisations in Sweden and Denmark, the LO-chiefs sought a compromise solution. After two rounds of negotiations and vote taking, the strike was finally brought to an end.[13] None could claim a victory, least of all the management side, despite the fact that wage reductions were achieved. Real wages, however, were not affected, for living costs dropped as well. More important, none could win, but everyone stood to lose from such wars of attrition.

This was perhaps the significance of the Menstad episode in 1931. It paved the way for a new spirit of mutual compromise between the parties in the labour market. The LO-leaders were concerned about a possible mass exodus of its members. But the same fear spread in the employers' federation NAF. New examination of its protocols and diaries brings out that the NAF-leaders fought tendencies among its members to resign membership, and sought ways to placate both the unions and its own members, directly in opposition to the official attitude of the Conservative Party to which, naturally, the employers' organisation affiliated itself.[14] This new conciliatory posture in NAF originated from the experience in the 1920s when the government tried to govern the labour market by legislative fiat. This was a total failure, hence the search for a new compromise. A formal expression of the new compromise was deferred, however, until 1935 when NAF and LO signed a lasting labour relations contract, the so-called 'Main Agreement' (Hovedavtalen).

Despite the bitterness voiced by organised labour in the twenties, the fact remains that after 1924 union workers improved their wages, till 1932 at least in real terms, for while nominal reductions occurred in those years, the cost of living fell more. Table 2.1 offers evidence that permits the reader to take stock of the situation. So does Figure 2.3; both bring out clearly that apart from the years 1922, 1926, and 1935 real wages for industrial workers were rising steadily. Each plateau, following temporary setbacks, was consistently higher than the earlier one. Some were worse off than the curve suggests, but some were similarly better off. Between 1919 and 1939 real hourly wages in industrial firms with membership in the Norwegian Employers' Federation showed a rate of growth of 2.1 per cent a year.

Yet labour conflicts and a spirit of confrontation dominated the domestic scene in the 1920s. Probably the threatening posture of organised labour reduced investments and risk taking on the part of capital owners and entrepreneurs. Another main factor responsible for reduced investments was the deflationary policies of the postwar decade.

Figure 2.3: Average Hourly Earnings for Men in Manufacturing (Current Kroner). The Cost-of-Living Index (1900=100) and Real Wages per Hour for Men in Manufacturing 1914-1939

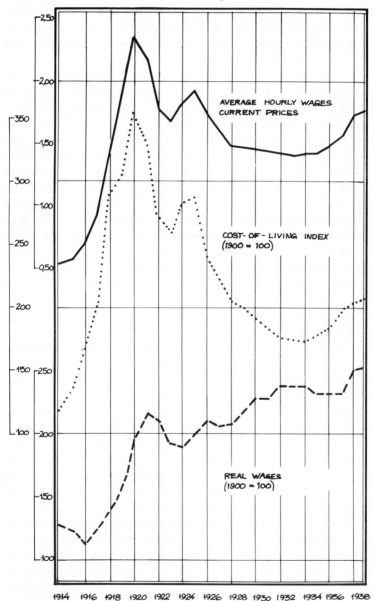

Sources: Gerhard Stoltz, *Økonomisk utsyn 1900-1950*, Oslo 1955, p. 177.
Erling Petersen, *Norsk Arbeidsgiverforening 1900-1950*, Oslo 1950, p. 671.

28   A Decade of Labour Conflicts

Notes

1 *Farmand*, 3 January 1920, p. 10.

2 Juul Bjerke, *Langtidslinjer i norsk økonomi 1865-1960*, Oslo 1966, pp. 29, 54. *Historisk Statistikk*, NOS XII, 245, Oslo 1969, table 17.

3 G. Stoltz, *Økonomisk utsyn 1900-1950*, Oslo 1955, tab. 15, p. 43.

4 An English account is Walter Galenson, *Labor in Norway*, Harvard UP, Cambridge, Mass. 1949, p. 18.

5 Knut Langfeldt, *Moskvatesene i norsk politikk*, Universitetsforlaget, Oslo 1961. Per Maurseth, *Fra Moskvateser til Kristianiaforslag*, Pax, Oslo 1972.

6 Edvard Bull, Jr. *Norsk fagbevegelse*, Oslo 1968, 4th ed. 1979, p. 61.

7 Edvard Bull, Sr, 'Die Entwicklung der Arbeiterbewegung in den drei skandinavischen Ländern'. *Archiv für die Geschichte des Sozialismus und der Arbeiterbewegung*, 10 (1922), pp. 329-61.

8 William M Lafferty, *Industrialization, Community Structure, and Socialism*, Oslo 1974, pp. 20-1, 146 and *passim*. Walter Galenson, *Labor in Norway*, pp. 60-1.

9 Hans Amundsen, *Norsk Jernbaneforbund gjennom 60 år 1892-1952*, Oslo 1952, pp. 109-33 The standard survey of the trade unions in Norway is Gunnar Ousland, *Fagorganisasjonen i Norge*, 4 vols., Oslo 1949, new paperback edition 1975.

10 See the new study of the strike and its motives by Synnøve Aarseth Barder, 'Storstreiken 1921', *Tidsskrift for arbeiderbevegelsens historie*, no 1, Oslo 1977, pp. 35-77.

11 W. Galenson, *Labor in Norway*, p. 109.

12 W. Galenson, *Labor in Norway*, pp. 111-13. *Labour Relations in Norway*, the ILO Committee & The Royal Ministry of Foreign Affairs, Oslo 1975, pp. 32-41, 121-6.

13 Per Ole Johansen, *Menstadkonflikten 1931*, Oslo 1977.

14 Svein Dahl, 'Norsk Abeidsgiverforening 1927/28. Tilbaketog og revurdering' *Historisk Tidskrift 1981*, no 1, pp. 1-25. Rolf Danielsen, *Høyres historie*; 3 vols. forthcoming, vol. 2, (The History of the Conservative Party 1884-1984).

3 THE DEFLATION POLICIES 1920-1928

The Deficits on the Trade Balance

The Scandinavian countries have traditionally had a large foreign trade, not least Norway, hence the export sector opens the door to an understanding of the economic situation in the entire interwar period.

During World War I the country built up a considerable foreign currency surplus abroad, as the war restricted the opportunities for imports. As a result, the liquidity situation was quite unusual. The external value of the Norwegian krone in turn rose, even beyond its gold value, despite a runaway inflation in the internal economy. The krone had been taken off gold in the opening days of the war in 1914.

Immediately after the war there was understandably a strong demand for replacements of stocks and new capital and consumer goods. Existing import bans or restrictions were also gradually lifted. In consequence imports relative to gross national product shot up to 48 per cent in 1919 as against an average of 36 per cent for the years 1910-14. It was a figure not surpassed till the late 1970s. Again it was 47 per cent in 1920, and dropped to the 30 per cent level thereafter.[1] See Figure 3.1. In absolute figures imports rose from 1,580 million current kroner in 1918 to a record 3,495 million in 1920. Exports on the other hand were 1,730 million in 1918 and 2,649 million kroner in 1920.

The import spree not only wiped out the wartime surplus on current account of 1,360 million kroner by 1919; the import hunger let loose the currency spectre that was to haunt the nation's economy and politics for a whole decade. Other European nations experienced similar problems, for everywhere the goal was to return to 'normalcy' after the war, that is, to return to the gold standard with a freely convertible currency at traditional gold values.[2] What distinguishes the Norwegian story then, is that the return trip lasted longer and cost more, in terms of lost economic opportunities, than elsewhere. The deflationary policies of the twenties lasted so long that Norway got next to nothing out of the general prosperity wave of the midtwenties. Table 3.1 reveals the trade deficits that in the final analysis lay at the root of the deflation of the twenties.

For ten consecutive years, shown in Table 3.1, the country accumulated a trade deficit. The shipping earnings, as noted, offset the wartime

Table 3.1: Imports, Exports and Trade Deficits 1915-1925
Million Kroner. Fixed 1910-Kroner

	1915	1916	1917	1918	1919	1920	1921	1922	1923	1924	1925
Exports	623	628	423	367	403	544	457	588	628	666	732
Imports	682	787	577	391	867	795	524	657	704	700	704
Deficit	– 59	–159	–154	– 24	–464	–251	– 67	– 69	– 76	– 34	+ 28

Source: NOS. *National Accounts 1865-1960*, Table 51.

deficits; however, by the end of 1919 these had been spent. Notably the huge imports 1919-20 created havoc in the trade balance and in the foreign exchange market. Dollar and pound sterling that recently had sold below par, now appreciated against the krone. Divorced from gold the Norwegian currency began to lose ground, and loss of confidence in its future hastened its downfall by mechanisms all too familiar. Importers bought forward, exporters postponed converting their holdings abroad; both created an abnormal foreign exchange shortage that squeezed the krone still more.

Already in 1920 the government was forced to float a loan abroad, the so-called currency loan of 100 million kroner, placed in New York on humiliating terms. The municipalities followed suit, notably Oslo and Bergen, which both took up loans of $5 and $4 million respectively at 8 per cent interest.[3] the bonanza over, the adverse signs surfaced almost everywhere in 1920, and at once, in bank failures, business failures, poor dividend reports, in debt problems, foreclosures, unemployment and curtailments of new stock issues. At this point one should remember the wage increases of an average of 24 per cent accorded by State Mediator Kristoffer Thinn earlier in the year. To implement a policy of deflation in that situation certainly was not easy.

A central figure in the deflationary policies of the 1920s was Nicolai Rygg (1872-1957), governor of Norges Bank from November 1920 till 1947. As central bank governor he was bound to play an active part; in a climate of weak parliamentary minority governments his influence could easily become decisive. For that reason it is worth noticing that Rygg was viewed as 'a strong man' at the time, a man of moral convictions, a nationalist, a pillar of conventional wisdom. The nation had sinned gravely; to atone for its sins it now was to undergo a moral cleansing. Rygg was called upon to administer the sacrifice.

Protecting Employment 1920-1924

When the currency troubles began in the autumn 1920, the central bank received the first petitions for help from the banks in the northern coastal districts, now threatened by a run from frightened depositors. Despite declarations to the contrary, Rygg felt that such help was in order. In principle a policy of deflation had been decided on before Rygg's entry; at any rate the bank's discount rate was raised to 7 per cent on 25 June 1920, the highest nominal rate since 1877. The notes in circulation were also reduced from the record 483 million in December 1920 to 410 million by the end of December 1921.[4] The discount rate of 7 per cent remained effective until 7 July 1921, more than a year later, when it was reduced to 6½ per cent. Against a rapidly falling price index (Fig. 2.3), this was a steep rise in the real price of money.

The above monetary measures pointed generally in the direction of deflation, showing Rygg's desire to bolster the external value of the krone. The emergency loans to banks in distress pointed in the other direction, reflecting Rygg's desire to protect jobs and employment by protecting firms and banks. The first goal, as it turned out, had to be postponed temporarily, in order to cushion the economy and the nation through the postwar slump. Thus, despite convictions and legislative backing, Rygg in fact, was responsible for a net supply of liquidity of 100 million kroner in 1921 and 50 million in 1922 and 1923.[5] This could hardly be called a contractive monetary policy. At best the bank accomplished a break with existing trends, which so far had been those of rapid increase in liquidity. Initially, this was the best Rygg could do.

In contrast, the Swedish authorities chose an alternative solution, a brief drastic depression (1921-2) involving high unemployment as weak firms, obsolete products and techniques were wiped out, but which allowed the Swedish Riksbank to declare convertibility at the old gold rate by 1922.[6] From this point on, Sweden developed a series of new growth industries and logged a satisfactory performance on the whole for the interwar period.

The Norwegian policy of protecting employment, intended as a provisional measure, was soon put on a more permanent footing. Legislation enacted in the so-called Administration Act of 24 March 1923, aimed at preventing a nationwide banking failure. Banks facing a liquidity crisis could apply for administration by the central bank. Administration meant that a new board of directors was appointed, old deposits were frozen, and new liquidity was furnished from the central bank in an understanding with the Treasury department. New deposits were to have priority over old. The general aim was to preserve solid banks, whose assets exceeded liabilities, but which were threatened by liquidity problems as a result of runs from panicky depositors. The earlier improvisations now turned out to be permanent.

One unintended consequence was to give depositors an incentive to move their savings from conservative banks and place them with banks under administration, where deposits obviously were safer. The law unintentionally rewarded speculation while punishing thrift, which should have bothered Rygg, whose views appeared to be moored in moral principles, rather than economic expediency.

Another consequence of the bank assistance was to undermine again the external exchange rate of the krone. Attention was increasingly drawn to the country's trade deficits, which continued at a high level, and naturally drove up the price of dollars and sterling. After a brief recovery in 1922, the krone in 1924 dropped to an all time low, with the pound selling for an annual average of kr 31.71 and dollars for kr. 7.20.[7] Par exchange under the gold standard was kr 18.16 and kr 3.73 respectively. The external value of the krone had thus dropped by 75 per cent against the pound and by 93 per cent against the dollar (Fig. 3.1). On the face of it, up to 1924 the deflationary policy to raise the external value of the krone had failed, and all the problems of 1920 remained. Worse, the year 1924 saw some of the serious results of the policies of deflation in the form of a number of bank failures. Of 67 banks that Rygg attempted to help, among them 20 savings banks, a total of 56 went into liquidation eventually, together with 50 other banks not under administration.[8] The bank crisis lasted during most of the decade. Its extent is attested by the following grim figures: the country had 195 private commercial banks in 1919, by 1930 the numer number was 145, and 105 in 1935.[9] In fifteen years half the country's commercial banks were wiped out. The commercial banks lost 1800 million kroner 1921-37, a sum that equalled their total assets in the latter year, and representing 37 per cent of their assets in the former.[10] This merely reflected the drop in all nominal values, including the banks' portfolio values, that was bound to occur as the deflation progressed. The fluctuations in the external value of the krone are shown in Figure 3.1, which covers the years 1914-30.

Figure 3.1: Average Exchange Rates for US Dollars and Pound Sterling at the Oslo Stock Exchange 1914-1930 (yearly averages)

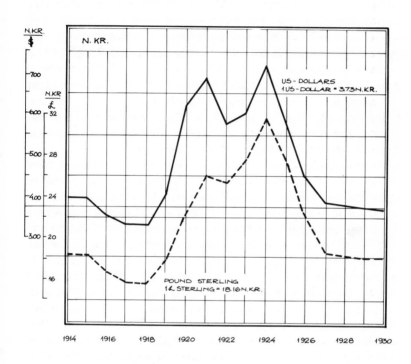

Source: *Historical Statistics 1968*, Table 271.

Protecting the Value of the Money 1925-1928

Mainly as a result of an improved foreign trade balance, the krone's exchange rate meandered upwards in 1925, from 55 per cent of its par value (100) to 78 per cent during the months February-September 1925, and the upward movement continued briskly in the following year. By December 1926 the krone exchanged for 95 per cent of its gold exchange value, a rapid and dramatic turn of events. In his annual report for 1925 governor Rygg, reviewing the causes for the upturn in 1925, noted that there had been no change in policies, nor in ultimate goals — the pressure just lifted of its own. What he referred to was that discounting by the central bank had not become overly contractive in the last year; in general it had been contractive since the ouverture in 1920, but exports of goods and services, notably shipping incomes, had reduced the recurrent foreign trade deficits. The year 1925 even saw a slight surplus (Table 3.1). Even the government was finally able to balance its budget and its accounts in 1925-6.[11] In consequence confidence in the krone returned in the money markets.

This was just what Rygg had been waiting for. When the flight from the krone abated, the banks got a breathing space, and Rygg a chance to cultivate the external value of the krone, a point that had been sidestepped so far. In the main he did this by publishing intermittent statements to the effect that the board of the central bank foresaw a continued appreciation of the currency. This was correctly interpreted as an invitation to currency speculation at zero risk; at any rate the banks suddenly faced a huge inflow of foreign capital, seeking short term gains in the rising price for the Norwegian krone rather than investment outlets in the Norwegian economy. Rygg so far had fought bravely to stem the fall of the krone, now he faced the task of preventing it soaring equally precipitously. While the first job proved a difficult challenge, this last one turned out impossible.

The government appointed a currency commission in September 1925, with the mandate to . . . 'evaluate the currency issue, and express an opinion whether the krone should be brought up to the old gold parity or be stabilized at a lower gold value, possibly in connection with its eventual devaluation'.[12] The commission published its report on 31 January 1926. As to the central issue of devaluation, the report remained as elusive as current informed opinion, stating that for the immediate future the policy should aim at a *de facto* stabilisation at the present level (of exchange), until with more experience the matter of an eventual devaluation could be decided.[13] In line with its recommendation the Treasury and Norges Bank set up a secret joint consortium in May 1926, whose task was to buy and sell Norwegian kroner at an agreed upper and lower limit and thus bring about an effective stabilisation. The goal was to freeze the price of the pound at 24 N kr. As an upper limit for its currency purchase risk Norges Bank staked 20 million kroner against 40 million by the Treasury.

In view of the inflow the amounts must have appeared deliberately inadequate beforehand. Second, Rygg issued another statement to the press in which he said that both the government and the bank board shared the current apprehensions attending stabilisation, but added that no such measure was intended . . . 'The central bank would continue to regulate the exchange rates in accordance with the natural conditions.'

Rygg's aversion for stabilisation below the legal gold parity, despite the cryptic language, is unmistakeable. The consortium did try to peg the price at 24 kroner to the pound till the middle of September. However, as later alleged by Rygg, the speculative inflow of foreign currency had by then reached such huge proportions that there was a renewed risk of inflation, a new fall in the external value of the krone, and almost certainly a prospective loss to the consortium. For these reasons the half-hearted attempts to stem the speculative raid were given up, with the result that the krone shot up almost to par (100) by November 1926. The formal return to gold was postponed till 1 May 1928, three years after Britain's return to gold and two years after Denmark's. Thus victory for conventional wisdom.

Rygg and his Critics

In retrospect, Nicolai Rygg succeeded in his long term goal: restoration of the traditional, legal value of the currency. This was the prime objective of any Western central bank governor. It was the cornerstone of the self-regulating system. With respect to the wisdom of the 'par policy' of the 1920s, Rygg was subjected to criticism both for deflating too much in 1921-2, and too little in 1923-4, and again for having deliberately let the krone be swept to par in a raid during 1926, which benefited only the speculators, at least in the short run. One tradition, originating in the 1930s, with historian Wilhelm Keilhau, makes Rygg the scapegoat of almost all the economic adversity that debtors of all categories experienced in the 1920s.[14] A timely reappraisal was attempted by Francis Sejersted in 1973, to the effect that Rygg in his day did what at bottom everyone else tacitly agreed was his job, to bring the country back on to the gold standard, and at the old value.[15] One group of objections has been raised time and again; it stems primarily from authors of a Keynesian persuasion which centres on the adverse economic aspects of Rygg's monetary policy. Why did Rygg so doggedly pursue a policy which in the short-run benefited none but speculators? In other words, why did he not devalue like Finland, or France? Since Norway eventually did so in 1931, this criticism gains added force. Was Rygg in fact, a prejudiced defender of the class interests represented by the creditor side of society?[16] From here the innuendoes degenerate into downright accusations of conspiracy, voiced at the time by the Labour press and later by leftist historians.[17]

The Hornsrud Government 1928

Basis for the conspiracy-accusations is Rygg's alleged action against Norway's first labour government in 1928.[18] At the Storting elections in 1927 the Norwegian Labour Party, now united again with the moderate wing, won 37.1 per cent of the votes, taking 59 out of 150 representatives. This made Labour the largest party in the Storting. Though unable to carry a majority in the Storting, and despite the mistrust that surrounded the party's policy, Labour's chairman Christopher Hornsrud was called by King Haakon to form the next government. The new ministry, appointed on 27 January 1928, was met with nervousness in business circles, and capital was reported to emigrate. The spectre of another bank panic re-entered.

To stem the flight of capital and the possible collapse of the banking system, a group of prominent bankers, shipowners and industrialists had already in 1925 organised a private company, Securitas Ltd, with a view to buying up bank shares and thus preventing their fall in the stock market. Capital was obtained by borrowing from Norges Bank, against guarantees provided by the participants. But the banking crisis continued, despite these efforts, so in 1927 the idea of government backing for continued support purchases was aired. Rygg fell for the idea. A central agency was to accept deposits from private sources and from Norges Bank and place them with banks squeezed by liquidity problems. A proposal for a central public deposit thus lay on the table when the Hornsrud cabinet took office on 28 January 1928. In its government declaration, however, the new cabinet signalled its anti-capitalist intentions with military bluntness. Not mincing its words the Labour government declared in part:

> The goal of the Norwegian Labour Party, as set forth in the party's programme, is to bring about a socialist order in Norway. The government realises that the political constellation at the moment prevents any far-reaching social changes, but it will in all its actions be guided by its concern for the interest of the working class and all the working people, and will facilitate and prepare the transition to a socialistic society.[19]

The declaration was all the more remarkable as the Prime Minister, Christopher Hornsrud, on taking office on Friday 28 January, said in an interview that another era of currency fluctuations must be avoided at all costs.[20] It is also remarkable in view of the comments printed in

Tidens Tegn, an influential Oslo newspaper, on the same day, which emphasized the need for moderation: 'Since the new cabinet is a victory for reformism, we would assume that the government wants to show its ability in positive work, and for that reason it must proceed with a certain amount of caution.'[21] But the Hornsrud government refused state guarantees for a central public deposit with government guarantees. Shortly thereafter, the leading opposition politician, Johan Ludwig Mowinckel of the Liberal Party (Venstre) proposed a vote of no-confidence, after first having conferred with Nicolai Rygg at Norges Bank. The Hornsrud government resigned on 15 February 1928, after a fortnight in power, the most short-lived ministry in the country's history. Mowinckel, who formed the successor cabinet, did not, however, press the plan for central deposit. The endangered banks, which now included the three biggest commercial banks, Den Norske Creditbank, Bergens Privatbank, and Christiania Bank og Kreditkasse, received instead fresh capital and support elsewhere, in part from British banks, authorized by the Bank of England, and were able for the time being to stay afloat. Thus the basis for the conspiracy theory.[22]

Amid all the outpourings that accompanied the events leading to Hornsrud's fall in 1928 and since, perhaps it will suffice here to point out that it was hardly politically wise for a revolutionary party to endorse the exclusive interest of one single class in a situation when it controlled a mere 59 out of 150 representatives in the country's parliament. The essence of the parliamentary game is, after all, to rule in agreement with the majority. Commenting on the socialist failure in Norway, *The Times* observed the obvious when it said that . . . 'Although it was the largest body in Storting, the Labour Party with fifty-nine places out of 150, could only provide a minority Government, and therefore it was clear that a moderate policy alone could obviate a successful attack by its opponents.'[23]

The Gold Standard and the Rule of Law

If one dismisses the conspiracy theory, the continued debate of the monetary events of the 1920s still appears legitimate. The question of why the country returned to gold, for all its historical hindsight, involved the economic fortunes of thousands; the issue dominated the scene for an entire decade, and speculators apart, the outcome must be considered a disaster in an economic context. An answer should be based on the motives of the actors and the information they possessed rather than on the insights and values of a later generation. This brings us to the validity of the context. The opinion here is that Rygg belonged to a world in which the value of the currency was a non-negotiable issue. The view, entirely conventional, harboured the conviction that money and monetary theory were best analysed in isolation, divorced from a consideration of the overall economy. The conviction rested on the liberal doctrine that the tasks of government were´set *ex ante*. The private sphere was private precisely because its boundaries had been drawn up beforehand, the public sphere was public by the same criterion. According to the liberal doctrine, moreover, savings, investments, borrowing, and all the economic decisions belonged to the private sphere. The yardstick for all calculations was the currency. If politicians were to tamper with its value as they thought best, private risk taking would dry up, private calculability would be lost, indeed, society would be subjected to tyranny. Against this background it was understandable that the currency was to be taken out of daily politics. Money was rather a constituent part of the social contract that made up the foundation of society.

The value of money, then, was thus not an economic, but a moral issue. Therefore its value should not be interfered with by either politicians or bankers. Rygg's course of action, set already in 1920, was merely in accord with the conventional world view. His was a generation that was not yet emancipated to the idea that interfering with the value of the money is only one among a bag of tools whereby the government achieves a set of stated policy goals, unbound by any commitment save expediency.[24] This interpretation, proposed by professor Sejersted, reconciles the paradoxical course of events, and explains why Rygg always seemed determined to do the wrong thing, particularly since he and his opponents knew of alternative lines of action. After all, France and Finland devalued.

On closer examination, however, his opponents, farmers and industrial workers, apparently had no practical alternatives. The Labour Party spokesmen, riding two horses, were caught in the dilemma that their demands for higher pay, at a time of falling prices for industrial goods, undermined the basis for industrial employment, hence the welfare of the workers they championed. The agrarian spokesmen offered no clear and responsible alternative till 1926, by which time stabilization, or a *de facto* devaluation, was official policy anyway.

Besides, the demands from the farm organisations were limited in scope to help farmers alone, among them unilateral debt reductions, which their party, Bondepartiet, accomplished by political log rolling in the Storting in 1934.[25] Other sectors increasingly criticised Rygg's handling of the speculative raid in 1926, but dissatisfaction with the speed at which speculators bid the krone up to par value begs the real question, whether opponents possessed any alternative. They had none.[26] In any case, whatever suggestions were offered, among them one from the economists at Oslo University, they all came at a time when the damage had already been done.[27] Finally, looking outside Norway, we see that most Western countries, large and small, returned to a gold exchange standard in the twenties, by way of a period of deflation. At best Norway was exceptional merely in the sense that, prior to the return, the inflation and the depreciation had been more violent, and had lasted longer than in other countries. By the same token, it is possible to reduce the responsibility Rygg had for the outcome. In his absence the country in all probability would have pursued a policy of deflation, by the same means, and with the same outcomes as those that were realized at the time.

Looking back from the perspective of the 1980s, it is easy to predict that no present government would have returned to the old gold standard once the currency had depreciated 95 per cent against the dollar, as was the case by 1924. But it is equally melancholy in retrospect to conclude, that given the insights and values prevalent at the time, Rygg must be exonerated. In a context of relative values and unintended consequences, the only world Rygg and his critics knew, he acted as the high priest of a national sacrifice, no more, no less, by which the nation suffered temporary discomfort in the hope that thereafter a golden age would return, to justify the pain.

However, on a deeper level the responsibility for a political course cannot be shirked by pointing to limited knowledge. Pontius Pilate has never gone down well in history. In the final analysis people will claim justly that Rygg — *de facto* in charge — should have sensed that the world had changed so much that the value of the currency could not be decided in isolation from the real economic situation, and having sensed it, acted upon the new insight. This is what distinguishes the statesman from the moralist, and why perhaps history contains so many of the latter and so few of the former.

Notes

1 Nos XII 163, *National Accounts 1865-1960*, SSB, Oslo 1965, Table 50, pp. 345-6.

2 In the Currency Act of 17 April, 1875, still valid, the Norwegian krone was defined as the equivalent of 0.40323 grammes fine gold. One kilo gold at the then

prevailing prices was defined as the equivalent of 2,480 kroner. On the basis of the weights above, pound sterling equalled 18.16, one US dollar 3.73 Norwegian kroner.

3 Nicolai Rygg, *Norges Banks historie*, II, Oslo 1950, p. 548.

4 *Statistical Survey 1948*, NOS X, 178, Oslo 1949, Tables 160, 161.

5 Nicolai Rygg, *Norges Bank i mellomkrigstiden*, Oslo 1954, p. 172. I owe this point to Tore J. Hanisch, 'Om virkninger av paripolitikken', *Historisk Tidsskrift*, 1979, pp. 240-68.

6 *Kriser och krispolitik i Norden under mellankrigstiden, Nordiska historikermøtet i Uppsala 1974, Møtesrapport*, Uppsala 1974, pp. 31-2.

7 *Statistical Survey 1948*, Table 153.

8 E. Engebretsen, *Norsk bankvesen*, Oslo 1939, p. 104, 195.

9 *Statistical Survey 1948*, Table 168.

10 *Historical Statistics 1968*, XII 245, Oslo 1969, Table 252.

11 *Historical Statistics 1968*, Table 234.

12 Report from the Currency Commission of 8 Sept., 1925, p. 3. Printed in Stortingets records, *Stortingets Forhandlinger 1926*, as Appendix to St. prp. no. 62, p. 3.

13 Ibid., p. 41.

14 Wilhelm Keilhau, *Norsk pengehistorie*, Oslo 1952, and his volume, *Vår egen tid*, Oslo 1938, pp. 432-3. The view is echoed by Erling Petersen, *Den norske Creditbank 1857-1957*, Oslo 1957, pp. 142-4, 255-8, and many others, notably by the editor of *Farmand*, the weekly business magazine.

15 Francis Sejersted, *Ideal, teori og virkelighet. Nicolai Rygg og pengepolitikken i 1920-årene*, Oslo 1973.

16 Øistein Hveding, review of Sejersted, *Historisk Tidsskrift* 1973, pp. 217-46.

17 Edvard Bull, *Klassekamp og fellesskap, 1920-1945*, Oslo 1979, pp. 90-3.

18 Ivar Arne Roset, *Det Norske Arbeiderparti og Hornsrud's regjeringsdannelse*, Oslo 1962, p. 77 – Wilhelm Keilhau, *Vår egen tid*, Oslo 1938, pp. 430-2.

19 Ivar Arne Roset, *Det Norske Arbeiderparti*, p. 77.

20 *Tidens Tegn*, 27 January 1928, p. 1.

21 Ibid., p. 2.

22 Einar Gerhardsen, *Unge år. Erindringer fra århundreskiftet fram til 1940*, Oslo 1974, pp. 222-4, for a repetition of the old view of a coup against the Labour Ministry, hatched by exra-parliamentary forces.

23 *The Times*, Monday 13 February 1928, p. 2.

24 This is the gist of the recent debate on Rygg and the money issues of the 1920s. See Francis Sejersted, *Ideal, teori og virkelighet*, cited above, Øistein Hveding's criticisms in *Historisk Tidsskrift 1973*, pp. 217-46. and Seiersted's rejoinder ibid., 1974, pp. 61-79. An elaboration of Sejersted's position is 'Demokrati og rettsstat – et perspektive på 1800-tallets politiske brytninger', *Historisk Tidsskrift* 1979, pp. 1-42.

25 Øistein Hveding, 'Gjeldsforliket mellom Bondepartiet og Arbeiderpartiet 1934', *Historisk Tidsskrift* 1979, pp. 326-57.

26 Åsmund Egge, 'Naeringslivet og paripolitikken', *Historisk Tidsskrift* 1974, pp. 80-8.

27 Hermod Skånland, *The Norwegian Credit Market since 1900*, Oslo 1967, pp. 161-2.

4 THE INVESTMENT PAUSE IN THE 1920s

Debts and Failure of Investments

The deflationary policies of the 1920s may have been inevitable, given the controlling assumptions among bankers and politicians at the time, but they failed to allay unrest among the industrial workers. We have earlier seen how the conflicts in the labour market in the twenties largely stemmed from the protests against wage cuts which the employers justified by falling living costs.There was another field that equally suffered. Investments tended to be postponed in line with the general contraction. Naturally, business, like any individual, is loath to borrow cheap and pay back dear. Moreover, the bank crisis reduced both willingness and ability among the banks to underwrite new loans. A third point must be noted. During the years 1922-4 the krone remained well below par, but like any *de jure*-devaluation this helped exports. Exports of goods and services were, in fact, buoyant in those years, perhaps contrary to expectations. Earnings made in exports could finance investments, and thus make a firm independent of banks and outside capital. Against this one should remember that the violent krone fluctuations hampered sensible calculations regarding the future. In the next three years, 1925-8, however, the krone appreciated quite drastically. As a result export earnings yielded far less in Norwegian kroner. The drive to par reduced profits, depressed spirits, and also eroded the chances for independent investments and management. Businesses became victims of their debts.

The twenties thus saw major segments of industry, due to shortage of working capital, being taken over by foreign interests. The take-overs usually involved the large, capital intensive companies that represented the most advanced skills and technologies. Debts also engulfed farmers, fishermen, and local government; indeed, problems of debt settlements preoccupied local politics for more than a decade. So they did internationally, as witnessed by the German war reparations to the Western allied governments.

Beginning with industry, we consider first some statistical data. Average share dividends on Oslo's Stock Exchange were 21.1 per cent in 1916, but dropped to 6.3 per cent in 1921 and 4.2 per cent in 1925.[1] The index of share prices for manufacturing stood at 39 in 1921

41

and climbed to par (100) as late as 1937.[2] Issues of industrial shares reached a record of 365 million kroner in 1918. In the following twenty years the figure rose above 40 million only twice, in 1923 and 1930, with 77 and 70 million kroner respectively. Bottom for the decade was 1927, when issues dropped to 11 million, precisely at a time when the speculators bid the krone to par. Only 1932 was poorer.[3]

Norwegian Industry for Sale

Next we turn to the take-overs that caught the headlines. Two new industries, the electrometal and electrochemical, based on the country's ample waterpower reserves and harbour facilities, went through extensive restructuring. In Odda in Hardanger on the west coast, the British-owned calcium carbide and cyanamide plants went bankrupt in 1922. Two years of austerity ensued. In 1924 Norwegian interests formed a new company, Odda Smelteverk A/S, which continued production of carbide. In 1937 after a record of poor earnings, British interests again resumed control. The other plant, near by at Eitrheim, was bought by the Belgian firm Compagnie Royal Asturienne des Mines in 1929. The Belgian firm started zinc production on the basis of an electrolytic method developed by the Anaconda Company of America. About 600 jobs were provided. A third industrial undertaking at Odda, in Tyssedal just outside, was an aluminium smelter, established in 1914 by Sam Eyde, Norway's Prometheus among industrial entrepreneurs at the outbreak of the war. This factory was taken over by the Aluminium Company of America (ALCOA) and British Aluminium Company (BACO) together with the French aluminium company Pechiney in 1922. With control of the markets the internationals saw to it that the plant in Odda could continue, but just barely. In the 21 years 1918-39 the stockholders received dividends only five times. The takeover required permission by the Storting, according to existing concession legislation. It was granted without fuss, for unemployment and unrest threatened the whole community of southern Hardangerfjord.

Another Eyde plant, Arendal Smelteverk of 1912, producing a silicon product (SiC) for the world market, was bought up by the Melltone Corporation, Pittsburgh, in 1928. The carbide firm, A/S Meråker Smelteverk of 1898, up in Trøndelag, was sold to Union Carbide Ltd, Canada, in 1928. The plant, which provided jobs for 500 men, switched to ferro alloys in response to new market signals, and established a name for itself in the alloy field. A/S Bjølvefossen, at Ålvik in Hardangerfjord, tells a similar story. Established in 1905 to utilize a local waterfall for carbide production, the company initiated production in 1916. The plant had 500 employees. In 1928 the Norwegian owners sold a controlling interest to C. Tennant Sons & Co. Ltd, a Scottish company. A/S Bjølvefossen now launched production of ferro silicon on an extensive scale, adding ferro chrome in 1934. Biggest in the alloy field in Norway was Electric Furnace Products Company Ltd, located in Sauda in the fjords further south. A controlling interest passed into the hands of the Union Carbide Corporation group in 1925, whereupon production was switched to alloys, notably manganese and chrome alloys, in all about 50 different products for the world's steelmakers.

Norsk Hydro, the biggest and most publicised of Sam Eyde's industrial undertakings, employing 4000 in 1917[4] went into partnership with the German industrial giant, I.G. Farben, in 1927. Pressed by its competitors, Hydro dropped its old nitrate processing method and adopted the German Haber-Bosch ammonia-based method, saving up to 70 per cent energy. In return I.G. Farben obtained 25 per cent of the Hydro stock. The agreement included the construction of a new nitrate factory at Herøya, Porsgrunn, to be financed by American loans. The new policy undertaken by Hydro represented an example of the international tendency to higher concentration in the chemical industry. The Herøya site was chosen for its excellent harbour facilities. The move from the original sites at Rjukan and Notodden, however, had negative social repercussions that went largely unnoticed. In retrospect short term lay-offs and technological innovation have tended to follow each other, but the transition costs this time fell perhaps too harshly on one side. At any rate, employment at the Hydro plants was reduced from 3456 in 1929 to 2056 by 1935 and Rjukan's population dropped by 29 per cent, down from 9277 in 1920 to 6560 in 1936.[5]

Capital shortage crops up again in the reconstructions of the aluminium industry. A case in point was the agreement in 1926 between the Norwegian company in Høyanger, Norsk Aluminium Company in the west fjords, and ALCOA, whereby ALCOA provided capital and market outlets in return for a 50 per cent interest in the company.

Similarly, the firms in the electro-technical industry, among them Elektrisk Bureau, established 1882, came under foreign control in the 1920s, due to lack of capital. In a futile attempt to reserve the home market for Norwegian workers the Storting in 1927 passed 'the ten per cent bill', which in effect added 10 per cent on foreign bids for deliveries to all high and low voltage installations. Placed at a disadvantage by discriminatory legislation, the foreign companies answered by buying up interests in Norwegian firms whereby they evaded the customs barrier. Thus the country, unable to isolate itself from foreign competition, got access to the best vintage technology and products. An American multinational company like ITT represented not only the most advanced cable products, it was also a pioneer in introducing time and motion studies to ensure the workers' acceptance of pay rates based on productivity performance.

The pulp and paper industry, the country's first large scale mechanized industry, was also affected by the deflation. It too suffered from the tendency to chronic saturation and oversupply, following Finland's and Canada's entry into the market. With modern plants constructed early in the 1920s, the latter were better able to absorb price reductions. The Norwegian firms, by contrast, now reaped the disadvantage of the first starters. Union Co, Skien, one of Scandinavia's biggest paper makers, paid no dividends on ordinary shares for twenty years. In the eleven years 1922-33 alone the company wrote off 45 million kroner. The repeated writedowns forced its bank connection, Centralbanken for Norge, into receivership in 1924 and final liquidation in 1928. Centralbanken for Norge was the country's largest investment bank, its demise an earthquake that served once again to undermine confidence in the financial institutions, both at home and abroad. In 1934 control over Union Co passed into the hands of Hambro's Bank, London. Follum paper mill was bought by British interests in 1927. The takeover price, 27.5 per cent of nominal value for the ordinary shares, offered an index to the situation.

The mining industry, already largely controlled by foreign interests, also underwent a period of write downs and refinancing, whereby the foreign-held share of the capital stock increased from an average 45 pre cent in 1919 to 74 per cent by 1936. Between the two dates the face value of all mining shares dropped from 146 to 70 million kroner. Since the index of share prices was 39 in 1921 against 88 in 1936, and the consumer price index 102 and 57, we may say that mining share capital remained static for fifteen years 1921-36. In fixed prices this represented full stagnation. Exports, notably of iron ore, picked up in the next decade (see Figure 4.1).

The sell-out wave also engulfed the match industry. In 1927 Ivar Kreuger, the world's match king, controlling the International Match Corporation, bought up the two largest Norwegian match factories. The purchase gave Kreuger a Norwegian market share of 95 per cent. Nestlé & Anglo Swiss Condensed Milk Co already controlled the con-

Figure 4.1: Value of Output from Norwegian Mining 1900-1947.
Current Kroner

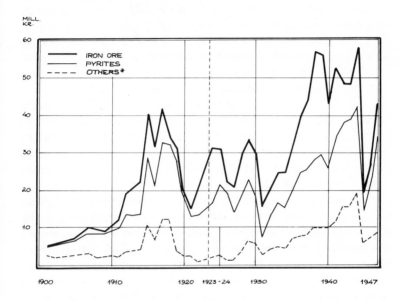

MILL.
KR.

Source: *Teknisk Ukeblad* 5 September 1949, p. 540.
*Molybdenite, Lead, Zinc, Ilmenite, Nickel, Copper, Silver and Cobalt

densed milk industry. In 1929 Lord Leverhulme and Unilever obtained
a controlling interest in the country's largest margarine company, Agra
Margarinfabrik, Oslo. In 1931 Unilever, UK, through an exchange of
stock extended its influence to the entire fats and oil industry. Already
in 1913 Lord Leverhulme of Port Sunlight had bought a working control of De Nordiske Fabrikker, Fredrikstad, the country's largest whale
oil processor. In 1924 DeNoFa began marketing the well known Lever
brands 'Sunlight', 'Lux', and 'Rinso', until then imported from England.
The biggest soap manufacturer, Lilleborg Fabrikker, Oslo, felt the
crunch. In 1929 a merger was agreed. In return ᶠ ₜ a part of DeNoFa's
stock, Lilleborg offered its competitor 50 per cent of its own. The take-
over, due to the concession laws, required government approval. Despite
criticism, this was given by the liberal government, headed by Mr Johan
Ludwig Mowinckel. Coming as a climax of a series of takeovers, the
matter caused a political crisis. Mowinckel resigned on 9 May 1931,
and was succeeded by a ministry from the Farmers' Party. The irony
was that the successor government let the concession stand, a loss of

prestige for a government that owed its existence to blocking just that concession.

As seen, the lack of capital strength in industrial companies paved the way for a veritable invasion of foreign capital into Norwegian industry towards the end of the twenties. That the key factor was lack of capital is illustrated by what happened in the tobacco industry. The firms here, notably J.L. Tiedemanns Tobaksfabrik, a family firm, rode on a wave of increasing sales and profits, which reflected the market expansion for cigarettes in that decade. As a result they acquired sufficient internal reserves to prevent BATCO, i.e. British-American Tobacco Company, from getting control of the Norwegian tobacco market. After fifteen years of industrial warfare BATCO teamed up with J.L. Tiedemanns Tobaksfabrik and launched a 50-50 firm, Norsk Engelsk Tobaksfabrik (NETO), to market the BATCO brands. This could not be called a victory for BATCO. Typically, Tiedemann's success stemmed from its ultra-modern advertising and marketing methods, now deployed in an American way against the British-American cigarette trust. In turn Joh. H. Andresen (1888-1953), Tiedemann's owner, ranked as one of the country's wealthiest men in the 1930s.

The above is not an exhaustive survey, but the sketch suffices to underline the far-reaching effects of the deflationary policies on the fortunes of Norwegian industry in the 1920s. In the aggregate, foreign

Table 4.1: Capital Stock in Norwegian Corporations 1919-1936, Mill. Kroner, and Foreign-held Share of the Total

	1919		1936	
	Total capital stock mill. kr	Foreign-held %	Total capital stock mill. kr	Foreign-held %
Mining	146	44.5	70	74.2
Manufacturing	1203	11.6	92.9	22.5
Water transport	1110	1.8	406	5.7
Financial institutions			336	1.5
Trade	1058	1.2	226	12.4
Others	162	7.4	56	1.8
	3726	6.7	2023	15.7

Source: Arthur Stonehill, *Foreign Ownership in Norwegian Enterprises*, Oslo 1965, pp. 44, 47.

capital by 1936 loomed quite large. See Table 4.1. In manufacturing the share of foreign interests increased from 11.6 to 22.5 per cent of total capital between 1919 and 1936. In mining the share held by foeigners increased from 44.5 to 74.2 per cent. Overall, foreigners owned 6.7 per cent of corporate capital in 1919 against 15.7 per cent in 1936. In absolute figures the foreign capital amounted to 250 million inflated kroner in 1919 against 318 million in 1936. Between the two world wars foreign-held capital in Norwegian corporate industry thus more than doubled. To set the above figures in perspective, we should remember that foreign-held capital in Norwegian industrial companies was 38.8 per cent in 1909, or 115 million kroner in absolute figures.[6]

Electrification halted

Water power construction also now suffered a setback. In 1922 generator capacity was 975 megawatts as against 1377 mw by the end of 1939. This gives a rate of growth of 2 per cent annually. But in the period 1900-20 the average rate of increase had been 11.2 per cent, or five times higher. Again in the years 1946-66 the annual rate of increase ws 6.2 per cent, or more than three times higher.[7] The figures expose the weakness of hydroelectric development: its near exclusive dependence on foreign markets. When the electrochemical market stopped expanding after the war, the power companies, notably the municipal companies, fell upon hard times, since alternative outlets for electricity were difficult to find. It was only during the late thirties that urban households came to use electric energy for purposes other than lighting. Besides, the gasworks had long since established their networks, and gas competed successfully with electricity in such fields as heating and cooking until the end of World War II. There were 17 gasworks in as many towns, the first dating back to the 1850s.

The retrenchment is underscored by the fact that NVE, the Norwegian River and Electricity Board, had one single construction assignment during the twenty years following its establishment in 1920. The project was the construction of Nore I power plant in Buskerud county during the years 1924-8. The project, financed mainly by the municipality of Oslo, provided welcome orders for the mechanical industry and electro-technical firms in an otherwise bleak period.[8] The majority of the power plants owned by local governments had been financed during the inflationary years with short-term loans. Deflation and drastically reduced sales of energy brought several power companies to bankruptcy. Their difficulties tended to drag down the local municipality as well. According to a survey in June 1929 the rural electricity companies had spent 481 million kroner on electrification, 431 million with the aid of short-term borrowing. At the same time their assessed value stood at 399 million, or less than outstanding debts. Raising delivery prices offered scant hopes, nor did the local tax revenue prospects show signs of improvement.

The solution was to bring political pressure to bear in the Storting. In 1927 funds were voted for the establishment of a state government bank for assisting municipalities in financial distress. The Norwegian Municipal Bank provided conversion loans at reduced interest rates and extended repayment periods. In this way the prior creditors, most often the local savings banks, were saved from bankruptcy through the default of their customers.[9] The municipal debt as noted earlier more than quintupled during the period 1915-25, up from 254 million to 1,501 million kroner.

Budget cuts in local and central government became the order of the day. Public investments languished, notably railway and road construction. Emergency works, a traditional antidote against unemployment, thus failed to win majority support in the Storting till 1935.

Crisis in the primary Sector: The Fisheries

The fisheries had enjoyed a favourable market situation during the war, while operating with state guaranteed minimum prices. For a time the fishermen had ample capital in their hands, and investments in boats and gear shot up. They owned 4937 decked vessels in 1914 as against 7710 in 1918 and 10929 in 1929.[10] The number of open motor vessels was 2472 in 1914 against 9432 in 1929.[11] Fishing capacity swelled mightily, but so did income expectations.

After the war fish products faced declining prices. The downward trend was not accompanied by a fall in the prices of inputs, gasoline, gear, and debt payments among them. The govenment was forced to assist in various ways. The measures came *ad hoc* in response to crisis symptoms; as yet there was no idea for a permanent system of state subsidies for the fisheries. In 1921 the gasoline price was reduced by an appropriation of 5 million kroner, the government paid for freight reductions, and the Storting voted 2.3 million kroner in support of purchases of new fishing gear. In addition, the Storting placed at the fishermen's disposal a guarantee of 1 million kroner for expected losses of gear during the stormy weather of March 1920. Finnmark, in the extreme north, obtained a special appropriation of 1.7 million kroner as government purchase guarantees during the spring and summer fisheries of 1921. More general government guarantees were introduced for exports of klippfish to offset losses in the uncertain export markets.[12] These amounted to 4 million kroner in 1927 and increased steadily.[13] The above suffices to suggest the general drift towards increased central government responsibility for fishermen's incomes in the twenties.

New technology and new income horizons now combined in a vicious circle. The result was to ensure chronic overproduction. To maintain incomes the fishermen doubled their efforts, only to press prices still further. The price for 100 kg klippfish was 35 kroner in 1924, but 13 kroner in 1926. The appreciation of the krone during the latter year tended to victimize particularly the debtors in the economy. The fishermen moreover almost alone bore the brunt of the battle, staged by the anti-alcohol movement, to turn the country into a nation of teetotallers. A consultative referendum in 1919 gave a weak majority for a ban on alcohol. In September 1921 the Storting passed a permanent ban on all liquor. The 'wine-countries', France, Spain, Italy and Portugal, immediately retaliated by cutting down their imports of Norwegian fish, which was boycotted until 1923, when Norway exempted wine with an alcoholic content of up to 20 per cent. After six years of moonshining, smuggling and illicit drinking, the crusade against alcohol appeared a failure. Another referendum taken 18 October 1926, confirmed the disillusionment among the voters: 531000 voted against continuance of the alcohol ban, 423000 voted for it.

At a time when the traditional fish products had a rough time, new ideas for new products spread more easily. The fishmeal and fishoil industries had their sunrise in the twenties, while porbeagle, caught on the banks outside Måløy, was introduced as a new export article abroad. The success of the new growth sectors attracted fresh capital and entrepreneurship, and provided a welcome opening for labour threatened by idleness. The fishmeal factories, by processing herring into edible fats and oil, removed some of the downward pressure on herring prices. On the whole, however, the entire fishing sector presented a picture of small agents, each helpless in the face of a disorganised market. This applied to exporters, processors and fishermen alike. In 1926, the fishermen set up a branch organisation, Norges Fiskarlag (Norway's Federation of Fishermen), a countrywide interest organisation that sought control over prices and quantities in order to ensure some security for the average operator or fisherman.

The efforts at cartellisation, however, became important only in the following decade. The government provided capital for a special fishermen's bank, Statens Fiskarbank (the Government Bank for Fishermen), established 1919. The bank offered easy mortgage loans for small fishing vessels. In addition, a government research agency, Det Norske Fiskeri-direktorat (the Norwegian Fishery Directorate), organised in 1900, helped in a variety of ways to spread knowledge of new methods and new gear, while conducting minor experiments of its own. The work proceeded cautiously, in order not to challenge the traditional forms of ownership and the seasonal nature of fishing in the northern coastal districts. As yet the Directorate's efforts were negligible, but its role as catalyst for innovations tended to grow as the amount of venture capital increased and continuous fishing replaced seasonal operations.[14]

Figure 4.2 shows how the enormously increased catches of the 1920s contrasted with declining total sales values. Landings increased from 484 thousand tons in 1920 to about a million tons in 1930, after which the volume stagnated for a decade. The doubling of volume was paid less and less, down from 97 million to 90 million kroner in 1930, which even allowing for the revaluation of the currency, still represents a decline in real terms. The divergent paths show up particularly if one compares 1916 with 1933. In the former year 80,000 fishermen received 162 million kroner for 515 thousand tons; in 1933, the nadir for the interwar period, they landed one million tons and were paid 69 million kroner.[15] The fishermen, moreover, saw no reduction of their numbers, which would have left those remaining with more to share; on the contrary, with America practically closed to unskilled labour from abroad, and the industrial sector at home in depression, the number of Norwegian fishermen tended to pick up in the interwar period. They numbered 107 thousand in 1920, including those with fishing as secondary occupation, and 102 thousand in 1930, but in 1939 the figure had increased to 124 thousand, up 22 per cent in the thirties.[16] In the extreme north, the situation deteriorated so much that outright cases of malnutrition or starvation were reported, notably among the coastal Lapps of Finnish descent in Finnmark.

Since about 90 per cent of the landings were destined for exports, the difficulties stemmed ultimately from declining market conditions abroad. Low income elasticities for food now combined with saturation of markets to reduce the buying power of the coastal population engaged in fishing, which still made up 30 per cent of the total population.

To cope with the situation the government and spokesmen for the fisheries in the next decade took steps to organise the various interests into strong organisations, backed by far-reaching cartel legislation. This proved the beginning of the later era of state subsidised fisheries.

Figure 4.2: Landings of Fish in 1000 Tons and their Value in Million
Kroner, Compared to the Value of Whale Oil Production 1914-1939

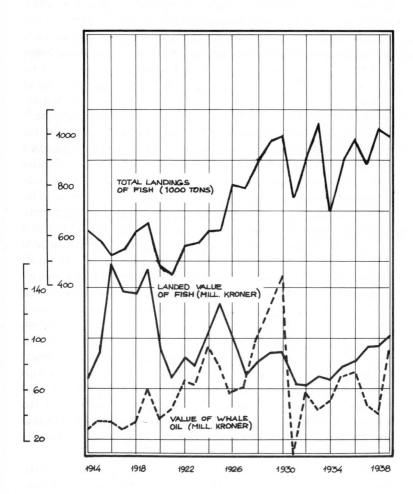

Source: *Historical Statistics 1968*, Tables 28, 29.

Agriculture's Structural Problem

The war had boosted both total agricultural production and the levels
of efficiency in terms of yield per land unit or annual milk volume per
cow. The threat of blockade had even resulted in orders from the

government providing for compulsory production. With the reopening of markets and trade routes after the war, grain prices fell and the farmers were hurt. Unlike the fishermen the agrarian interest was able to organise collective action immediately.

The Liberal Party of 1884 (Venstre) had served as a useful vehicle for nineteenth century political emancipation. Now that the political demands had long since been met, the purely economic interests of the agrarians needed a separate organisation. In 1896 they had set up Norsk Landmandsforbund (The Norwegian Federation of Agriculturalists), an interest organisation, on the pattern of Bund der Landwirte (1892) in Germany. The situation in 1920 called for more direct political action. The result was the establishment in 1921 of Norges Bondeparti, a farmers' party, which immediately began campaigning for corn protection and state subsidies for agriculture. Political pressure came from the producer rather than the consumer side. At the Storting elections in 1921 the new party won 17 representatives, polling 110,000 votes (13.1 per cent) mostly from the old Liberal Party.

In ideology conservative and nationalist, the Farmers' Party mainly voiced the economic interests of the upper strata of rural society, notably in the counties of Oppland and Trøndelag, which also presented the strongest signs of class differentiation. The party's affiliation to the Landmandsforbund, from 1920 rechristened Norges Bondelag (Norway's Federation of Farmers), was very strong; the party's chairman, Johan Mellbye, was also chairman of Norges Bondelag. The smallholders, long the political base of Venstre, the old Liberal Party, had banded together a few years earlier to set up their own interest organisation, Norsk Bonde- og Småbrukarlag (1913) (The Norwegian Federation of Farmers and Smallholders), to seek political influence for the smallholders. The programme favoured the consumer interests rather than those of the producers. The latent conflict between Venstre and Norges Bondeparti surfaced time and again, and eventually paved the way for the farm party's compromise with the left, with Labour in 1935 whose voters, beside the farmers, may have been most adversely affected by the interwar depression.

The economic reality was that with some exceptions the country by now had achieved almost 100 per cent self-sufficiency in food. Bread grain, that is wheat, tended to come from the USA and Canada, when normal trade routes reopened. An increase of farm incomes in real terms could be achieved by widening the market for farm products. Exports, however, were not a likely outlet for surplus production, since other industrialised nations were in a situation similar to

Norway's. All tended to reserve their internal markets for the produce of their own farmers, and increasingly farm imports were restricted to types of food where shortages existed. Canadian wheat exports to Europe are a case in point, another is Danish food exports to Britain, 55 per cent of Denmark's commodity exports. Reducing the number of farmers might be another solution. This would become more imperative if the farmers continued, as they had done in the past, to raise productivity levels through qualitative improvements of the input factors. (See Figure 4.3.) At this point the low income elasticities for food stuffs must be recalled. Typically they fluctuated around 0.4 to 0.5 for grains, potatotes, meat and around 0.6 for milk, fruit and vegetables. This meant that if the consumers increased their incomes by 10 per cent, demand for food would go up by a mere 4-5 per cent. Income increases, in other words, would only to a small extent be attracted to farm products. The agrarian economy had reached a point of general and lasting saturation.

In retrospect one notices a gap between the political definition of the agricultural problem and the economic definition sketched here. This explains why contemporary observers exaggerated what politics and politicians could do. The political composition of the Storting tells part of the story; a majority of its members still had a rural background. The figures for occupational distribution point in the same direction: 35.8 per cent of the work force was registered in primary occupations in 1930, of which 26.1 per cent was in agriculture, the rest in forestry, fishing, and whaling, but they produced only 16.7 per cent of the gross national product that year.[17] Perhaps the sheer weight of history was decisive for the inability to see demand and supply of farm products together. At any rate the longterm prospects of the agricultural sector were not stated at all, or when stated, expressed in misleading terms. Thus there was much talk of the profitability of agriculture, when in reality the issue at stake was subsidies or transfers to farmers.

The twenties thus witnessed a double attack on the farmers. Like other debtor groups they were hurt by increased debt payments, following the deflationary policies in the 1920s when the krone appreciated its internal value by something like 55 per cent. The debt as a percentage of assessed farm values was 44.5 per cent for middle farmers, and 50 per cent for smallholders in 1932,[18] or 45.2 per cent as an overall average, as against 37.9 per cent in 1914.[19] In addition, the farmers laboured against the constraints of a permanently saturated market. The irony was that any increase in production or productivity

Figure 4.3: Yield Per Decare, 5 Year Moving Averages 1900-1967
Feed Units*

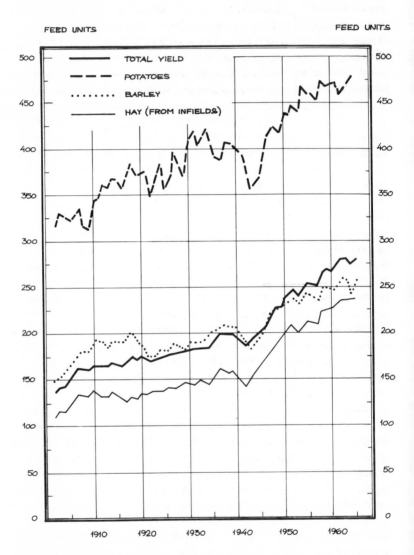

Source: *Historical Statistics 1968*, p. 128.
*1 Feed Unit (F.E.) = The Nutritional Value of 1kg of Barley.

merely served to erode still further their income situation. The population figures offered dim hopes: the nation counted 2.6 million inhabitants in 1920 and 3.2 million in 1946, which yields an average rate of growth of 0.8 per cent annually. Hence the farmers could not expect rescue from a widening home market. Moreover, jobs were difficult to obtain in industry, and increasingly, the free labour market in the USA closed up after 1920. The usual avenues of escape failed in the interwar years. The resulting desperation surfaced in the next decade in political movements to both the right and left end of the spectrum.

Farm Support Programmes

In the 1920s the farm support policies vacillated between market economy measures and purely social relief programmes. It was typical of the transition period. Initially, the farmers' spokesmen demanded programmes for reducing farm debts, to offset a rising debt burden, due to a higher valued krone. Indeed, the government owed them relief, for they had no responsibility for the war time inflation, when they had borrowed money cheaply. Mental barriers at first prevented any positive response on this score. After all, outright debt liquidation smacked of Bolshevik radicalism, from which most farmers recoiled.

Another demand was permanent support for domestic grain producers. Temporary measures had been in effect during the war. In 1927 a state purchasing agency was set up. By legislation in the following year the present state agency, Statens Kornforretning, obtained a monopoly on all imports of grain and flour. Retail and wholesale trade at home remained in private hands. The agency was bound to buy all home-produced grain at prices above those in the international grain markets, and the costs were debited against the national budget, i.e. the taxpayers. The producers also received subsidies for the quantities consumed on the farm, to offset any price gap. By later legislation the support programme, which proved permanent, included purchases of fertilisers and cattle feed concentrates.

A third feature was state aid for creating new smallhold farms, the beginnings of which may be traced back to the 1850s. From 1920 the settlement programme got under way, with fresh government funds, up from 21,000 additional decares of fully cultivated land in 1921 to an annual 72,300 decares new land in 1930. Legislation in 1927 gave the local municipalities the right to expropriate suitable land for the settlement programmes. The extent of internal new cultivation was impressive. State aid resulted in 1.2 million decares of fully cleared farm land during the years 1920-50. By comparison the country's total farm area, fully cleared, ranged between 7.2 million and 8.3 million decares.[20] A welcome new line for the smallholders in the west fjords was fox farming, the raising of blue and silver fox and mink, for fashion-conscious ladies at home and abroad. Not surprisingly with so much new land brought under cultivation at a time of saturation, the income gap between farmers and income earners in other sectors was bound to increase. Table 4.2 illustrates the gap and hints at the deterioration in the terms of trade for farm products.

Table 4.2: Gross Domestic Product at Current Prices per Person Employed. Ratios between three main sectors for selected years 1865-1960.

Ratios between sectors	1865	1875	1890	1900	1910	1930	1950	1960
Manufacturing: agriculture	2.70	1.86	1.85	1.68	1.73	2.46	1.85	1.93
Services: manufacturing	1.43	1.55	1.79	1.91	1.47	1.24	1.36	1.33
Services: agriculture	3.91	2.88	3.30	3.20	2.55	3.05	2.53	2.57

Source: Juul Bjerke, *Trends in the Norwegian Economy*, Table 25.

Table 4.2 shows that in 1910 gross productivity per employed person in manufacturing was 70 per cent higher than in agriculture, but 150 per cent higher in 1930. The potential gain from transferring labour from agriculture to sectors with higher productivity also inched upwards. Estimates of the transfer gains for the decade 1930-9 suggest that these may have amounted to 33 per cent of the annual GNP growth per person of the economically active population.[21] The costs to the taxpayers of the farm support programmes were as yet modest, but they point to the farmers' ability to organise in defence of their interests. The next decade saw their near total departure from the market economy.

Notes

1 *Historical Statistics 1968*, Table 267.
2 Ibid., Table 266.

3 Ibid., Table 264.
4 Kristian Anker Olsen, *Norsk Hydro gjennom 50 år*, Oslo, 1955, p. 277.
5 Ibid., pp. 278, 391, 392.
6 *Fabriktaellingen i Norge 1909*, NOS V, 147, Oslo, 1911, vol. 1, p. XXXI.
7 *Historical Statistics 1968*, Table 147.
8 Johan Vogt, *Elektrisitetslandet Norge*, Oslo, 1971, p. 110.
9 Dag Karmly, *Norges Kommunalbank 1927-1977*, Oslo, 1977, p. 20.
10 *Historical Statistics 1968*, Table 116.
11 Ibid., Table 116.
12 *Farmand*, 5 January 1922, p. 18.
13 K. Fasting, *Vintersildsoga, Norges Sildesalslag 1930-1960*, Bergen 1960, p. 160.
14 Leiv Norstrand, *Fiskeridirektoratet og den tekniske utvikling i norsk fiske på 1900-tallet*, Historical Institute, Univ. of Bergen, forthcoming.
15 *Historical Statistics 1968*, Table 120.
16 *Historical Statistics 1968*, Table 115.
17 Juul Bjerke, *Langtidslinjer*, Tables 20, 21. Einar Hope, *Naeringsøkonomiske oversikter*, 3 vols, Oslo, 1972, vol. I, p. 85.
18 Nicolai Rygg, *Norges Bank i mellomrigstiden*, Oslo, 1954, p. 528.
19 *Statistical Survey 1948*, NOS X, 178, Oslo 1949, Table 67.
20 *Historical Statistics 1968*, Tables 82, 85.
21 Preben Munthe, *Sirkulasjon, inntekt og økonomisk vekst*. Universitetsforlaget 1976, p. 312.

5 THE PROBLEM OF GROWTH AND STAGNATION

What Went Wrong in the 1920s?

Looking back at the situation sketched above in major manufacturing industries, and at the lot of the fishermen and the farmers, one is perhaps tempted to conclude that the decade of the twenties was one of unbroken gloom. This was not the case: the twenties saw the rise of a series of growth industries, among them pelagic whaling, the introduction of motorpowered ships, new electrical household goods, advertising, and new consumption patterns associated with the automobile, cinema, radio, bicycle, and the outdoor culture of sports and recreation. Internationally, these developments gave rise to a number of new industries. They may be termed growth industries, by virtue of their rates of growth of employment, turnovers, productivity levels, and their superior returns to labour and capital. The 'sunrise' industries in the twenties, notably in the United States, illuminate the structural tensions inherent in the process of economic development. Their checquered rise in Norway in the interwar years provides an opportunity to say something about the general and specific forces that shaped the course of economic development in the period.

Looking back on those years, the present generation is conditioned to view the economy through Keynesian eyes. According to Keynesian economic theory that gained ascendancy after World War II, the question of sustained economic growth and full employment was simple. Given the necessary powers the authorities either alone or with help from the private sector, would be able to keep effective demand in line with current production, if necessary by resorting to deficit budgeting. Growth could in theory be planned and implemented by bureaucrats trained in economics at a university. At bottom growth was a matter of stimulating demand. The locus of interest clearly was on the demand side. This view tended to underrate the importance of new inventions and technological innovations for economic growth. By contrast, the Harvard economist, Joseph Schumpeter, Keynes' contemporary, who most consistently emphasised the role of innovation and entrepreneurs for new investments and growth, failed to capture the headlines. His views were nearly forgotten for twenty years, following World War II. And yet when the two are juxtaposed, one easily observes a missing premise in the Keynesian doctrine. The tacit but false premise is that people tend to ask for the same goods *ad infinitum.* This is contrary to experience. Demand patterns do tend to shift. The shifts are linked to changes in personal incomes in a well known manner, and conveniently expressed in figures for income elasticities. By the same token they are causally linked with the sequence of the rise and fall of new products and new industries, as described by the Schumpeterian system. To come to grips with the events in the interwar economy, then, one has to make a distinction between old sectors with saturated demand and new sectors in which potential demand lies dormant. The latter may be turned into growth sectors if capital, innovations, and entrepreneurial skills are deployed.

So much for the general economic mechanisms visible in the interwar years. As for the specific causal sequences observable in the Norwegian economy, no single explanation is likely to carry conviction. The view argued here concerning the forces of growth and stagnation, may thus be taken as a plausible point of view. It runs as follows: when the escape of surplus labour to America was brought to a permanent halt in the twenties, an important condition for growth disappeared. On one level the ban meant that the transfer of workers from sectors with low pay to sectors with higher returns was barred. For the Norwegian economy capital formation was impeded. The immigration ban in the United States meant in effect that the primary sector began to pile up labour. The workers trapped in rural areas tended to bring down the whole national income level. The alternative route of escape had been employment in industry at home. But owing to a variety of difficulties, the home industrial sector absorbed few additional workers in the fifteen years 1920-35. (See Table 5.1). According to Table 5.1 total manhours in industry amounted to 317 million in 1920, but as late as 1935 the figure was only slightly higher at 326 million. Population figures by contrast suggest that 183,000 young persons of working age entered the labour market in the decade of the twenties and 285,000 persons the following decade. The figures for industrial manhours and total available work force contrast sharply.

At this point we should remember the difficulties that faced the manufacturing industries in the 1920s. It was industry which previously had provided most of the capital and jobs for the new recruits to the labour market. But owing to difficulties in the export markets, deflation and currency fluctuations, investment opportunities and earnings, generally, were limited in these years. Therefore, the home economy was on the whole unable to generate either markets or buying

Table 5.1: Indices of Production in Selected Industries (1900 = 100) and Total Manhours in Industry 1900 − 1939 (in Millions)

Year	Iron & metal	Wood industry	Pulp & paper	Textiles	Food & beverages	Metal extrac- tion & mining	Chem- icals	Man hours (million)
1900	100	100	100	100	100	100	100	223
1910	137	87	197	130	125	310	336	303
1915	198	92	266	146	151	929	804	372
1920	239	96	254	103	153	490	822	317
1925	233	99	325	121	160	1,300	639	306
1930	301	98	376	148	163	2,050	1,480	309
1935	316	97	396	186	175	2,360	1,420	326
1939	457	135	450	223	210	3,390	1,830	391

Source: G. Stoltz, *Økonomisk Utsyn 1900-1950*, SØS nr. 3, Oslo 1955, p. 195; *Historical Statistics 1968*, Table 130.

power for newer goods. A breakthrough for the mass consumption articles occurred only after World War II.

The outcome stemmed either from lack of capital or lack of entrepreneurs, the closing-up of traditional markets, or a combination of these factors. Shortage of risk capital acted as a brake on new investments, and hence on the normal structural shifts that occur when input factors are transferred from stagnating to expanding sectors. The lack of risk capital, however, points further to the absence of entrepreneurs and markets, both at home and abroad. Indeed, one may push the quest for causes one step further and argue that the signs of stalling observable in the interwar economy were ultimately due to the disappearance of export markets for traditional export products. However, the view that stagnation symptoms were due to a single cause may prove misplaced. In order to bring out more clearly why, we turn to a review of two central growth sectors in the interwar years, whaling and shipping.

Whaling: a New Growth Sector

Both whaling and shipping are old trades of the country, but in the interwar years they showed all the characteristics of new growth sectors. They did so by virtue of a series of inventions and innovations whose linkages to the rest of the economy provided outlets for considerable amounts of capital and labour.[1] Their development contrasts sharply with the performance recorded by other sectors.

The ban against whaling in Norwegian coastal waters, effective from January 1904, had goaded the hunters to seek out new whaling grounds. Far a brief period they hunted off Spitzbergen, Greenland, Jan Mayn, the Shetland and Faroe Islands. The war of 1914-18 had brought a pause. The new era started elsewhere however, in the Antarctic, and the beginning came in 1905. In that year Chr. Christensen (1845-1923) of Sandefjord sent his whaler 'Admiralen' to the distant waters of the Antarctic to hunt the big blue whales off the coast of the British-owned Falkland Islands. The 'Admiral', originally a steamship bulk carrier of 1517 gross registered tons built in Britain in 1869, had been fitted out with a boiler and storage tanks so that the whale carcasses could be processed to oil on board, the ship subsequently returning to Europe with the oil after the hunting season. The 'Admiral' was in fact a shorebound floating factory. The oil found an expanding market in the armament industry. Around 1910 new methods for hardening the oil opened new prospects of using whale oil in margarine and soap at competitive prices for the world market. The expedition was a success, and soon Christensen was followed by neighbours, whalers from Sandefjord, Tønsberg, and Larvik. The towns became for a time a world centre for the new industry. In 1911 the Norwegians accounted for 77 per cent of total world production. The value of whale oil processed by the Norwegians in that year was 36 million kroner. The figure compared well with total landing value in the fisheries, which amounted to 54 million kroner.

Expeditions to the Antarctic were resumed in 1919, and the earnings were rumoured to be excellent. The bonanza profits lured capital and men into the industry. With capital available the entrepreneurs could underwrite risks and experiments. The time was ripe for inventions. Some sort of linkage was present, for the number of patents taken out in whaling culminated with the peak of investments.[2] At the same time prices fell. The squeeze reinforced the search for new cost-saving technology. The patents plotted in a diagram present a bell-shaped graph, or the typical S-shaped curve, which portrays a life cycle for both a product and a business sector, roughly during the period 1900-60.[3] One major innovation was the hauling-up slip, patented by Petter Sørrle in 1922. The slipway made it possible to haul the whale, tail first, directly onto the aft deck, where the men could flense the carcass and then drop the blubber directly into the boilers. Another innovation was the oil separator that replaced the older method of distilling. A third was the evaporator unit which made it possible to distil fresh water out of seawater. A fourth novelty was the radio that enabled the ships of the whale expedition to keep in touch regardless of distance or weather.

As a result the factory ships were emancipated from their earlier dependence on the British authorities in the Falkland archipelago. It was no longer necessary to ask permission to land their carcasses on British territory for processing or request to anchor in shorebound waters. The new technology turned whaling into a fully pelagic business, a business adrift in the open seas. Money was poured back. New special ships were ordered with tonnage up to 20,000 gross tons, against 1,517 tons for the 'Admiral'. When Anders Jahre's 'Kosmos I' of 19,000 tons put to sea in 1929, she was Norway's largest ship, and the world's largest cargo ship. Processing capacity soared, up from about 600 barrels circa 1914 to 2,500 barrels per day in the late twenties. Inevitably the success of the Norwegian companies, among them Pelagos, Tønsberg Hval, Kosmos, and Rosshavet, attracted foreigners into the field. Foremost among them were the Japanese, followed by the British and Germans. As a consequence the Norwegian share of whale oil production fell from 65 per cent of the world total in 1927 to 45.8 per cent in 1936, and by 1938 Norway's share of Antarctic catches was a mere 29.9 per cent.[4]

Skilled gunners were reported to make up to £5,000 in one season; ordinary crew made less. Until 1930 the whole business basked in financial success. In that year, the record for the interwar period, 6,400 Norwegian men in the Antarctic produced whale oil valued in total at 150 million kroner. The output per man was of the order of 23,500 kroner. Compare this figure with those in the Norwegian fisheries. In the same year 74,000 fishermen, participating in the major commercial fisheries, hauled up fish valued at a total of 90 million kroner. The average per participant was thus 1,216 kroner, or twenty times less than in whaling. In fact, for several years in the twenties six thousand men in whaling achieved almost twice as much in total sales as 70-80,000 fishermen. The uneven development, seen in Fig. 5.1, was only less spectacular in the thirties. Overhead expenditures were far higher in whaling than in the fisheries, yet there can be no doubt that returns to labour and capital were considerably higher in whaling. The income gap was probably an extreme example of the gap between best and second best resource use; if so, it illustrates vividly the way in which economic growth occurs, that is, in the appearance of new lines of activity outside existing firms, products or technology. These new businesses, utilising a technological innovation, have high productivity levels, growth, and superior returns to productive factors. Thus, they help to raise the average level of incomes for the entire economy.

Figure 5.1: Number of Patents taken out in Whaling (A) and Prices of Whaling Products (B) 1880-1968

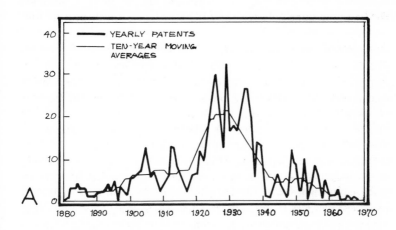

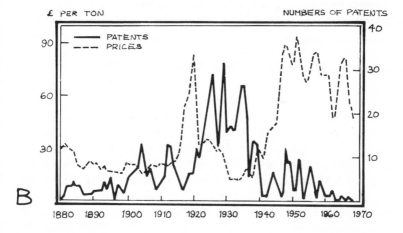

Source: Bjorn L. Basberg, 'Patents, Innovations and Technological Development in Norwegian Whaling 1880-1968', in *World Patent Information*', Vol. 3, No. 1, pp. 19-22, 1981.

The whaling industry illustrates the Schumpeterian prediction that crisis or depression is overcome by innovation. A recent study of the industry shows that throughout the period 1880-1970 there has been a negative correlation between prices and patents, see Fig. 5.1. The price decline was most pronounced in the 1920s, but the number of new patents, indeed the peak in patent activity also occurred in that decade. The coincidence supports the hypothesis that responses to falling prices and depression generally spark the attempts at cost-cutting by way of patented new technology. The secular long term trend in patents taken out in the whaling industry 1880-1970 is clearly bell-shaped. Its form suggests the life cycle for the patents, the product and the industry.

In the interwar period whaling, though admittedly of restricted dimensions in the overall economy, possessed just the right mix of ingredients: a new resource, new technology, initial high returns to capital and labour, and strong linkages with shipbuilding and engineering. Reality fits the description to 1930, when the symptoms of glutted markets and collapsing prices signalled the end of the sunrise era. In that year the Dutch-English oil trust Unilever, organized in 1929, refused to buy any whale oil. After a dead season, the whale companies resumed activity in 1932, this time on a more modest level, as the participating nations agreed on a total catch with quotas allotted to each. The aim was to preserve the whale stock and stabilize the whale oil market. A warning had been sounded, which became stronger as time passed, that whaling was a predatory business which threatened the ultimate extinction of a whole animal species.

Shipping conquers new Frontiers

The transition from sail to steam was far from completed in 1914. Sail still accounted for 24 per cent of the merchant fleet, or 610,000 tons out of a total of 2.5 million tons. The course was clear, however. Sails were on their way out. The shift to steam meant a farewell to the old assets — cheap labour and second best technology — which had enabled the Norwegians to carve out a footing in international shipping, in the cargo business at first and later in the overseas liner trade. The role of low cost nation on the high seas now passed to the Greeks and the Finns.

The 1914-18 World War involved the loss of 2,000 Norwegian sailors and 1.3 million tons, or nearly half the entire merchant fleet. On the other hand, the war speeded up change. During hostilities the nation had come to appreciate that the fleet was the country's main asset both as a source of income and as a bargaining counter in securing supplies essential to the home economy from the Western powers. The experience boosted self respect and national pride. The shipowners emerged from the war with more self confidence. The seamen, who had served in the front line, came away with the expectation that they deserved a new deal. They had recently unionized and had therefore greater bargaining power. Both were ready to strike a new bargain.[5] The insurance money waiting in Britain of 979 million[6] kroner, which within a time limit could be reinvested tax free, made a new departure possible and perhaps necessary, for the seamen's unions now basked in a wave of national sympathy.

During subsequent years the merchant fleet underwent substantial changes that influenced all sides of the shipping economy.[7] In the first place total tonnage more than doubled, up from 1.9 million tons in 1919 to 4.8 million in 1939. At a time of retrenchment elsewhere, and declining freight rates generally, capital clearly found satisfactory deployment in ships. Risk capital in shipping loomed large even in the overall economy. During the years 1932-9 alone the taxable value of ships owned by the country's 350 shippng companies went up from 320 million to 1,492 million kroner.[8] A quintupling of shipping capital over a five-year period represents a yearly rate of growth of 24.6 per cent. By comparison, total fixed real capital increased from 10.1 billion to 18.9 billion kroner in these years, a rate of growth of only 2.5 per cent per year.[9] In the midst of depression it is thus clear that real capital in shipping increased at an unprecedented rate. Manpower requirements lagged behind; in 1919 the ocean going fleet employed 23,600 men, in 1939 just over 32,000 men, of whom 90 per cent were Norwegian citizens. Hence, shipping easily ranked as the most capital intensive sector of the economy.[10]

Next, the shipowners changed the traditional policy of operating second-hand tonnage at low freight rates, and manned by sailors at minimum wages. Instead they moved into the fast growing oil market. The switch to the tanker market accounts for the rapid expansion of tonnage. By 1939 Norway had acquired one of the world's largest and most modern fleets of tankers, trailing third behind the United States and Great Britain. The shipowners found new openings in the international liner trade, in the heavy lift and refrigerator and cold storage transports. All these required high class tonnage, capable of operating over the world's distant oceans and climates. 'Speed and service', the motto of the Wilhelmsen shipping company, could well be said to apply to Norwegian shipping generally.

Third, the new fields meant that the fleet came to consist of mostly new, specialized, and fast-going vessels, embodying the latest technical novelties. In 1939 the fleet had an average age lower than that of any other, with one fourth of the tonnage less than five years old. At the same time the average tonnage of the ships increased. The chief innovation was the introduction of the diesel engine as propellant in place of the steam engine. Its origins go back to the patents taken out in the 1890s by the German engineer Rudolf Diesel. Burmeister & Wain, Copenhagen, in 1912 patented a marine diesel engine, which was installed the same year in a larger vessel, M/S Selandia of 7400 dwt. In the same year Akers Mech. Works, Oslo, obtained a licence for the new marine diesel engine. Technically and commercially the Selandia was a success. Depending on distance, the savings in fuel costs over coal were up to 30 per cent. Diesel oil required less storage room on board, which left more space for cargo. Moreover, the diesel propulsion system required fewer engine men, and eliminated the toil of the old coal stokers. Bunkering time in ports was also reduced. The country's conversion to diesel, not unnaturally, was swift: 60 per cent, or 2.8 million tons out of a total of 4.6 million gross tons, consisted of motor vessels by 1939. Of this tankers alone made up 1.9 million tons, or about one fifth of the world's tank tonnage. Norway had acquired a seaborne empire, and the country's economic centre of gravity moved still closer to the sea, to the world of the ship.

Fourth, the transition to first class tonnage meant higher initial capital costs and higher operating costs. Going from steam to diesel, the shipping economy moved into a capital-intensive phase. This is remarkable against the background of depression and capital shortages that generally prevailed. The key to success was the long term charter contracts which became popular among the big international oil companies in the late twenties. The Norwegians eagerly sought these charter contracts, at a time when international prices were falling and the business horizon was dark. Hiring off tonnage for up to ten years at a fixed monthly rate(even though low),promised security in an uncerain world to the shipowner and his creditors alike. This was also a period when the shipbuilding industry offered easy credits to customers in order to maintain activity and employment. Both factors played into the hands of the risk-taking entrepreneurs, able to see the opportunity. The normal arrangement offered by Swedish or British yards was that the shipowner put up 30 per cent, the remaining 70 per cent being provided by the builder against a priority mortgage on the vessel. The practice rested on confidence in the shipowner's record of his earlier performance. The shipyard kept the men employed, while the shipowner obtained first class tonnage that could be paid off by future operating earnings which were guaranteed by means of long-term contracts with the oil companies.

British yards built 27.1 per cent, Swedish yards 18.1 per cent of the new tonnage delivered to Norwegian shipowners in the years 1914-39.[11] Norwegian yards by contrast built a mere 16.1 per cent. The bulk of the latter consisted of small vessels, vessels for local passenger traffic or whale catchers of 500-600 gross tons. The average size of the Norwegian deliveries was thus a modest 875 gross tons as against 5,670 tons from the Swedish yards. The failure of the Norwegian shipbuilding industry stemmed in part from strained labour relations which eroded confidence, lack of credit facilities, in part absence of berths capable of accomodating the bigger hulls, and protective duties, notably from 1927, that reportedly raised the costs of materials above those of competing foreign yards. For these reasons the linkage effects of shipping were reduced. There was for a time serious talk of forbidding Norwegian shipowners to contract for ships abroad as a means of boosting the shipbuilding industry at home, but nothing much came of it. The industrial multiplier effects of shipping were reaped particularly by Sweden, whose shipbuilding firms now elbowed themselves into a front runner position on the experience gained through Norwegian orders. Once again we are reminded of the importance of foreign capital in under-writing investments in Norway. With foreign credits up to 75 per cent of building costs, the shipowners did not encroach upon the savings and capital generated by the home economy. It is time to consider a few figures illustrating the unique position of shipping in the Norwegian economy at the time, (Table 5.2).

Table 5.2 shows that freight earnings from shipping in relation to the gross national product, ranged from 10 per cent to roughly 18 per cent in the years covered. In this respect Norwegian shipping occupied a unique position. A mere 2 per cent of the economically active population, 25-30,000 men, contributed roughly 10 per cent of the national cake. An even more important index, investments, also underscores the importance of shipping. Column 6 in Table 5.2 shows that investments in ships exceeded one quarter of total gross investment in several years. In 1930 for instance ships represented 255 million kroner, 25 per cent of total gross capital formation, against 154 million for dwellings, 127 million in industry and 87 million kroner in agriculture.[12]

Concluding these observations on growth and stagnation, we may perhaps say that the economy in the 1920s presented a range of stagnating sectors, among them agriculture, fisheries, construction and a number of industrial branches. The pressure on earnings was reinforced by the protectionist tendencies abroad, banking crises at home, mone-

Table 5.2: The Norwegian Merchant Fleet, its Gross Freight Earnings. Gross Domestic Product, Gross Domestic Capital Formation and Investmets in Ships, Absolute Figures and in % of GDCF (Current kroner). Selected Years 1900-1939

Year	Total tonnage 100 gr tons	Freight earnings Mill. kr	Gross domestic product Mill. kr	Gross domestic capital formation Mill. kr	Investments in shipping Mill. kr	In % of GDCF
	1	2	3	4	5	6
1900	1925	144	1115	208	39	18.7
1910	2161	410	1435	263	51	19.4
1915	2662	475	2594	513	139	27.0
1920	2430	1280	7500	2297	640	27.9
1925	2783	484	5633	1052	224	21.3
1930	3883	411	4377	1005	290	28.4
1935	4071	430	4362	923	135	14.6
1939	4846	776	6253	1600	294	18.4

Sources: *Historical Statistics 1968*, Tables 61, 65, 175, 195. *National Accounts 1865-1965*, NOS XII, 163, Oslo 1965, Table 7 col. 5.

tary difficulties, and the rigidities in the labour markets introduced by the trade unions. The resulting contraction of investments in the public and private sectors barred excess labour from moving out. The squeeze on average income levels and consistently high unemployment was aggravated, since escape to the United States was halted.

Offsetting these tendencies was the swift rise of new growth industries, notably whaling and shipping, geared to the international economy, and a broad range of consumer goods industries oriented toward the home market. However, the income- and employment-boosting effects of these were not strong enough, at least not in the interwar period, to balance the depressive tendencies of the stagnating sectors; hence the impression of a general stalling of the economy.

Notes

1 Arne Odd Johnsen & Johan Tønnessen, *Den moderne hvalfangsts historie. Opprinnelse og utvikling*, 4. vols. Oslo, 1959-1970. Johnsen has written vol. 1, Tønnessen vols. 2-4.

2 Arne Odd Johnsen, *Norwegian Patents relating to Whaling and the Whaling Industry*, Oslo 1947; Bjørn Basberg, *Innovasjonsteori, patenter og teknologisk utvikling i norsk hvalfangst 1880-1968*, Norwegian School of Economics,

Bergen 1980.

3 Bjørn Basberg, 'Patents, Innovations and Technological Development in Norwegian Whaling 1880-1968', *World Patent Information*, vol. 3, No. 1, 1981, pp. 19-22.

4 *Statistisk-økonomisk oversikt over året 1939*, Central Bureau of Statistics, Oslo, 1940, p. 39.

5 Johan Schreiner, *Norsk skipsfart under krig og høykonjunktur 1914-1920*, Oslo, 1963.

6 Hermod Skånland, *Det norske kredittmarked siden 1900*, Oslo, 1967, p. 104.

7 Johan O. Egeland, *Kongeveien, Norsk skipsfart fra århundreskiftet til Den annen verdenskrig*, 2 vols., Oslo, 1973; Kaare Petersen, *The Saga of Norwegian Shipping*, Oslo 1955.

8 Wilhelm Keilhau, *Skipsfartens betydning for Norge*, Oslo, 1948, pp. 101, 102.

9 *Historical Statistics 1968*, Table 73; Juul Bjerke, *Langtidslinjer*, Table 7 (1938-prices).

10 *Historical Statistics 1968*, Table 56.

11 J.O. Egeland, *Kongeveien*, II, 429.

12 *National Accounts 1865-1960*, pp. 100-2.

6 CRISIS AND CARTELS 1930-1935

The End of an Epoch

The international economy suffered a variety of ills in the 1920s: an uneven expansion in productive capacity both in agriculture and industry, the burden of international debts, high customs tariffs and a distribution of gold that became more unbalanced as time passed. After the Wall Street crash in October 1929, the international dis-equilibrium worsened rapidly. The American short-term loans to Austria and Germany were called up. The governments of these countries, in attempts to stave off chaos, suspended gold exports in June 1931. Nervousness now engulfed the pound. On Monday 21 September 1931, after heavy withdrawals of gold, the British government suspended the gold standard, after six years of painful efforts to maintain the pound sterling at the old gold parity. The devaluation sent shock waves throughout the world.

On 27 September Norway followed the British example and left gold. A similar decision was taken by the Swedish government the same day. Denmark, having suspended gold exports already on Tuesday 22 September, waited until 29 September, and Finland until 12 October.[1] The British market absorbed 25 per cent of Sweden's exports, 26.5 per cent of Norway's commodity exports and over 55 per cent of Denmark's total exports; hence their decision to follow the pound was understandable. Still, the decision, while economically sound, was a psychological blow. Stable money was not only a national symbol, it was a bulwark against anarchy, its devaluation therefore a breach of the social contract. It was indeed the end of an epoch. It signalled the departure of the old self-regulating system, set up after the Napoleonic wars more than a century earlier. The Rechtsstaat-idea suffered another blow.

Norges Bank immediately raised its discount from 6 to 8 per cent. The action was traditional and signalled its determination to stem the possible flight of capital during the sterling crisis. Panic must be avoided. The stock exchange also stayed closed on the famous Monday 21 September and subsequent days. The exchange rate of the pound dropped about 10 per cent in relation to gold and the dollar. Norges Bank followed the pound but at a lower peg so that the krone at year's end had gone down about 20 per cent against the dollar and 10 per cent against the pound. Caution was indeed called for. During the summer of 1931 the country experienced the bitterest labour conflict in its history that culminated in the 'Menstad battle'.

In the late autumn the public received another shock. The country's two biggest private banks, Den norske Creditbank in Oslo, and Bergens Privatbank, announced that owing to the need for further write-offs on loans to shipping and industry in particular, and the need for fresh reconstruction capital, they had applied for a letter of respite for three months from the government. On 15 December 1931 the moratorium was given in accordance with the country's bank law.[2] New claims were to take precedence over old ones. By this provision the banks were able to continue operations, and the creditors stood a reasonable chance of avoiding losses, as situation reports published shortly afterwards showed that their share capital was safe. The gamble was successful, the currency was not influenced, nor did the event unleash another general bank crisis. Together the two banks had one third of all loans to manufacturing firms. Norges Bank accordingly offered credits and provided deposits for the two banks in distress. The aid reached a total of 150 million by the end of 1933.[3] The Central bank also reduced its discount rate gradually to more normal levels, to 4½ per cent in May 1932 and 3½ per cent in May 1933.[4] The pound sold for a mere 16.50 during the sterling crisis in September 1931 as against the par value of 18.16, but as noted, Nicolai Rygg gradually let the krone go down about 10 per cent against the pound and 20 per cent against the dollar.[5]

The devaluation or depreciation of the N. krone was continued on an informal level during the following years, in the shadow of the pound's downward movement. By 1933 Norway had joined the sterling bloc at a rate of 19.90 for the pound, or about 10 per cent below the pre-devaluation rate. This exchange rate was consciously maintained as the sterling-bloc countries continued their monetary decline against gold. By 1939 the Norwegian krone had depreciated by about 50 per cent against gold. When World War II broke out in September 1939, the krone was tied to the dollar, temporarily at a rate of 4.40 as against 3.73 during the gold standard era before September 1931. The initial hope, harboured in some circles, of boosting exports through depreciation, was soon dispelled, for most countries devalued eventually, and the effort soon turned into a race of competitive devaluation.

In 1936 new legislation was passed that enabled Norges Bank to influence the krone's exchange value by means of open market operations, through the selling and buying of government securities. The legislation was patterned on the Federal Reserve System of America, but it came too late and was used to a very modest extent. Indeed, currency questions and price fluctuations, that had embittered the atmosphere in the twenties, disappeared in the thirties. Monetary issues were henceforth overshadowed by fiscal issues.

Indicators of Depression

The figures for the overall economy illustrate the extent of the depression. It is worth underlining that the GNP statistics have been worked out retrospectively. Lack of adequate figures was a handicap in the interwar years. Gross national product dropped from a high 4.4 billion kroner in 1930 to 3.8 billion in 1931 and rose thereafter. Not till 1936, however, did the country surpass the level of 1930. Investment, another key indicator, declined from 1,005 million kroner in 1930 to 649 million for the year 1932. (Note that the price level remained constant.) This was the bottom, but it took four years to recover the 1930 level. Exports, a third key variable, showed a similar course. The turn occurred in 1931, but recovery took another four years. Only in 1936 did export values exceed those of 1929. The comparison is a little misleading, for meanwhile all prices continued to fall until the middle of 1935. In short, total value creation in Norway fell by 12 per cent, gross capital formation by 34 per cent, and total exports by 22 per cent.[6]

Germany and the United States fared much worse. Another symptom underlining the moderate impact of the crisis here is that Norway escaped a national bank disaster, which now ran its course in Germany and above all in the United States. Nor did the money volume show any contraction. The volume of notes in circulation was 312 million kroner in 1930 as against 334 million in 1931, 315 million in 1932 and 327 million in 1933.[7] The cleaning-up of the credit system apparently was over before the international depression set in.

Unemployment figures offer more revealing evidence. The unemployment rate for organised workers was 15 per cent in 1929, and rose rapidly to a record of 33.4 per cent at the trough in 1933. But again the percentage had been 17.6 per cent in 1921 and 25.4 per cent in 1927. Altogether 110,000 men were unemployed in 1933. The Hundseid ministry (1932-3) of the Farmers' Party gained notoriety by issuing departmental menus for unemployed paupers in rural areas.

These food stamps, specifying in calorific values the nature of public charity, were to replace cash payments. The aim was to keep relief expenditures down to acceptable levels. The numbers on the dole peaked as late as 1935 when 158,000 persons received social relief. Total net payments for relief purposes paid out by local and central government, were 46.5 million kroner in 1931 and 56 million in 1935. The expenditures kept rising till 1940.[8] Urban unemployed families meanwhile ran up arrears on rents and taxes which were often not settled until years later during the war. Some were undernourished, no doubt, but people did not starve.

One is reminded here of demographic statistics. The thirties, like the previous decade, saw the last of the massive age groups enter the labour market, 183,000 in the 1920s, and 285,000 new recruits in the thirties. The figures suggest that even under normal conditions some unemployment would have been unavoidable.

In the area of unemployment we seem to be faced with a chronic and intractable phenomenon. The scars of humiliation left by the crisis determined voting and party affiliations for two generations afterwards. Unemployment became the bogus word. It still remains so, forty years later. The experience of the thirties hastened the welfare legislation that was enacted in that decade and later. It was above all out of the trauma of mass unemployment in the 1930s that the welfare state was born.

The Economic Problem

Though conflicting and often baffling, there were ample signs that the economic machine was out of gear. To start from below, for the worker the depression meant a loss of wages, for the business firm a loss of profit, for the owner of capital, an incentive to take flight into new areas where potential demand would offer some return on capital so redeployed. For the national economy the depression involved a waste of productive resources, including skills, complex capital and entrepreneurship. On a still more aggregated level, for the world economy, the depression caused a sharp contraction of world trade down from $5.4 billion in 1929 to $1.9 billion in 1933, a deterioration of the terms of trade for primary producing countries, and a return to national economic isolationism.

One may also consider the time dimension. There was a short-term perspective and a long-term view, each offering a partial definition of the crisis. The lack of a general comprehensive crisis theory at the time is well known by now. It explains in part why effective political measures were slow in forthcoming. Events tended to push governments rather than vice versa. The short-term problem was how to get people back to work. Existing theory offered little or misleading guidance. The controversial John Maynard Keynes, however, was well known, and in both Sweden and Norway academic economists like Bertil Ohlin, Gunnar Myrdal and Ragnar Frisch toyed with the idea of radical government intervention in the economy. Various proposals were aired. They usually centered on a crash programme of public works financed by central government borrowing in the domestic capital market. Via the multiplier, a new piece of jargon, the investments would generate an increase in total income. This would allow increased savings and a new round of investments, at the same time as government would be able to collect more taxes and repay its debts. Once the push provided by government had been given, the economy would spiral out of the contraction by well-known feed-back mechanisms. At a time when the majority of countries had gone off gold, the Keynesian recipe won increasing acceptance, at first among labour parties in Europe, but soon also in America. By the end of 1932, thirty-two countries had suspended gold payments. The major remaining countries soon followed. The United States devalued on 20 April 1933, France at the end of September 1936.[9]

By going off gold, governments were no longer constrained as under the gold standards to limit the money volume in accordance with a fixed value of a currency, freely exportable and convertible into gold. Despite the inflationary implications, a relief programme of public investments through government deficit spending won sympathy at a time of mass unemployment. From the Soviet Union came word of Stalin's first five-year plan (1928). The new US president, Franklin Roosevelt, launched the New Deal in 1933. In the same year two Norwegian authors, Ole Colbjørnsen and Axel Sømme, published a tract titled 'En norsk 3-årsplan. Veien frem til en sosialistisk planøkonomi.' [A Norwegian three-year plan. The road to a socialist planned economy.] The book offered a Soviet-inspired porgramme for a public works offensive to combat unemployment and promote rapid economic growth. In one form or another political pressure forced the governments of the various industrial countries into a more active role in the economy. The change meant that monetary policy, control of which so far had been in the hands of central bankers, now became the province of politicians. The time perspective was shortened to momentary tasks. Most voters were convinced that the crisis was one of under-consumption, reflecting lack of effective buying power. Mental barriers were broken, the interventionist state took hold, justified by mottos such as 'national self help', or 'work for all'.

Traditional economic theory also contained a long-term view. According to conventionl thinking the depression was a normal temporary downswing that represented a maladjustment between production and demand in a number of markets. Given time the disequilibrium would disappear by ordinary self-adjusting market forces without government intervention. The condition for recovery was that productive inputs, including labour, should let themselves be pushed around to meet market demands, as reflected in prices customers were willing to pay. This view had been in reasonable accord with economic realities in the world of nineteenth century capitalism.

The advent of trade unions and mass production techniques in one sector after another, however, had since rendered the prescription increasingly obsolete and the remedies increasingly inappropriate. It is apparent that the system lacked a crisis theory and guidance for emergency action. With the tacit consent of governments for example, business responded to saturation with cutbacks in production instead of cutbacks in prices The labour press exploited the point. After all, the unions, by resisting wage cuts, merely acted as a monopolist in a market. Most markets had been captured by monopolies, anyhow, so why not the labour market? Besides, the economic crisis was not temporary, it persisted. Apparently Marx was correct in predicting that capitalism was on its way to its programmatic ruin. Again, critics pointed to the disintegration of the international gold standard. The United States experienced an inflow of gold in the 1920s, and particularly after 1930. According to the conventions of the gold standard, this inflow should induce an increase of the US money volume which would force up prices and wages. As foreign goods became relatively cheaper, US imports would increase. However Congress enacted custom tariffs which prevented the entry of foreign goods. And the dollar, which according to existing legislation was to have 34 per cent gold coverage, soon had a gold backing of more than 100 per cent, as the federal government, despite the gold inflow, took steps to prevent monetary expansion.

However irrelevant the conventional theory seemed in 1931, its implication that input factors had to be periodically redeployed in line with exhaustion of demand in saturated markets, remained valid, at least in the longer-term perspective. But its spokesmen provided no immediate practical guidance. They appeared almost paralysed by their insistence that the government should balance its budget and cut back expenditures. The psychological advantage lay with the advocates of the active state.

The following sections throw light on the forces that halted the downward movement, and the next chapter analyzes those that were responsible for recovery. They will show what Keynesian policies amounted to in practical politics in Norway in the 1930s.

Cartels and Monopolies in Agriculture and Forestry

Looking back, the depression presented two sets of forces at play: on the one hand the eroding forces affecting the sick industries, on the other, the expansionary tendencies seen in the growth industries. Considering the former, they saw their markets contract and their prices tumble. They sought refuge in cartels and monopolies, trying at the same time to secure state support for their purposes. For the Norwegian chemical and metallurgical industries, facing a temporary glut, tariffs or cartels were a payable proposition. For farmers and fishermen, coping with an inelastic demand or permanent saturation, this strategy seemed only a stepping-stone to monopoly. Accordingly, they campaigned for salvation outside the market.

Their efforts were aided by the force of tradition, the mystique of the soil or the *Blut und Boden*- fantasies then in vogue in Germany. The soil touched a romantic nerve everywhere at a time of industrial unemployment. Nobel laureate Knut Hamsun wrote 'Fruits of the Soil' (Markens Grøde) in 1917. The royalties typically went into land. Catching the mood, Trygve Gulbranssen, an unknown tobacconist in Oslo, wrote a trilogy in the 1930s on the fortunes of an ancient, proud yeoman family from the dark, eastern backwoods. Drippingly romantic, the trilogy scored the biggest commercial success recorded so far in Norwegian publishing history. Gulbranssen's books 'Beyond sing the Forests' (Og bakom synger skogene) sold 100,000 copies in Norway in the 1930s. They were also translated into 30 languages with a total sale of over 8 million copies by 1965.[10] Literary critics have never forgiven Gulbranssen his success with the readers.

The vogue contained an anti-liberal, anti-urban tendency that has run quite strongly in the country's history. The antipathy against a secular culture gained strength from the resentment felt among the rural population, now no longer the dominant social group in society. In the case of Hamsun the anti-capitalist sentiment had affiliations with Nazism, but for the majority of farmers anger centred on the effects of the deflation.

One signal of the difficulties in the countryside was the number of foreclosures and forced sales of real property. Of the latter about 4,000 were reported in 1927 as against 6,985 sales in the bottom year 1932.[11] The sales affected above all the small-holder group; indeed 90 per cent of all forced sales in 1932 pertained to recently acquired properties of less than 5 decares, or about one acre. Next, the sales occurred mainly in the eastern districts. It was a regional, not a national problem. The situation was far better in the west and in the south, where agriculture was already a part-time activity. Moreover, in eighty per cent of the cases the property was returned to the owner and his family. Another sign of crisis was the protest organisation, Bygdefolkets Krisehjelp (The Rural Crisis Support), that attracted members, at one time 12,000, for a purely negative programme of drumming up local sympathizers to chase away those who turned up to bid at auctions. The organisation fanned an atmosphere already loaded with fanaticism. After all, the country had 186,286 registered farm holdings over five decares (just over one acre) in 1929 and 197,260 holdings in 1939, up by about eleven thousand.[12] Besides, the Rural Crisis Support tarnished its image by collaborating with Quisling's new fascist party, Nasjonal Samling, at the Storting elections in 1933.[13] Afterwards support from earlier members eroded quickly.

By hasty legislation, 6 June 1930, the Storting passed measures to promote the sale and distribution of farm products. The legislation gave the farm co-operatives a monopoly for handling agricultural products on the home market. Voluntary co-operation had failed to bring all farmers together in a strong monopoly organisation. The major dairies united in a national organisation in 1931. This was followed by the meat and pork organisation later the same year. A national egg central, operated by the producers, came in 1929. The agro-cartels soon comprised both meat and milk products, eggs, fruit and vegetables. Additional legislation was rammed through in the Storting which in effect banned imports of meat, milk and egg-products, though not grain. The ban proved permanent. The general idea of the farm co-operatives is seen in the structure of the Norske Melkeprodusenters Landsforbund, (The Norwegian Milk Manufacturers' Federation).[14] Organised in eight regional dairy districts, the milk co-operatives, dating back to 1881, set up a national marketing board that henceforth took over the distribution of milk. Milk at the time represented 40 per cent of total farm income. The fresh milk was sold at a uniform price to the consumers. Surplus milk was held off the market and processed into dairy products. The board through the local co-operative held back part of the proceeds paid to each individual member. The deductions went into a national equalisation fund, operated by the board. In this way all farmers participating in the co-operatives obtained a uniform price for their efforts, regardless of transport distance or use made of the milk. The consumers benefited from a stabilisation of fresh milk deliveries throughout the year.

Surpluses were exported when possible at dumping prices by the central marketing board, which, by tapping the equalisation fund, was able to bring down the export prices as much as was needed in order to offload the surpluses abroad. The milk co-operatives were compulsory in practice, since those farmers who did not join, were also forced to contribute to the equalisation fund. The law thus invested a private corporate agency with the right to tax. However, dumping proved inadequate, and market surpluses tended to pile up. The dilemma was solved in 1931 by additional legislation that provided for compulsory mixing of surplus butter into margarine, in an understanding with the margarine industry, which also built up a cartel organisation around this time. The dairy producers may be said to have been successful. The downward drift of milk prices was arrested 1931-4, but at a level probably a good deal higher than the assumed price in a free, unregulated market. In this way the traditional farming structure in Norway was maintained. The third party, the customers, were not heard. The arrangements in Sweden and Denmark were similar. The success of the farmers' market regulations has since been invoked as a model for a corporate economy that allegedly has proved viable without the profit motive.

The forestry industries also witnessed defensive cartellisation in these years of depression. World War I saw timber prices soar from an average of 14 kroner per m^3 in 1914, to 56.50 kroner in 1920. From then on timber prices tended downwards for the next 15 years. The downward trend reflected the situation in the export markets, to which both forest owners and their workers were spectators. None were as yet organised in nationwide interest organisations. Unemployment, reduced wages, and strike breakers became the order of the day in the forest communities. Class conflict was even more bitter here than in the towns. Several intense labour conflicts occurred. They were increasingly bitter after 1927, when the forest workers against considerable resistance were able to set up a national union within the national Federation of Labour (LO). Notably the Randsfjord lake region, forming the upper parts of the Drammen river system, witnessed prolonged conflicts, during which the state police squads, organised to stave off attacks on strike breakers, were reported to act with unwarranted brutality. The forest workers' union attracted members also from the farm workers. In three years their union ranked third in membership, with 13,960 members out of a total of 144,000 members in LO in 1931.[15] In response the employers set on foot the Norwegian Federation of Forest Owners in 1929. National bargaining and national tariffs now replaced local negotiations. Still, unionisation could not prevent the wages in forestry from falling for yet another few years. A lasting upturn occurred only after 1935.

The forest owners commanded weight in a country where nine-tenths of the total productive forest area were privately owned as against one-tenth by the central government.[16] Moreover, most forest properties were relatively modest. The magnate group here with forest holdings exceeding 1 million acres, could be counted on one hand, among them Lövenskiold, Mathiesen, and Treschow, whose ownership dates back to the eighteenth century. Co-operation soon took hold among the forest owners, in joint industrial ventures, marketing and sales organisations. These proved lasting.

The Cartel Movement in the Fisheries

Voluntary action also failed initially, in the fisheries. The power of the central government was needed in order to insure compliance with new regulations deemed necessary for all. By far-reaching legislation, initiated partly by the fishermen themselves, but more often by the central government, all the major fisheries were brought under stringent controls regarding prices, production and marketing arrangements. The process stretched over the years 1930-8. The general aim was to stabilise prices through adjusting supply to demand. Moreover, the political influence of the fishermen dictated that legislation would insure the continuance of the traditional decentralised structure of the fisheries, with participation of a mass of small-time fishermen. These overall demands coloured the nature of the resulting cartel and market regulations. By several steps a national interest organisation, Norges Fiskarlag, was established 1926-38, which obtained a monopoly on all first-hand deliveries of fish to the various processing interests. The crucial legislation was the Raw Fish Act of 1938. The various export organisations were brought together in national sales cartels, among them the canned goods industry. Norwegian trawlers already in operation were allowed to continue to land their catches, but further trawler participation was halted by a system of concessions. This was to protect the small scale operators. Foreign trawlers were forbidden to land their catch for any processing purpose in Norway. To prevent further speculative capital entering a depressed trade, a registration system was introduced that restricted ownership of fishing boats to bona fide fishermen.

By and large the level of technology in the fisheries was frozen by legislative fiat on the insistence of the majority of fishermen who rejected a future as wage labourers. Market regulation, however, failed to provide a decent income; so beginning *ad hoc* in the twenties, the central government drifted into a policy of subsidising prices so that the fishermen received non-market prices for their catches. The minimum price guarantee included cod at first, but by degrees the subsidies were extended to other types of fish.

Cartellisation in Industry

The autarchic tendencies in industry took the familiar forms of protective tariffs and cartel agreements. Free trade had traditionally been the dominant policy of Norway, though some modifications had occurred in 1897 and 1905, in response to protectionist tariffs elsewhere. The onrush of foreign goods at dumping prices after 1920 led industrialists to defensive countersteps. New tariffs in 1922, 1923 and 1927 provided some protection for home manufactured radios, bicycles, grammophones, steel and textiles. The tariff rates averaged 20-25 per cent of value to customers and in view of the subsequent imports, cannot have been prohibitive. With its large export sector, Norwegian manufacturing interests have never believed in self-sufficiency. The steps in the 1920s were considered temporary bulwarks against unfair trading practices among their foreign customers. In this light one should view the 'Ten Per Cent Rule', voted in the Storting in 1927. Henceforth foreign firms bidding for orders in the electro-technical industries in Norway, were to have 10 per cent added to their offering price. The alleged reason was that foreign bids contained elements of dumping.

Price agreements among industrialists date back to the 1890s. Saturation of markets for pulp and paper in the 1890s had even resulted in Scandinavian cartel organisations. Similar national price cartels came in beer and tobacco around 1900. As yet no legislation existed in regard to competition, marketing practices, advertising or price fixing. The decade of the twenties saw two legislative landmarks here. In 1922 the Storting passed the Unfair Competition Act. The central aim was to

foster competition by outlawing specific trade and advertising practices which experience at home and abroad had brought into focus,
notably tie-in contracts, gratuities, collusion or other forms of price
fixing intended to restrict competition. In 1926 the Storting passed the
Act Controlling Trade Practices in Restraint of Trade. This act commonly called 'the trust law', unintentionally reversed the earlier trend.
The act provided for a permanent trust control board, an executive
director, and a secretariat. Wilhelm Thagaard (1890-1970) was
appointed as the first director. He had earlier been in charge of the
war time public price controls. The new legisation gave Thagaard wide
discretionary powers to review prices and cartels, call for periodic
reports of old and new price agreements and institute legal proceedings
in cases of manifest abuse. Much thus depended on how the anti-trust
law was to be practiced.

Thagaard took the view that the rise of monopolies had rendered
competition as a means of social control permanently obsolete.
Competition might well be replaced by public price control boards,
the members of which might include consumers' representatives. In
some cases where competition was deemed negative, firms could be
forced to join hands. This was the idea of compulsory trustification.
Thagaard accordingly thought it his duty to register and monitor existing cartels rather than prosecute them. There were 73 cartels in 1923
and their figure exceeded one hundred before 1928. They soared to five
hundred in the 1960s. The trend towards cartellisation thus went on
wih the tacit and sometimes open consent of Thagaard, who had no
difficulty in equating his views with that of the general good. His influence became notorious for a generation and culminated in the late
forties with the postwar price regulation system which he operated till
1952.

Norwegian industry and shipping also participated in international
cartels as well, for nitrates, steel, tankers and others. The method of
approach may be illustrated by the tanker pool. The International
Tanker Owners Association Ltd, Intertanko, was organised in London
in 1934. The pool, representing 95 per cent of the tanker tonnage that
competed on the free market for oil transports, counted among its participants most of the Norwegian tanker operators. The pool acted as a
common bargaining and hiring agency for tonnage. The philosophy
was to hold back tonnage in order to maintain rates that at least
covered the costs of the tankers that sailed and the lay-up costs of those
that lay idle in the buoys. This was achieved by contributions from the
tankers employed to a common lay-up fund, operated by Intertanko.[17]

Another facet of economic nationalism in the 1920s was the 'Buy Norwegian' movement. Firms vied with each other other in selling products of national origin. Agreements on special stamps of origin were concluded for a number of products. Appeals to patriotism thus supplemented the tariff in protecting Norwegian manufactures.

Experience was to show that while the market regulations proved pervasive and permanent for the primary sector, the trust movement in manufacturing in general failed to shield industrial firms from market forces. At best the textile and garment industry enjoyed a few peaceful years in the decade of the thirties. The new regulations of the labour market that came in 1935 will be dealt with in the next chapter.

Notes

1 Nicolai Rygg, *Norges Bank i mellomkrigstiden*, pp. 424-535. Hermod Skånland, *Det norske kredittmarked siden 1900*, pp. 170-8; *The Economist*, 26 September 1931, pp. 547, 553; 3 October 1931, p. 600.

2 *Farmand*, 19 December 1931, p. 1130.

3 Erling Petersen, *Den norske Creditbank*, pp. 266-74; *Kriser och krispolitik i Norden under mellankrigstiden*, Uppsala 1974, p. 35.

4 *Historical Statistics 1968*, Table 248.

5 *Farmand*, 19 December 1931, p. 1076.

6 *National Accounts 1865-1960*, Table 1, pp. 64-5.

7 *Historical Statistics 1968*, Table 247.

8 Ibid., Table 316.

9 A.G. Kenwood & A.L. Lougheed, *The Growth of the International Economy 1820-1960*, London, Sydney, 1971, pp. 207-9.

10 Kjølve Egeland & Tordis Ørjasaeter, *Mellomkrigstid*, Oslo, 1975, p. 289.

11 *Historical Statistics 1968*, Table 326.

12 *Historical Statistics 1968*, Table 75.

13 Kaare Frøland, *Krise og kamp. Bygdelfolkets krisehjelp* Universitetsforlaget, Oslo & Bergen, 1962.

14 Berge Furre, *Mjølk, bønder og tingmenn*, Oslo, 1971.

15 Gunnar Ousland, *Fagorganisasjonen i Norge*, vol. II, pp. 481-2.

16 *Historical Statistics 1968*, Table 103.

17 J.O. Egeland, *Kongeveien*, Oslo, 1968, vol. II, pp. 300-8.

7 MARKET FORCES AND RECOVERY 1931-1939

Breaking the Downward Spiral 1931-1932

National income statistics throw light on the question why the down-turn movement in the economy was arrested. They show to begin with that while total consumption fell between 1930-4, the fall was more pronounced for some items than for others.[1] Expenditures on fruit, vegetables, bread, sugar, cigarettes increased, while those for snuff, chewing tobacco, meat, fish, and dairy products declined. The trend for milk was reversed from 1934. Proceeding to other household expenditures, we note that while the total declined, some items fell more than the average, some remained neutral and a few actually increased. In the latter group were such new items as aluminium casseroles, electric cooking appliances, light bulbs and furniture. With a yearly growth rate of 7.5 per cent annually in the decade 1930-9, expenditures on household durables ranked number one among consumption categories, followed by transport 5.8 per cent and food 3.4 per cent. The electric durables were the harbingers of a new age and a new consumption pattern. Other signals of shifts were expenditures on health care and personal care. Doctor's bills and hospitalisation were largely covered by taxation, hence the increases here point to pharmaceuticals, cosmetics, visits to the hairdresser and beauty treatment. They reflected new ideals, and the means to realise them.

An entirely new item was the radio. After a test period, a monopoly of broadcasting was transferred to the present company, the Norwegian Broadcasting Corporation (NRK). It based its operations on listeners' fees and started regular service in 1925. Soon local manufacturers competed with imported sets. Sales shot up from zero in 1925 to a total of 77,000 in 1930 and 423,500 by the end of 1939. By that date there was one set for every second household. Prices tumbled from around 200 kroner for a set in 1925 to 79 in 1936. This was 'the people's radio' of NRK design. The radio represented the rise of a new growth sector based on electricity. Among the pioneers was Vebjørn Tandberg (1904-78) who started radio production 1933. The radio was accompanied by electric stoves, refrigerators, sewing machines, electric irons and others, though expansion was far more modest for these than for the radio. Synthetic textile fibers enjoyed rapid expansion a bit later in the decade. From 1935 a brand called 'cell-wool' was maufactured by the Notodden factory A/S Kunstsilkefabrikken. Though one or two cars were made in Norway in the pioneering days before 1910, the motor car remained an import article. Automobiles numbered a total of 41,900 in 1929 and 99,400 in 1939, including buses, lorries, and private cars. The latter alone almost trebled in the period, as did motor-cycles. Auto repair shops were a fast growing line.[2] Sports wear and smartly designed working garments were other new items, together with the bicycle, the weekly illustrated magazine, the gramophone and the cinema.

In other words, one should look at the changes in composition rather than at the total size of consumption expenditures. The national income figures, when disaggregated, suggest a far-reaching shift in consumption habits. The changed pattern of demand also provides a simple explanation as to why the downturn was checked. It was halted to the extent that the supply side of the economy moved out of saturated markets into new growth industries. These tended to be profitable lines with new products experiencing rapid sales, produced by new firms, and run by new entrepreneurs, making their way up beside existing products and firms. The case of the porbeagle fisheries illustrates the situation. First hand value soared from 54,000 kroner to 712,000 kroner in the years 1926-37. In the midst of depression, this yields a rate of growth of 26.4 per cent per year, against a negative growth for the fishery sector as a whole, down from a total of 94 million current kroner in the former year to 92 million in the latter.

The ongoing transformation, though lacking the force of a later period, was noticeable in the crafts. Makers of carriages, barrels, sails and ropes dropped out of sight. Hat makers, another traditional handicraft, saw their orders restricted to top hats which were still used for funerals of prominent persons, of which there still were a limited number. The pneumatic drills, operated by mechanical air pressure, also began to undercut the ancient drill and hammer worked by muscle and brawn. The navvy, the classical proletarian figure, who had bored the nation's tunnels, dug its road and railway beds, moving mountains in the process, was increasingly faced with obsolescence. The navvy – 'rallaren' – started his last journey, out of history, into poetry. So did the memory of his back-breaking toil.

Electricity and the small electro motor, by contrast, provided the opportunity for new industrial ventures in new regions far away from the older industrial centres. There was a trend both of diversification and decentralisation, e.g. bicycles at Sandnes outside Stavanger, ready-to-wear-garments and furniture on the Møre coast. In these local villages trade unions were absent. Every one knew each other. Traditions of thrift and skills now found outlets in new, cheap goods, oriented to a local market and local needs. In the towns the first departmental stores appeared. They competed with the '75 øre-bazaars', selling household items even to customers on the dole. Advertising was a growth industry. The cinema and 500-700,000 coloured weeklies spread the modern notions of culture and comforts. Films fired the desire among the viewers to imitate, mostly middle class ideals. The ideal of a contented union proletarian somehow never caught on.

The statistics for entry and exit of industrial firms do not offer precise information as to what actually happened. But the pioneering study by Frøystein Wedervang does reveal an increase in new industrial establishments in the thirties.[3] Looking at the period 1930-48, the author found 341 outgoing against 595 incoming firms from 1930-3. In the next period 1933-7, however, 303 firms folded while 1,083 new establishments entered registration, (i.e. firms with over 12,000 man hours annually). Net additions thus averaged 84 new firms 1930-3 against 195 new firms 1933-7. The last period 1937-48 covers the war and cannot be made comparable. The figures for that period may thus be ignored here. The upshot is that there was doubling of new business ventures 1933-7 compared to the years 1930-3. And the new entries tended to be small scale ventures with modest capital requirements. The evidence, such as it is, points to the pervasive influence of ordinary demand signals.[4]

If the turn was due to normal market forces, one would expect the downward spiral to have been broken before parties and politicians woke up to agree on any common action. The national income figures provide information. The key variables to consider are total value creation (GNP), capital formation, and exports. It appears that GNP and exports turned the corner in 1931, and gross capital formation in 1932. All the indices agree that the key variables reached bottom in 1931-2 after which a long recovery or convalescence got under way. It should be recalled that the national income statistics were constructed retrospectively; the first series, covering the years 1930-9 and 1946-51, were published in 1952. However, contemporary opinion had precise information available on the movements of at least some key economic variables, including exports. A case in point is the index of industrial production, worked out by the Central Bureau of Statistics from 1928 and listed below. With 1938 = 100 the industrial production index for the years 1928-35 was as follows[6]

Year	Export industries	Home market industries	All industries
1928	71.5	68.7	69.5
1929	80.4	75.8	77.4
1930	79.2	77.7	78.2
1931	56.4	62.9	60.2
1932	76.7	69.5	71.8
1933	79.1	69.6	72.6
1934	77.6	74.8	75.7
1935	86.4	82.0	83.4

The index figures for total industrial production fell from 78.2 in 1930 to a bottom of 60.2 in 1931, and rose thereafter. Export industries and home market industries, though not behaving in the same way, all turned the corner in 1931. Despite the unanimous statistical evidence, however, part of which was available to contemporaries, the view arose at the time, and persists in popular imagination to this day, that enlightened economic policies, notably those alleged to have been introduced by the Labour Party from 1935, were the proximate cause of recovery.[7] This view amounts to little more than a myth, though if unemployment is used as a yard stick, depression persisted throughout the decade Research into party programmes at the time will thus hardly yield anything worthwhile in answering the economic problem under review here.

Next, we turn to the factors that sustained convalescence once the crisis point had passed in 1931-2.

Recovery Period 1932-1939

Expansion of the Home Market

In analysing the recovery period 1932-9, a good start is to consider investments. This will be followed by a brief note on foreign trade and public sector expenditures. Figures for the main types of capital formation are offered in Table 7.1 and Figure 7.1.

Table 7.1 indicates that in 1930, at the onset of depression, new ships towered as the biggest investment item. They dropped from 290 million kroner in 1930 to 63 million in the bottom year 1932, but rebounded quickly, so that by 1937 ships were again the second largest investment category. As noted earlier, the linkages of shipping to the rest of the economy were weakened in the 1930s as the ships were mostly built and equipped at foreign yards and sailed in international

Figure 7.1: Gross Fixed Capital Formation 1930-1939. Selected Industries. Million Current Kroner

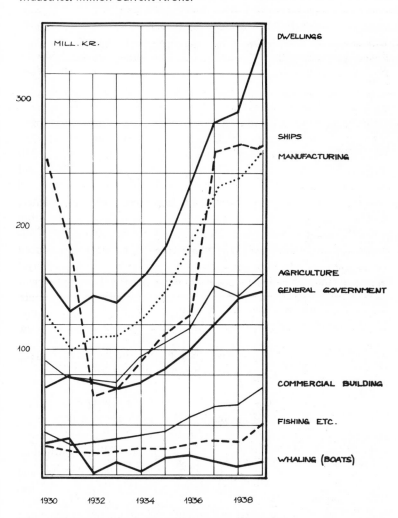

Source: *National Accounts 1865-1960* Nos XII, 196, Table 7.

waters. It has been estimated that 36 per cent of gross freight earnings were spent abroad in 1937, as against 38 per cent in 1938 and 51 per cent in 1939.[8] Indeed, in the interwar period the fortunes of the fleet, employing about 27-30,000 men, suggest that Norway in some respects relapsed into a dual economy with enclave characteristics. The impulses

Table 7.1: Gross Fixed Capital Formation 1930-1939. Selected Industries. Current Kroner in Millions

	1930	1931	1932	1933	1934	1935	1936	1937	1938	1939
Agriculture	87	77	76	75	94	106	116	151	144	160
Fishing	23	19	18	20	21	21	26	28	27	41
Whaling	27	29	1	0	4	13	16	11	8	10
Manufact- uring	127	99	110	112	124	146	181	229	237	261
Electricity supply	27	26	26	32	30	29	34	38	49	52
Trade	10	7	7	6	8	12	18	24	25	27
Commercial buildings	31	26	28	27	31	35	46	56	57	69
Dwellings	154	129	142	137	157	179	230	283	291	350
Mercantile fleet	290	186	63	68	87	135	128	256	263	294
Railway transport	43	41	39	38	40	47	53	59	64	65
General government	75	78	75	69	75	86	101	119	142	145
Total gross investment*	1005	741	699	654	771	923	1081	1414	1473	1600

Source: *Nasjonalregnskap 1865-1960*, Nos XII, 163, Table 7.
*As some minor items are ecxluded, the figures do not quite add up.

for recovery must be sought elsewhere, despite the fact that shipping represented from 16 per cent to 25 per cent of total capital formation in the decade.

The most conspicuous type of investment was private construction of dwellings and commercial buildings. This made up 18.4 per cent of gross capital formation in 1930, but increased to 24.6 per cent in 1932, and culminated at 26.2 per cent of the total in 1939. Construction, unlike shipping, had very strong linkages within the home economy. It was labour intensive rather than capital intensive; most of the input factors, moreover, stemmed from local resources, including cement, brick, wood, glass and metal fittings, and the buying power generated accrued almost entirely to producers in the home market. For these reasons, it seems probable that building and construction were the most important factors in sustaining recovery.

Statistics for manhours in construction point in the same direction. After a series of weak years in the 1920s, with 18 million manhours in the bottom year 1927, private construction rallied to around 25 million manhours in the depression years 1930-3, after which it doubled to 50 million by 1939.[9] To gauge its importance one should recognise, however, that with a 48-hour week and 40 working weeks per year, construction still represented only about 26,000 man years in 1939 against 32,000 for shipping. In addition, public sector construction, roads, railways among them, should be added to the figures cited above. Overall, total manhours in construction were 50 million in 1930, against 95 million in 1939. Public sector work showed a doubling between 1930 and 1939, or about the same as the private construction sector. Road work totalled 9.5 million manhours in 1930 against 20.9 million in 1939, and railways 4.3 million and 5.7 million manhours in the respective years. These figures represented 28 per cent of total manhours in both years. The figures alone serve to dispel the idea of a massive countercyclical government campaign against unemployment in the thirties.

Another time series, involving new finished rooms, including kitchens, also sheds light on the alleged importance of construction in bringing about a recovery. The figures, compiled from 1928, may be used to check exaggerated notions held regarding the extent of new building activity in the thirties. Net additions of new rooms in towns with more than 5,000 inhabitants were as follows:[10]

1928	8.223 rooms	1934	16,028 rooms
1929	11,918 "	1935	18,216 "
1930	12,433 "	1936	24,964 "
1931	12,249 "	1937	20,319 "
1932	17,231 "	1938	18,130 "
1933	13,803 "		

Construction of new homes culminated in 1936 with just about 25,000 new rooms being added; however, in the depression year 1932 a total of 17,000 rooms were also added, more than the two following years and almost as much as in 1935 and 1938. The evidence is thus not at all straightforward, but at least it underlines once again the limited effect that government financed construction can have had in sustaining the recovery.

Turning to the other capital formation categories, table 7.1 indicates that manufacturing loomed as the second most important investment sector, while agriculture trailed a good deal behind. Fisheries were a minor investment area, ranging between 3.1 and 1.8 per cent of total capital formation in the decade, trailing behind electricity supply and railway construction.[11]

Foreign Trade

As for the role of exports, we have already observed that in the 1930s shipping incomes had only a modest influence on the level of activity at home. Since shipping incomes traditionally represented as much as 50 per cent of total exports, one would tend to believe that exports cannot have been a strong recuperative factor in bringing the economy back on its feet. Other evidence tends to strengthen the view. Avoiding numbers this time, we turn to Figure 7.2. This provides a survey of sorts of total commodity exports 1930-9, total freight earnings from the merchant fleet and the export performance of major commodity groups. The obvious point again is that the turn around occurred in 1931, both for gross freight earnings and total commodity exports. Looking at specific items, we note that timber, i.e. sawn and planed goods (15) dropped steadily, oils and fats (13) stagnated, as did fish products (2), while freight earnings, paper (18) minerals (21), and metals (22) maintained their levels and even expanded considerably, notably metals and freight earnings.

The graph underlines also the abnormal size of freight earnings in the Norwegian economy. In the years 1937-9, for instance, they equalled or exceeded total commodity exports.

To evaluate the role of exports in the 1930s, we note that their share of GNP declined, down from 39.1 per cent in the decade 1915-24 to 28.7 per cent the following decade 1925-34. The reduction suggests that the pull from foreign markets that had buoyed the economy earlier, notably 1900-20, now fell off. A symptom of this is that Norway ran up a surplus on its current account balance, in the present century, a very rare thing indeed. Thus in the decade 1925-34 annual exports averaged 1,241 million kroner, imports 1,210 million, yielding an export surplus of 31 million annually, corresponding to + 0.7 per cent of GNP. In the next decade the surplus similarly amounted to an annual 89 million, or + 1.9 per cent of GNP.[12] The verdict is that to the extent that we can talk of recovery in the thirties, this cannot have been export-led. See Fig. 7.3 that traces the long run movements of imports and exports and the dramatic downturn that occurred in the interwar years. Despite the export surplus, recovery, such as it was, cannot have been export led. The verdict rests, first, on the observation of the severe contraction that occurred in foreign trade in the decade relative to total output; second, on the observation that shipping earnings and other services represented more than 50 per cent of exports, and that between 36 and 51 per cent of the freight earnings were spent abroad. The export surplus nevertheless stimulated recovery.

Figure 7.2: Exports of Total Commodities, Freight Earnings in Ocean Shipping and Export Values for Selected Commodities 1930-1939. Million Current Kroner

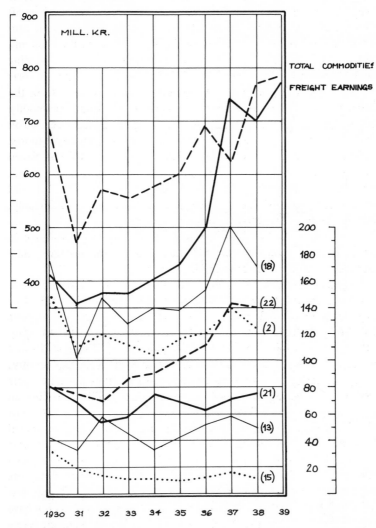

(2)   Edible animal products
(13)   Fats, Oil, Rubber
(15)   Timber
(18)   Paper
(21)   Mineral products
(22)   Metals, crude and semi-manufactured
Source: *Historical Statistics 1968*. Tables 153, 195.

Figure 7.3: Exports, Imports of Goods and Services in % of Total Output (GNP) 1865-1977

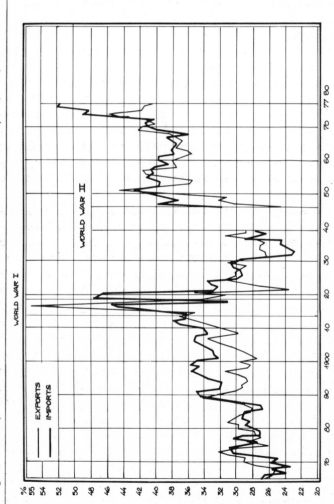

Source: Nos. *National Accounts 1865-1960*, and Nos. *Økonomisk Utsyn*

The Role of Government

The third influence to be considered is the role of government in com-
bating the depression. Anticyclical policies by government were well
known; after all, roadwork and railway building from the 1860s
onwards had been inspired by periodic waves of unemployment. But
anticyclical spending by local and central governments was always considered as makeshift improvisation, intended to bring the economy out
of a temporary embarrassment. Providing jobs for people did not count
among governmental responsibilities. Keynes is justly remembered here
for his work, that was interpreted as having theoretically justified deficit
programmes by the central government. Various plans for a crisis programme began to circulate after 1931, but the Kolstad and Hundseid
minority ministries, 1931-3, both from the Farmers' Party, though
representing rural Norway in distress, failed to consider more unortho-
dox plans for a major deficit budget campaign. The Hundseid ministry
was followed by the third Mowinckel government in March 1933. The
last Liberal premier, Johan Ludwig Mowinckel, like Herbert Hoover,
did too little too late. Although his government did undertake crisis-
measures, including increased appropriations for roads, railway construction and electricity, these tended to be counterbalanced by budget
reductions elsewhere. The expansionary effects amounted to very
little.

In the end the two arch enemies, Labour and the Farmers' Party,
voted down the Mowinckel minority cabinet in March 1935 and saw to
it that Labour formed a new ministry under Johan Nygaardsvold
(1879-1952), with the support of the Farmers' Party. In return the new
government promised to meet the central demands of the farmers.

In view of the fact that it was the recent Kolstad's Farmers' government that had included Vidkun Quisling as defense minister, the
Farmers' Party volte-face in 1935 was something of a sensation. It confirmed what was observed elsewhere, however, that Quisling and his
Nazi-party, organised in 1933, had particular appeal in rural areas
among strata threatened by proletarisation. But one should also recall
that a similar political compromise between social democrats and
farmers had already been made in Sweden in 1933, and was also under
way in Denmark. For a time the slogan 'Town and Land, hand in hand'
won popularity with the mass of the voters.

Labour had taken 69 out of 150 seats in the Storting elections in
1933 on the platform 'The nation back to work'. Together with the
farm bloc, Nygaardsvold had the backing of a comfortable majority, but
like the Hornsrud cabinet in 1928, he was unable to govern effectively

alone. Unlike Hornsrud, however, Nygaardsvold stepped easily on doctrinaire socialist manifestos. A member of the Storting from 1916, Nygaardsvold, a former sawmill worker from Hommelvik in rural Trøndelag, was a seasoned veteran of Norwegian politics. His jovial appearance created an air of confidence. Besides, as shown already, the economic crisis was in fact over. The task was to combat unemployment. The means Nygaardsvold easily found within the existing constitutional framework. Mowinckel had proposed 43 million in crisis appropriations. Originally, Labour had wished to double this, but settled for 30 million extra, with the help of the farmers.[13] The central government expenditures on current account for 1935-6 totalled 384 million kroner.[14] Of this, total crisis appropriations amounted to 76 million, or about 20 per cent.

The theoretical reorientation suspected in the figures, however, was apparent only, for the government was compelled to levy some new taxes, and cut down elsewhere in the budget, so that the expansionary effect was negligible or nil. Direct taxes were increased by 13 million. To this was added a sales tax, levied at 1 per cent of over-the-counter value of all sales to consumers. The following year came a 25 per cent interest tax on capital income, at the same time as income tax rates were made more progressive. All this redistribution of income was wholly predictable, given the party's past and its following. No echo from Cambridge is discernible. For as long as the new government measures were financed through taxes, it merely meant that buying power was transferred from one group to another. No extra buying power was created. To make the issue clearer, we consider the government deficits in the budgets, their size, and the national debt. Table 7.2 traces the development of government finances in the thirties.

The data indicate that an upward trend set in for central government revenue from 1932/3 and for expendiures from 1933/4. After the trend shift both incomes and |expenditures increased, the former slightly more than the latter. As a result the account was settled with a surplus every year after Nygaardsvold took over in 1935 until the outbreak of war 1940. In per cent of gross domestic product the government expenditures fluctuated around 8 per cent. No upward trend is visible. The shift in 1939 was due to war appropriations. Hence the Labour Party's programme for an economic counter defensive against depression turned out to have had only a slight effect on the overall level of economic activity. Expansion of expenditures in one direction was matched by reductions in others. This was in order to maintain budgetary balance, so that on balance the aggregate multiplier effect was on the face of it

Table 7.2: Central Government Revenue and Expenditure 1930-1939.
Absolute Figures in Curent Millions and in % of GDP

	Revenue	Expenditure	Surplus + Deficit –	Capital- expenditure	Total expenditure	In % of GDP
1930-1	330	313	+ 17	60	374	8.5
1931-2	317	313	+ 4	48	361	9.4
1932-3	259	254	+ 5	56	309	8.0
1933-4	278	242	+ 36	61	302	7.8
1934-5	293	268	+ 24	73	341	8.4
1935-6	350	298	+ 52	86	384	8.8
1936-7	413	323	+ 90	99	422	8.7
1937-8	474	375	+ 98	96	472	8.5
1938-9	533	426	+ 107	146	567	9.7
1939-40	562	591	– 28	123	714	11.4

Source: *Historical Statistics 1968*, Table 233; *Nasjonalregnskap 1865-1960*,
Table 49.

negative. Despite this GNP now grew at a rate of 4.6 per cent per year
1934-9, against 0.6 per cent for the years 1930-4.

Nor are Keynesian ideas discernible in the national debt in these
years. The central government debt was 1,565 million in 1930 and
1,464 million in 1939, which means that there was a slight reduction,
quite the opposite of what pump priming, inspired by Keynes, should
have amounted to. Debt service ranged between 33 and 38 million
kroner annually. Also the municipalities reduced their total debt in
these years.[15]

Far more important, though generally overlooked, was the decision
in 1936 to increase the money stock by 75 million kroner, up from 250
to 325 million.[16] In 1939 the circulating note issue, not covered by
gold, was increased again, this time by 100 million.[17] In three years
the volume of notes in circulation was thus increased by 60 per cent, up
by 28 per cent.[18] The increased note circulation stemmed from net
sales of currency by the public and the banks to the central bank.
Though not by conscious design, this was in effect Cambridge rather
than Hommelvik. From this simple floating of paper money came the
perceptible inflationary wind that stimulated investments and buying
power among consumers. It was not the result of budgetary policies.
The consumer price index climbed 20 per cent in five years, up from
54.3 in 1934 to 63.8 in 1939.[19] Annual price increases averaged 3.3 per
cent in that period, which foreshadowed the postwar trend of controlled inflation. Prior to this prices had been falling for fifteen years.

A sense of relief that the worst was over prompted the government to propose new social welfare legislation that had been sidestepped for twenty years. Old age pensions were voted in 1936 and unemployment insurance in 1938. They were compulsory, but included as yet only industrial workers. It was in a way the urban industrial society that set up new security nets under its members in place of the old nets of the agrarian society that had crumbled. They must be counted land marks in social history. A minimum income was henceforth a right, not a charitable gift. The employees paid about one third, employers another third, and the state the remaining third. At the same time state subsidies to farmers and fishermen increased. Generally they were given in aid of investments, production, or price reductions. Subsidies under these headings amounted to 15 million in 1930, 28 million in 1935 and 59 million kroner in the last peace year.[20] Included here were subsidies for grain paid by the Grain Monopoly of 1928, aids to tilling of new soil, building of roads, potato cellars, siloes, potato subsidies, price stabilisation subsidies on milk, milk products and margarine, and subsidies to the cod and herring fisheries. The social relief items in the national budget also expanded substantially after 1935.

The Main Agreement 1935

The sense that one no longer had one's back against the wall also prompted the parties in the labour market to mutual concessions. In 1935 LO and NAF signed a Main Agreement whereby the two antagonists in effect formally recognised each other's legitimate interests and powers, and agreed on a code of behaviour that henceforth became binding for both.The main idea was that LO recognised NAF's legitimate demands in regulating work and working procedures. In return NAF accepted LO and its legitimate right to organise unions and bargain collectively through elected representatives. The agreement was valid for the following five years. With occasional revisions and additions, it has regularly been prolonged since. In popular imagination it took its place as a social contract beside the Constitution.

The immediate background for the compromise was a astrike among miners at Folldal Copper mine that led the employer to contest the union's right to collective resignation on behalf of striking workers.[21] In practice this right had been recognised by employers and their organisation NAF since 1900, but the legal rules, notably the voting rules regarding new contract proposals, were less than explicit. Too often union bosses insisted on speaking for all the workers when in fact the union organised only a minority. Why not individual contract? Indeed, old time liberalists tended to speak of 'freedom of contract' where LO spoke of 'strike breakers'. The Folldal company, insisting on individual rather than collective contract before re-admitting miners, took its case to the Supreme Court, which, in an unexpected ruling in February 1934, declared in favour of the company. The verdict in effect questioned the existence of the entire union system that had evolved during more than half a century. It was perhaps a sign of increased maturity that after the verdict the union-chiefs, rather than going on the barricades, sat down with the NAF board to hammer out a compromise. The LO-chiefs promised that pay and working contracts should henceforth be decided through secret ballot. NAF assured in return that in the future the unions were to bargain collectively for the workers. The compromise covered the Folldal case, and in effect voided the recent Supreme Court verdict.

Summing up the 1930s

The Main Agreement was signed in March 1935 in the very same month that Nygaardsvold formed the second Labour government. Together the events inaugurated a new era in Norway, or did they? Analysis of the economic programmes of the Labour government suggests that the transition to socialistic rule in 1935 meant little in the way of radical measures. Fiscal policy was orthodox. Unemployment persisted. As late as 1938 an average of 22 per cent of union workers went without work. In 1939 one out of every five workers was still unemployed (see Table 2.1). The means of production had not been taken over by workers' soviets. Words like 'state capitalism' or 'a planned economy' were heard more seldom. The economic and political power structure remained unchanged.

But economics is not all. Psycychologically, and in the longer perspective, the Nygaardsvold government did represent a watershed. In important respects the interventionist state replaced the older liberal conception of the tasks of government. Responsibility for the total level of activity was increasingly seen as a matter of political leadership. Moreover, organised labour left its revolutionary jargon and joined the nation. They were now the nation, its government their government. Symbols like the national banner soon appeared side by side with the red banner in May Day parades. A spirit of conciliation was abroad in

the land. Undoubtedly, statistics had a hand in it. Trade union membership, which had been as low as 84,000 in 1922, stood at 140,000 in
1930, a massive 224,000 in 1935 and 357,000 four years later (Table
2.1). Labour polled 40.1 per cent of the votes in 1933, and 42.5 per
cent in 1936, the last election before the war. A 'bandwaggon effect'
was indubitably at work. Besides, it was soon generally recognised that
a Labour government was a guarantee against wild-cat strikes.

When so much is said, the signs of continuity are easy to perceive.
It was the Liberal Party, not Labour, that introduced direct taxation to
the national government in 1892 and the male franchise in 1898. It
represented majority demands in a largely rural society. In the same
light one may view the bills for old age pensions and unemployment
insurance now introduced by Labour. These reflected dominant social
demands in an industrial society. If a comparison is made, which
depends on one's view of the relevance of politics, one would necessarily say that the male franchise in 1898 was the more radical step, and
that the social welfare legislation of the thirties was a mere echo of the
real radical reform of 1892 when direct taxation was introduced. In
effect from that year it was merely a matter of time until welfare
legislation for the majority, paid for by the minority, would find its
way to the statute book. In this fundamental sense the events in 1935
represented continuity rather than radical departure.

Finally, as for the economic impact of the Labour government, it
is evident that it failed to bring the nation back to work. In a way it is
thus misleading to speak of recovery of the economy in the last prewar
years. The home market orientation documented above lacked sufficient force to haul the economy fully out of the slump. Only war
resulted in full employment, in Norway, as in other industrial countries.

Notes

1 *Nasjonalregnskap 1865-1960*, Table 1.4.
2 *Historical Statistics 1968*, Table 207.
3 Frøystein Wedervang, *Development of a Population of Industrial Firms*,
Universitetsforlaget, Oslo, 1965, pp. 159-63.
4 This is also the general conclusion of a study carried out under the supervision of professor Francis Sejersted at the Institute of History of Oslo University.
A recent anthology, containing the main results, is Francis Sejersted, ed., *Vekst
gjennom krise. Studier i norsk teknologihistorie*, Universitetsforlaget, Oslo, 1982.
5 *Nasjonalregnskap 1865-1960*, Table 49.
6 CBS, *Statistisk-økonomisk oversikt over året 1936*, Oslo, 1937, pp. 36-7.

7 For an example: Ted Hanisch, *Hele folket i arbeid*, Pax, Oslo, 1977.
8 J.O. Egeland, *Kongeveien*, II, p. 453.
9 *Historical Statistics 1968*, Table 150.
10 CBS, *Statistisk-økonomisk oversikt over 1939*, Oslo, 1940, p. 43.
11 NOS *Nasjonalregnskap 1865-1960*, Table 7, p. 106.
12 Juul Bjerke, *Langtidslinjer*, Table 27 (current kroner).
13 Helge Nordvik, 'Krisepolitikken og den teoretiske nyorientering av den økonomiske politikken i Norge i 1930-årene', *Hist. Tidsskr.* 1977, pp. 289-317.
14 *Historical Statistics 1968*, Table 234.
15 *Historical Statistics 1968*, Tables 234, 236, 239.
16 N. Rygg, *Norges Bank i mellomkrigstiden*, p. 578.
17 Gunnar Jahn, *Norges Bank gjennom 150 år*, Oslo, 1966, p. 292.
18 *Nasjonalregnskap 1865-1960*, Table 49, p. 342.
19 *Historical Statistics 1968*, Table 285 (Base year 1949 = 100).
20 *Nasjonalregnskap 1865-1960*, Table 18, Note p. 153.
21 Jardar Seim, *Hvordan Hovedavtalen ble til. Staten, organisasjonene og arbeidsfreden 1930-1935*, Oslo, 1972.

8 THE WAR ECONOMY 1940-1945

Outbreak of War 9 April 1940

Germany attacked Poland on 1 August 1939 whereupon, treaty bound, Britain and France declared war on Germany.[1] The reactions in Scandinavia were similar to those in 1914. In line with its Scandinavian neighbours Norway declared neutrality. The Nygaardsvold government began a cautious build-up of stocks to meet a possible blockade. The Soviet Union's war on Finland in the winter 1939 brought the spectre of war and blockade nearer home. Coffee and sugar were rationed that winter, and private firms, sensing the course of development, also bought up stocks and supplies of raw materials. Some belated steps to strengthen the country's military preparedness were also taken. The government, however, like the military and the voters, was mentally unprepared for war. The country had not been engaged in war since 1814. The Labour government with its anti-military ideology suffered additional qualms. Yet responsibility for the country's defence rested squarely on its shoulders.

At any event, despite the repeated and unequivocal warnings, the government and the country were taken by almost complete surprise when German invasionary land, sea and air forces, under the command of General Nikolaus von Falkenhorst, attacked Norway on 9 April 1940. The German attack force counted 12,000 soldiers. Even the general call to arms over the broadcasting systems that morning was bungled. With mostly defeatist officers, obsolete weapons, inadequate supplies and communications, the Norwegian forces offered only scattered resistance while generally retreating northward. The Germans captured the main towns, ports and airfields immediately in the south. The invaders also commanded the air space, and their troops were able to press forward, despite resistance from Norwegians and Allied auxiliary troops who arrived on 14 April at Namsos and Åndalsnes.

The Germans had less than full control of the country north of Trondheim, where the Luftwaffe was unable to provide air support. The German marine had taken Narvik on the morning of 9 April, but in two daring counter attacks on 10 and 13 April the British navy sank all the 10 German war ships in Narvik harbour. Allied French, Polish, British and Norwegian forces later recaptured the town on 28-9 May.

Resistance began to pay off. Moreover, despite repeated German attempts to grab the royal family and the members of the government, the King, Crown Prince Olav and the Government escaped to the north. This was important, for at an emergency meeting at Elverum on 9 April, called by the Storting's President C.J. Hambro (1885-1964), the attending members of the Storting had given the Government a clear constitutional mandate as the rightful government of the country. If they desired an arrangement like that recently set up in Denmark, the invaders would have to deal with the King, representing sovereignty. Failing that, they would have to rule by military force.

Despite these bright spots, the Allied military campaign in Norway was called off on 7 June after two months' fighting. The background was the disastrous collapse on the west front in France where the German blitzkrieg had started in the meantime. The Allied troops at Narvik were urgently needed in the defence of France. King Haakon, Crown Prince Olav and the Government sailed from Tromsø for England on 7 June on board HMS Devonshire, to organise continued resistance.[2] The Norwegian gold reserve, valued at 240 million kroner, was also safely brought to England on board Devonshire. Thus, the German plan for a Danish arrangement failed in Norway. In retrospect the Norwegian government's resolution to continue resistance provided a rallying point, if any was needed, for moral self-respect. It took its toll. Casualties of the two months' campaign reached about 5,000 dead soldiers and civilians, comprising 1,038 Norwegians, 3,000 Germans and 1,000 Allied soldiers. Besides, a number of towns had been reduced to a rubble by German bombing, among them Kristiansund, Ålesund, Åndalsnes and Elverum.

Occupation

Meanwhile, the civilian population, trapped in occupied territory, was subjected to German military rule. The rule was tightened as time went by. In the early confusion Vidkun Quisling, head of Nasjonal Samling, the Norwegian Nazi party, tried to grab control, but was easily pushed to the sideline. He was not the stuff Führers are made of. Instead the population and the local civilian authorities in occupied territory took orders from the Administrative Council (Adminstrasjonsrådet) headed by Chief Justice Paal Berg, set up at the instigation of the German Army commander, General von Falkenhorst, on 15 April. It was a makeshift body only, that dealt with routine matters to stave off civlian chaos. When its members proved unco-operative, Hitler sent Josef Terboven to Norway as Reichskommissar (24 April) to set up a puppet government. The members of the Administrative Council and the Presidency of the Storting, called in to negotiate, stiffened their opposition.[3] They were adamant on the central issue of the deposition of the King in London, on which the Germans insisted. The Reichskommissar feared correctly that the loyalty King Haakon commanded might prove disastrous to Hitler's plans for integrating the country into the larger German system in Europe.

The negotiations for a 'Riksråd', a pro-Hitler Norwegian civil government, failed. The Administrative Council was sent home on 25 September 1940, the Storting having been dissolved a little earlier. From then on Terboven ran the country as a Reichskommissariat.[4] The civilian administration continued apparently as before, with Terboven as political leader, answerable to none but Hitler himself. The arrangement was ideal for a political terrorist. The system had not a thread of legitimacy. Its authority rested on bayonets. Quisling's party, Nasjonal Samling, had 4,200 members in August 1940, 24,000 at the end of that year, and attracted 43,000 members at its best in November 1943, after considerable advertising and propaganda. Membership at its peak thus amounted to 1.4 per cent of a population of 3 million. That is, the overwhelming majority felt that sovereignty rested with the King in England and his exiled government. With the organisation of the 'Kommissariat Ministers' in September 1940 the political situation froze as far as the distribution of power was concerned. Members of Nasjonal Samling, Quisling's party, gradually filled the top positions in the civilian administrative network, notably the police, though the three most important ministries of the *pro forma* government after September 1940, were headed by non-party members. They were the Department of Trade, the Department of Provisions and the Department of Finance.

On 1 February 1942 Quisling was put in charge of a 'national government', and assumed the title 'Ministerpresident', but real power, including the approval of 'laws', remained in the hands of the Reichskommissar.[5] Von Falkenhorst, head of the German military forces in Norway throughout the war, was ultimately under the political authority of Terboven. The entry of unqualified Nazi members into the administration, attempts at nazification, censorship, and the beginnings of unlawful arrests, gradually called forth legal, and soon illegal resistance, from all political and professional organisations, ranging from the parties, the trade unions, the Supreme Court, the University, the Boy Scout Federation, and the sports and athletics associations. Resistance was characterised by strong unity. There was one co-ordinated civilian and one centralised military branch of resistance (Mi.org.), both welded together as a single force by an executive committee that represented the Home Front leadership and was acknowledged as such by the London government in 1941.[5]

The Merchant Marine

Unlike other exiled governments, the Norwegian government in London was not a beggar. Aside from the central bank's gold reserves, it based its existence on the freight earnings that stemmed from a government-owned shipping company, the Norwegian Shipping and Trade Mission (Nortraship), organised by shipowner Ingolf Hysing Olsen in London, shortly after the outbreak of war in April 1940. From July 1940 it had a New York office as well, headed by shipowner Øivind Lorentzen. During the war Nortraship had offices in 30 other ports in all four parts of the world. Manned by 1,100 employees, Nortraship, the world's largest shipping company, owed its existence to an agreement, signed 20 November 1939 between the shipowners' association, Norges Reder-forbund, and the British government, whereby the shipowners, unable to operate their ships from occupied Norway, placed them at the disposal of Allied service for the rest of the war.[6] Anxious to secure tonnage and prevent their opponents from getting control over this vital asset, the German authorities in June 1940 sequestered 26 Norwegian ships in occupied France and French Africa and controlled the coastal fleet in Norway, about 240 smaller vessels. Most of the modern ocean-going fleet, however, despite orders issued over the occupied broadcasting headquarters in Oslo, sailed for Allied ports – about 1,000 ships, totalling four million gross tons and manned by 30,000 Norwegian sailors.[7] The charter agreement had come about at the request of the Norwegian government, wishing to secure Allied supplies in return for Allied use of Norwegian tonnage, much as in World War I. Lloyds had most of the insurance, and Hambro's Bank most of the mortgages for the ships, hence the arrangements were worked out in an atmosphere of mutual trust.

The crews sailed in all war zones, in the Atlantic, in the Murmansk convoys; they saw action in Malta, Egypt, Greece, the Far East, and Dunkirk. They took part in the Allied landings in Sicily, Normandy, Morocco, Madagascar, the Pacific Islands, and Finnmark. Above all, the sailings to Britain were vital. In 1941 Norwegian vessels represented 40 per cent of foreign tonnage entering British ports. During the war 19 per cent of all oil transported to Britain came in Norwegian tankers; in the fateful period 1941-2, when the military outcome hung in the balance, the Norwegian share was 30-40 per cent. The fleet was worth more than a million soldiers, according to Foreign Secretary Eden in 1941.

Losses were substantial. If one included the sailors who were killed in war action between September 1939 and April 1940, a total of 4,000 Norwegian seamen lost their lives during World War II. This was the same as the number of casualties suffered by the Norwegian army and the resistance movement during the entire war. One should remember that the seamen were never drafted or conscripted, they were on board by personal choice. Crew members who survived the torpedo nightmares often suffered nerve problems. The Seamen's Church, operated by the Seamen's Mission, achieved new significance in the war years. Material losses were also heavy. The overall shipping losses suffered by Nortraship was 461 ships. In gross tons the country lost 2.3 million out of a fleet of 4.3 million gross tons, or 47 per cent of registered tonnage at the outbreak of war 1940. Both maintenance and repair had suffered, hence the tonnage that did survive was of poor quality. Overall value depreciation was close to 60 per cent (1939 kroner).[9]

On the other hand, Nortraship by the end of the war had earned a surplus on current account of approximately 2.6 billion N kr. The final account for the company worked out by 1963, showed a total gross profit of almost 2.8 billion.[10] This included 58 million for the whale fleet, accumulated interest, and gross profits from the fleet's wartime sailings.

The Nortraship settlement comprised compensation both to the home fleet (226 ships) and the 901 overseas merchant ships. The claims included compensations to the participating shipping companies for the requisitioning of their ships, shipping losses, amortisations, contributions to diverse seamen's funds, administration and sundry expenditures for a total of 1,953,684,410 N kr. Nortraship thus made a net profit of 819 million kroner which accrued to the Norwegian state. Of the insurance claims of 1,387 million kroner, Nortraship paid 47 million while the rest was covered by the foreign insurance companies. The sailors' pension fund was allotted 186 million. For their settlement money the shipping companies paid normal taxes, worked out retrospectively, for a total of 300 million kroner. The Nortraship settlement was without parallel the most extensve economic transaction in the country's history.

The Nortraship Secret Fund

Then there was the secret Nortraship Seamen's Fund. The origin of the fund was due to the initiative taken by Nortraship's director Øivind Lorentzen in June 1940.[11] When Norway became an ally of Great Britain, following the German occupation, the British government demanded that the agreed war risk bonuses to Norwegian sailors, sailing in war zones, should be cut down to the levels of British sailors. A general wage freeze had been put into effect in Britain, and the authorities there feared unrest among British seamen if it became known that an Allied wage group had been granted substantially better conditions. In this situation Lorentzen persuaded the British shipping authorities to transfer the risk payments into a secret seamen's fund for the duration of the war, the proceeds of which were to be . . . 'used in the best interests of Norwegian sailors after the war'. By 1 January 1947 the fund had 43.7 million kroner.

In 1946 the four seamen's unions advised that the Nortraship fund should be used to provide pensions for widows and children of deceased war sailors besides providing pensions for war-disabled seamen. This view prevailed in the Storting, which in December 1948 passed a government bill along the above lines. Groups among the war sailors rejected this scheme. Their spokesmen argued that providing social security pensions for sailors was a natural government obligation, in view of their commitments to the national war effort. This social obligation had nothing to do with the secret Nortraship fund. These premiums, as the original statutes made clear, were simply delayed compensations payable direct to those sailors who had sailed in the war. In court disputes that ensued, both the Oslo town court (1951) and the Supreme Court (1954) decided in favour of the government. Bad conscience lingered, however, and in the late 1960s public opinion favoured resumption of payments to war sailors. Though generous, the compensation money of 155 million kroner, voted in the Storting in April 1972, hardly allayed bitterness that had grown during twenty years. The original fund was kept intact for the benefit of war sailors and their survivors. At the end of 1978 there remained 19.3 million kroner.

The shipping sector normally loomed large in the Norwegian economy; in the war it assumed vital importance. It represented in normal years 25 per cent of gross capital formation, earned 50 per cent

of total exports of goods and services, covered the deficits on commodity imports, and its capital made up 12-15 per cent of total real
capital. In the war the fleet enhanced its importance. It enabled the
exiled government to pay cash for aeroplanes, materials and its own
administration, for its training grounds, for social work among its seamen, and for most of the office space it used. The government made
little use of the American Lend and Lease Act, ran up no new national
debt, and the shipowners participating in Nortraship arranged for
payments to all creditors on the day.[12]

An Ersatz Economy

When normal trade channels were closed, demands had to be satisfied
either by imports from German controlled Europe, by increased
exploitation of internal resources, or by redeploying resources so as to
increase overall self-sufficiency. First, one should remember imports
for which no substitutes existed: bread grain, fats, rubber, cotton,
metals, sugar, phosphate, bauxite, alumina, fertilizers, coal and
coke, petroleum, gasoline, and fuel oils. In normal prewar years there
was an average import of 300,000 tons of bread grain, 70,000 tons of
phosphates, 3,000 tons of tobacco leaf, 300,000 tons of various metals,
90,000 tons of sugar, 300,000 tons of petroleum and gasoline, 3 million
tons of coal and coke, and 3,000 tons of cotton. Some of these imports,
most of which had come from overseas countries, at first could be
bought from Continental Europe. Morally, Germany was bound to
arrange for grain imports, lest the civilian population starve to death.
Other items, such as coal, lubricants or petrol fuels, were necessary for
the maintenance of the civilian industry. Machinery, bauxite and aluminium would soon become important as German plans for hydro-based
industries unfolded.

Second, increased utilisation of internal resources helped cover the
needs of consumers and producers. Farmers and fishermen came into
their own again. Despite expectations, however, total crops, expressed
in standard feed units, stayed below the pre-war level in all the war
years, down from an average of 1,893 million in 1935-9 to an average
of 1,662 million 1940-4, a fall of some 12 per cent.[13] Lack of manpower and phosphorus fertilizers account for the disappointing
outcome, but the statistics most likely under-report the real crop
figures. Throughout the war there was a black market in food. The
farmers were in a strategic position, improving their position in the

economy relative to other groups, and also absolutely. It was also part of the Nazi ideology to extol the peasants. One indication of their recovery is the figure for total farm debts, which dropped from 1,314 million to 1,044 million kroner during the war. Their debts relative to their assets averaged 40.3 per cent in 1940, and in 1946 20.3 per cent.[14] Another indication is the control figures for slaughtered animals, maintained by the occupation authorities with increasing ferocity during the war years. While an average of 185,000 cattle were reported annually in the five years 1935-9, the figure dropped to a yearly average of 63,000 cattle in the years 1940-5, down by two thirds.[15] A similar dramatic drop in meat deliveries through official, price-controlled channels occurred for calves, sheep and above all pigs. Annual deliveries of pigs before the war were about 320,000 pigs, in 1943 the figure was down to 5,087. Imports of concentrated feeds in agriculture, including proteins and carbohydrates, dropped overall to one third of prewar levels. Concentrated feeds were indispensable. Their virtual disappearance explains the drop in the figures for slaughtered animals. Another indispensable ingredient, hydro saltpetres, containing nitrogen, was of course manufactured at home. Consumption doubled, from 10,00 tons in 1940 to 21,500 in 1945.[16] The black economy, as is evident in the figures, concealed a good deal of farm production. The Germans also purchased quantities of meat direct from farmers. Figures for these purchases were reported after the war.[17]

Another bottleneck, aside from feed concentrates, was manpower. To increase agricultural production youths of recruiting age were called into 'labour service', operated by the Nazi government. The scheme was intensely unpopuar for that reason. To avoid service the young men in growing numbers fled to Sweden to join the Norwegian police troops being organised there, or sailed to England across the North Sea. The 'Shetland Bus' was a familiar word in those days. Increasingly the young also went underground and joined Mil.org, the military arm of the resistance movement, operating on Norwegian territory during the war. About 40,000 young men had gone into hiding in the forests by the end of 1944 to join the Mil.org. Another 50,000 fled to Sweden, where the young men were enjoined to serve in the Norwegian police troops organised there. About 3,300 people escaped across the North Sea to Great Britain. The Norwegian regular army in Britain counted 4,000 men, the navy 7,500 men and the air force 2,600 men, many of whom had fled from Norway to get into active service.[18] Manpower shortages were thus a bottleneck in agriculture as well as in the fisheries.

The third solution to the break-up of normal trade channels was to develop substitutes. The era of *Ersatzwaren* was at hand. Autarchy was a national-socialist ideal. In daily life it was a matter of irritation, and making the best of the situation. Thus, when petrol and coal virtually disappeared from domestic consumption, households turned again to the nation's birch forests for heating their homes and fuelling their cars. Cars ran on gas generated by wood or carbide burners mounted on the back. By 1945, 22,000 gas generators were in operation.[19] When meat became scarce urban people showed renewed interest in the art of rearing pigs and rabbits, and the growing of tobacco, vegetables and potatoes either in the back garden or on rented plots outside the towns. 'Villa pig' was only one of the current neologisms of those years. Cellulose fodder was produced by the forest product industry to replace imports of feedstuffs. A special plant was built by Borregaard at Sarpsborg.

Fish replaced meat to an unusual degree. However, total fish landings did not increase; they had been around 1 million tons in the last prewar years, but hovered around 700,000 tons during the war.[20] In view of the doubled need, the fall in landings looks curious. The reason is under-reporting. To prevent excessive requisitions by the Wehrmacht, it was common practice, according to professor Gerhard Meidell Gerhardsen who worked out the statistics on herring fisheries during the war, to report catch figures below the real amounts. Once the personnel at the Central Bureau of Statistics had gained the confidence of the occupation authorities, they had no scruples about doctoring the figures. The figures for landings in the *Statistical Yearbook* for the war years are therefore too low. Since the same figures are reprinted in *Historical Statistics* 1968, it follows that the present fisheries statistics under-report the amounts landed in the war years. According to professor Gerhardsen, the same sort of doctoring was done to the figures for agricultural production.[21] Despite repeated urgings and extra tobacco rations for fishermen, the numbers participating in the major cod, mackerel and herring fisheries showed no increase. Their number was 59,000 in 1939, against 32,000 in 1945.[22] Substitutes abounded: copper and nickel coins were replaced by iron and zinc coins, herring oil was used as surrogate margarine, cod liver oil as a health panacea, black sardine tins replaced the aluminium tins, surrogates replaced soap and detergents, leather soles were replaced by wooden soles, cotton by a synthetic fibre called cellull-yarn. Shoes made of fish skin remained an indelible memory for a generation, as did turnip dinners, B-soap and fish cakes made of mackerel.

Industry spontaneously rose to the occasion. In addition to those mentioned above, there were surrogates for tea, cream, coffee and tobacco. An echo of industrial ingenuity is observed in the statistics for industrial establishments, which increased 16 per cent, up from a total of 4,449 establishments in 1939 to 5,160 for 1945. [23] No serious study has yet been made of the innnovations and adaptations achieved by industry during the *Ersatz* years.

The German Industrial Projects

The reason why, despite the obvious need for food, the labour supply in agriculture and the fisheries declined during the war, must be sought in the higher pay available at German construction and building projects. Though a stain on the record, the fact remains that German war projects attracted at one time up to 150,000 workers. And the country had its quota of 'barrack barons', entrepreneurs who unpatriotically made a fortune when ideally they should have been engaged in guerilla actions against the invaders. However, the problem of a *modus vivendi* with Wehrmacht was an unavoidable issue. It began on the first day of the war when the Germans in Oslo, after the sinking of their cruiser *Blücher*, asked for a burial place for 1,000 dead soldiers. Whether one thinks of coastal passenger traffic, black-out routines, the maintenance of air raid defence, or fire protection, one is bound to conclude moreover that it was not always possible to draw clear lines between normal civilian work and work benefiting the enemy, directly or indirectly. It suffices here to note that it was the war, represented by the German occupation, which finally brought about full employment.

Not all the German projects concerned military fortifications. In the first war years the German authorities in Berlin entertained ideas for a complete economic reconstruction of Norway as part of the New Germanic Order in Europe, whereby Pan Germania was to become self-sufficient both in terms of raw materials and markets.[24] Economic and strategic views coalesced into far-reaching industrial vistas for a future autarchic Europe, united under Nazi Germany and bound together by corporative, representative assemblies, rather than parliamentary assemblies. Norway, an outlying part, was to be a military sronghold, hence Trondheim, Bergen and Narvik would have to be heavily fortified. Additionally, Norway had ample resources of cheap water power energy, metal ores, and a peasant population ideal from the point of view of racist ideology. Her economy would be reconstructed to serve the Grossraumwirtschaft of the future. Electricity production must be expanded, and energy transported over Kattegat to Germany. Aluminium, iron, zinc, pyrites, and ferro-alloy production was to be greatly increased. The Svalbard coal reserves were to be exploited, and ship building was to be encouraged. Transport systems, notably the railway system, would be expanded and made more effective. Also the Norwegian railway track was to be made standard gauge and electrified, to reduce its dependence on coal imports. To implement these ideas, diverse plans for industrial projects in Norway were submitted by the large German industrial firms to the Berlin government in 1940 and 1941.

Koppenberg's Aluminium Plans

The most ambitious of the industrial projects was the develpment of the aluminium industry in Norway, to supplement Luftwaffe's needs for aluminium in aircraft production. Norway's assets were icefree fjords, cheap water power, and deep sea harbour waters upon which the first wave of electrometal and electrochemical industries had been based. Norway's first aluminium smelter, A/S Stangfjord Elektrokemiske Fabrikker, dated back to 1906. This plant was situated in an isolated fjord on the west coast in Nordfjord. A second smelter, A/S Vigelands Brug near Kristiansand, started up 1907. Det Norske Nitridaktieselskap (DNN), near Arendal, was incorporated 1912. It was promoted by Sam Eyde. The company's capital was 75 per cent French-owned, the rest owned by A/S Elektrokemisk, the mother company of several electrometal establishments, notably Norsk Hydro of 1905. Det Norske Nitridaktieselskap built its second aluminium smelter in 1914 in Tyssedal, Hardanger, outside Odda, with electric energy from A/S Tyssefaldene, a power company in which Elektrokemisk held a stock majority. In 1914 the Storting gave concession for A/S Høyangfaldene, in the Sognefjord. Originally financed by Norwegian venture capital, this company registered a new company, Aktieselskapet Norsk Aluminium Company (NACO), the following year and in 1917 A/S Nordisk Aluminiumsindustri, Holmestrand in the Oslofjord, to refine the crude metal into household goods and tins for the canning industry. A final smelter, the A/S Haugvik Smelteverk, Glomfjord in Nordland county, originated during World War I as a private power company, but was bought by the government in 1918. After delayed negotiation, the Aluminium Corporation Ltd, a British company, started aluminium production at Glomfjord in 1927, with cheap hydro energy delivered by the government-owned power plant in Glomfjord.[25]

In an international context Norway's aluminium production had not been particularly important before 1914. Exports of ingots exceeded 10,000 tons in 1923. A record year was 1929 when 29,600 tons were exported. In the 1930s the volume fluctuated, down from 23,700 tons in 1930 to a bottom of 13,600 tons in 1932, and by 1938 exports again touched the earlier record of 29,000 tons. Productive capacity was higher, about 37,000 tons.[26] Relative to world aluminium production Norway's exports represented 11.8 per cent in 1924, 10.3 per cent in 1929, and the share fell to 4.7 per cent in 1937. Norway ranked sixth among the world's aluminium producers at the outbreak of war.

Foreign capital, mostly British, French and Canadian, had controlling interests in all the aluminium plants. German capital was not involved. Being foreign-owned, the Norwegian aluminium plants could be sequestered by the German occupation authorities that much more easily. On 14 April 1940, five days after the German invasion, Direktor Koppenberg of the Junkers Aircraft visited the country as representative of Reichsmarshall Göring, Commander-in-Chief of the Luftwaffe. The purpose of his visit was to settle formalities in transferring control of British and French ownership in the aluminium industry into German hands. On 10 May Göring appointed Koppenberg his trustee under the terms of the German Four-Year Plan, to conduct the necessary negotiations with the aluminium producers in occupied Europe and prepare plans for expansion. In October 1940 Koppenberg presented a two-stage plan for Norway. The plan foresaw expansion of alumina, aluminium, and magnesium production. Magnesium, a light metal, was used as a component of light alloys for aircraft engine casing and the tubes used in incendiary bombs. A new factory was to be set up at Herøya, near Norsk Hydro's plants. The expected output levels were gigantic. Alumina production would increase from 18,000 tons to 203,000 tons annually, and aluminium output from existing levels of 28,000 to 119,000 tons per year – all in about one year. Magnesium output was to be raised from scratch to an annual 10,000 tons. At a second later stage, when the aluminium factory had started operations, aluminium production would increase to 243,900 tons.[27]

The Koppenberg programme, moreover, entailed an increase of hydro-electric energy production, in part by increasing capacity of existing power plants, in part by constructing new dams and new hydro power plants. To assess the size of Koppenberg's electrification plans, we note that they represented a yearly estimated production of 725,000 KWh or 725 MWh as against Norway's total electricity production in 1939 of 10,468 GWh.[28] Total construction costs for the entire two-stage programme, including electricity, alumina, magnesium and aluminium, were estimated to run up to 1,218,250 RM, which at the nominal exchange rate of 166.66 N kr to 100 RM, amounted to a grand total of 2,033,330 kroner. By comparison the gross national product of Norway in 1939 amounted to 6.3 billion kroner.[29] According to Direktor Koppenberg's time schedule, aluminium production was expected to reach 60,000 tons per year by April 1942, 170,000 tons by October 1943, and by June 1944 the final level of 240,000 tons would be reached.

Responsibility for the actual implementation of the plans was entrusted to the German company, Nordische Aluminium Gesellschaft, soon to be known as Nordag. The stock majority was held by Bank der Deutschen Luftfahrt, which in turn was owned by Germany's Air Ministry. Koppenberg in these matters voiced the interests of Gøring and the Luftwaffe. Von Falkenhorst, the military commander, meanwhile pressed for the construction of 90 coastal batteries, new airfields, barracks for almost half a million German soldiers, U-boat bunkers in Bergen and Trondheim, the construction of the railway line from Kristiansand to Stavanger and the continuation of the line from Trondheim to Mo in Nordland county. A clash over priorities arose.

Other German Projects

The German schemes listed above went far beyond the fiscal and real resources of Norway. In meetings with Wehrmacht representatives in the autumn 1940 Terboven provided statistics showing that the *per capita* occupation cost was about 0.50 RM in France against 1 RM in Norway. According to the Reichskommissar, there was a threat of uncontrolled inflation if the projects were to be financed simply by printing Norwegian paper notes. Military and civilian German interests thus collided, which led to considerable delays. As 1940 and 1941 went by, the plans had to be scaled down.

As it turned out the German industrial plans proved largely illusory. At Herøya A/S Nordisk Lettmetall, a German controlled company, started work on a huge magnesium plant in spring 1941. At one time the work force exceeded 4,000 men. In addition, 2,000 men were at work in the Mår river, further upland in Telemark, boring tunnels, constructing dams, erecting pylons and stretching the wires for transmitting the electricity down to the Porsgrunn region and to Herøya on the coast. The magnesium plant was deemed strategic and on 24 July 1943 Allied bombers in a precision air raid damaged the works so much that the Germans gave up the entire project As for aluminium, Nordag began a gigantic project in Årdal in the bottom of the Sognefjord, to harness the Tyin waters and construct an alumina plant and aluminium smelter there, but the plant was still under construction by the end of the war. The aluminium smelter at Glomfjord suffered a commando attack by British troops on 21 September 1942. Alumina supply proved a constant bottleneck, owing in large part to lack of German shipping space, a neglected point in the Koppenberg aluminium plans.

Also Hydro's heavy water plans at Vemork, Rjukan, proved a disaster for the occupation authorities. Heavy water, a by-product of Hydro's nitrate production, was used in atomic fission experiments as part of the larger German ambition of producing nuclear weapons. In order to forestall a German break-through in this sensitive area, Norwegian and Allied authorities in London approved of sabotage action against Vemork, Hydro's Rjukan plant, since the plant was nearly immune to air raid attack. In the famous raid of 27 February 1943 members of the Norwegian Linge Company succeeded in damaging the factory at Vemork and destroying 500 kilos of heavy water. When production was resumed, Allied bombers damaged the plant again, after which the Germans finally resigned. The remaining 600 litres of heavy water were to be shipped to Germany in February 1944; however, the Linge Company in a second sabotage action sank the ferry that transported the heavy water across the Tinnsjø lake. After this all heavy water plans were relinquished in Norway.

Another strategic material was molybdenite. The Knaben mines in Vest Agder county were the only Western suppliers outside the United States. To secure stable shipments of this vital alloy for current armaments production, the German authorities, represented by Org. Todt, expanded operations at Knaben. Allied air raids, however, in March and November 1943 damaged the molybdenite mines extensively, and later local sabotage actions crippled production for the rest of the war.

Looking at the metal production record for these years, with the exception of ferro-silicon, the conclusion is clearly one of decline deespite the grandiose projects of expansion (Table 8.1). Overall, mining volume declined by 54 per cent between 1938 and 1944.[30]

Of lasting value, by contrast, was the completion in 1944 of the Stavanger railway and the northern railway to Mo completed 1942. One would say the same of the airfields at Fornebu and Sola. However,most of the occupation monuments represented poor value for money spent. Air raid bunkers for soldiers and for submarines, barracks and fortifications of all descriptions, camps for military and civilian prisoners could hardly be of lasting economic value for a peace time economy. Thus,

Table 8.1: Metal Production 1939-1945 (Tons)

	Aluminium	Zinc	Nickel	Copper	Ferro-silicon	Molybdenite
1938	29035	46523	8467	10547	42185	775
1939	31130	45917	9121	10458	39538	722
1940	27780	17229	3732	6730	39051	480
1941	17528	6464	1370	5017	54304	389
1942	20498	7693	949	4597	54723	624
1943	23514	15376	872	2014	84231	386
1944	20035	11777	1474	937	66321	420
1945	4608	9228	1555	1692	15987	130

Source: *Historical Statistics 1968*, Tables 141, 142.

speaking of the aggregate economy, the war years largely represented a waste of productive resources. For some individual industrial companies, however, the war represented a period of brisk activity, high nominal profits, and abnormal liquidity, as maintenance expenditures had to be postponed due to the impossibility of getting replacements. This brings us to the two central aspects of the German war economy: wartime controls and the methods of financing the German occupation.

War-time Controls

On the same day as war broke out between Germany and Poland in 1939, the Norwegian government introduced a temporary ban on price increases. However, when import prices rose, some increases were permitted. This in turn led to wage increases negotiated by LO and NAF, and approved by the price control authorities in January 1940. On 10 February 1940 a general price regulation ordinance was introduced. The precepts were based on the premise of continued neutrality. War on 9 April created a new situation. More drastic measures were called for. On 27 April the Administration Council decreed a general price freeze. Later precepts issued on 14 December of the same year codified the policy of a general price freeze for the remainder of the war. The main rule was that no one without legal permission was to charge prices higher than those in force on 8 April 1940. Permission for any increase, regardless of input prices, was given on an *ad hoc* basis by the Price Directorate. The prices were henceforth fixed by legal fiat as maximum prices. These pertained in principle to the price of all intermediate and final goods.

To police the price regulations an extensive bureaucracy came into being, with the Price Directorate as supreme authority and the county directors (fylkesmenn). assisted by local control boards, as regional authorities. A special price police was entrusted with the daily task of overseeing that the current rules were followed, and reporting any one who failed to comply, in which case special price courts heard and decided disputes involving price violations.

Attempts to freeze prices entailed parallel attempts to bind wages. Since wages made up a sizeable share of production costs, any wage increases necessarily led to increases in prices and vice versa. To prevent uncontrolled inflation, wages accordingly had to be regulated as well. It came as no surprise when the Administration Council on 23 May 1940 issued a decree of a general wage freeze. The decree banned any increase of wages beyond those in force on 9 April 1940, unless permission had been obtained from the Department of Social Affairs. For strategic wage earners pay raises were awarded in 1941, 15 per cent for fishermen in North Norway, 12 per cent for agricultural workers, 10 per cent for forestry workers over and above the basic rates.[31] Miners also received increases. However, for most wage earners in manufacturing and handicrafts wages were cut by 8 per cent on 1 June 1940. At that level they were frozen for the remainder of the war. The wage freeze policy was undermined by the German pay offers. In order to lure workers to their construction projects, the Wehrmacht at first offered wages five to six times higher than Norwegian employers in similar fields. Hourly pay in mining and manufacturing, including overtime and bonuses, averaged 1.72 kroner for 1940, as against 2.32 kroner per hour in the building trades, but the Germans were reported to be offering 10-12 kroner per hour in summer 1940. However, the price and wages policies in force during the war were generally successful in containing inflation, as indicated by the modest increases recorded in the cost-of-living index (Table 8.2).

Table 8.2 offers excerpts of the cost-of-living index 1939-45, which reveal the extent of price inflation during the war. From August 1939 to August 1941 the index rose by 40 per cent, from 100.8 to 140.5, but for the remainder of the war it increased only by a further 8.8 per cent to 152.9. A comparison between March 1940 and February 1945 gives a yearly rate of inflation of 6.2 per cent. Statistics on wages in mining and manufacturing suggest a 9.3 per cent increase in average hourly earnings between the first quarter of 1940 and the yearly average of 1943.[32] This corresponds well with the modest price increases noted above.

Table 8.2: Wholesale Prices and Cost of Living in Norway 1939-1945.
(1938 = 100)

Month	Wholesale prices	Cost of living index
August 1939	98.4	100.8
March 1940	130.3	113.6
August 1940	136.0	116.8
February 1941	152.9	133.7
August 1941	167.3	140.5
February 1942	170.6	144.7
August 1942	172.9	147.8
February 1943	174.3	149.2
August 1943	175.2	151.2
February 1944	175.6	151.7
August 1944	177.4	152.8
February 1945	177.6	152.9

Source: *Kjell Aukrust & Petter Jakob Bjerve, Hva krigen kostet Norge*, Oslo,
1945, p. 82

Price and wage controls were supplemented by other war time
regulations, above all a national system of rationing, the beginning of
which antedated the outbreak of war (9 April 1940). The decree of 23
May 1940, introducing a wage freeze, also empowered the central
authorities, viz. the Department of Social Affairs, to forbid strikes and
lock-outs. Another decree of 12 September 1940 authorised the Price
Directorate to fix maximum dividends. Rents were included in the
system of price controls, as were bank rates. Farmers, fishermen and
industrial firms had imposed delivery quotas.

As for foreign trade transactions, steps had been taken in autumn
1939 to centralise settlements to and from abroad. On 20 May 1940
the Administration Council in Oslo ordered all importers and exporters
to apply at the central bank or its branch offices for export or import
licences in connection with foreign currency transactions. Provided they
could procure a certificate of permission for the import from the
Department of Trade, a licence for the necessary currency would be
granted.[33] The decree in effect centralised all payments in foreign
exchange into the hands of the central bank, at the same time as control of imports and exports was centralised in the hands of the Directorate for Foreign Trade within the Department of Provisions. The system
of bilateral trade and payment agreements was known before the war.
By 1939 Norway had concluded such payment agreements with
Germany, Spain, Italy, Greece and Turkey. Additionally, eight coun-

tries were put on this list in the year 1940, bringing the total to 13 payment agreements. The payment agreements later came to include most European countries.[34] A separate office, the Clearing Institute, was set up within the central bank for dealing with currency licencing. The general idea was to balance accounts with each trading partner, as gold had disappeared as the medium of settlements.

By the above trade and currency regulations the country in relation to the outside world was run as a single firm for the remainder of the war. Together with the other controls they turned the economy into a fully centralised command economy, in which consumption, prices, wages, rents, bank rates, dividends and foreign trade transactions were placed under central administrative regulation. The edifice expanded continuously. It provided the model for the continued controls maintained by the Labour government in the postwar period. By 1944 the value of foreign trade had dropped to a mere fifth of the 1938 level. Germany, which bought 15.5 per cent of Norway's commodity exports in 1938, in 1944 took 80.9 per cent. Conversely, while Germany was point of origin of 18.4 per cent of Norway's commodity imports in 1938, by 1941 the share was up to 67 per cent at which level it remained for the rest of the war.[35] Most of Norway's foreign trade was channelled through German firms, whose profits now included, not only a monopoly element, but also those of the middlemen.[36] A cloud of suspicion still lingers over the German-controlled payment settlements of the war years.

Financing Occupation

To pay for its upkeep the Wehrmacht on 10 April 1940 announced over the Norwegian Broadcasting System (NRK) that the German troops would use Reichskreditkassenscheine as means of payment. Their value was set at 100 N kr to 60 RM, or 100 RM to 166.66 N kr. At that rate the Reichsmark or the Reichskreditscheine was overvalued by about 34 per cent.[37] They were declared legal tender for all transactions. Similar Reichskreditscheine appeared in occupied Denmark, Belgium, the Netherlands, Luxembourg, France, and Poland. The paper money was issued by a central Reichskreditkasse in Berlin, organised in October 1939.[38] To provide the Wehrmacht in occupied Norway and Denmark with means of payment, the Ministerrat für die Reichsverteidigung issued an order 3 May 1940 whereby the Reichskreditkasse gave a loan of 500 million RM to the German Reich. The sum was increased to 3 billion RM on 15 May 1940, when the Wehrmacht faced bills for its upkeep in Belgium, France, the Netherlands and Luxembourg. The Reichskreditkasse had no capital. The bank obtained cash for its operations simply by issuing notes with no other guarantee except their being lent to the German Reich. The Reich on its side had not guaranteed the paper notes. Thus, the Wehrmacht, by an easy swindle, forced its way to a free note emission right in occupied territories.

The German paper notes came into circulation on 9 April 1940. They found their way to the banks and from there to the Norges Bank. The board of directors of the central bank, too crippled by the sheer enormity of the events to call out against gangsterism, deemed it necessary to take up the Reichskreditscheine in circulation, and open an account for the Wehrmacht's further cash needs, whereby the bank provided Norwegian notes in return for IOUs from the Wehrmacht, preferably from one central agency. An agreement to this effect was worked out in May 1940 in negotiations with Reichsbankdirektor Rudolf Sattler of the German Reichsbank, sent up from Berlin. Apprehensions lingered among members of the board, so to clear the constitutional side, the Directorate of Norges Bank obtained written declarations from the Administration Council on 4 June 1940, and from E. Sandberg, head of the Department of Finance, following the dissolution of the Administration Council on 25 September 1940, to the effect that the political authorities carried full responsibility for the credits granted by the central bank to the occupation authorities in Norway for the duration of the war.[39]

At this early stage the directors of Norges Bank had no idea of the size of the German monetary needs. This grant of credit was the origin of the German occupation account. Up to 7 May 1945 the Germans drew from the account a total of 11.7 billion Norwegian kroner. It was never the intention of paying back these 'credits'. The issue of Reichskreditscheine disappeared in July 1940. Net debit outstanding by the end of the war was 8 billion N kr. as 'the state' had paid in on various occasions 3.1 billion taken in through taxation. The balance of 0.6 billion represented amounts in cash held by the occupation authorities as of 7 May 1945. The total cost of the occupation forces of 11.7 billion amounted to a staggering 2,320 million per year and an average of 193 million per month. One should recall that the peacetime government of Nygaardsvold had had difficulties raising 80 million extra for the whole budget year 1935-6. That sum, as seen, was less than half of what the Wehrmacht expropriated for itself every month for five successive years. The appropriations demanded by the Wehrmacht over the government budgets|were as a rule veiled behind bland budget titles, or drawn from secret accounts. Nor was the Wehrmacht account at Norges Bank widely known. This was no coincidence. According to Terboven's representative at the central bank, Reichsbankdirektor Rudolf Sattler, the advantage for Germany of proceeding according to protocol was that 'this awakened on the Norwegian side, the hope that the Deutsche Bank would later accept responsibility for a great part of the Wehrmacht demands'.

Inevitably the circulating issue showed a massive increase, up from 575 million kroner on 31 December 1939 to 1,040 million by the end of 1940. The German drawings upon the central bank drove the note issue up to 1,528 million in 1941, and 2,578 million by the end of 1943. By 7 May 1945 the note issue was 3,039 million kroner.[41] During the five occupation years the note volume thus showed a fivefold increase. What if the Directorate of Norges Bank at any one stage had refused to provide printed money? No doubt, Terboven would have had his own printing personnel provide the paper money.

Another dimension of the war burden in Norway is obtained by comparing the Wehrmacht's drawings with the costs imposed on other occupied countries. A calculation by the Bank for International Payments in Basle estimated the burden of the occupation payments from Norway and other countries to Germany in the first two years of the war. The figures are rendered in Table 8.3.

Table 8.3: Occupation Payments by German-occupied Countries 1940-1942

	Mill. kr	Kroner per inhabitant
France	32.680	779
Belgium	9.790	1,171
The Netherlands	12.160	1.401
Denmark	2.180	797
Norway	5.410	1.842
Total	62.220	—

Source: Aukrust & Bjerve, *Hva krigen kostet Norge*, Oslo, 1945, p. 29.

While *per capita* payments of the German occupation 1940-2 were 779 kroner in France, 1171 kroner in Belgium, they amounted to 1842 kroner in Norway. The figures do not take account of the value of

German war booty or expropriations taken without payments; still, there can be no doubt that in these years the occupation burden fell heaviest in Norway.

War Profiteering?

Attempts have been made to insinuate that Norwegian industry at large experienced a profit and investment bonanza during the war.[42] The charge is levelled, not at the notorious war profiteers whose behaviour was examined by the law courts after the war, but at the established industrial companies and organisations for commerce and industry. With a class bias implied,the allegation is that bourgeois society in Norway rather favoured Hitler inasmuch as he fought the Soviet threat and helped to keep the industrialists' order books full. After all, business is business.

The superficial basis for such a wholesale indictment is the behaviour of nearly all groups and organisations in the first months of the war. In the postwar trials of suspected war profiteers cases were cited of municipal authorities urging private entrepreneurial firms to take German construction orders, even at a time when fighting still went on. The attitude among private as well as public leaders was that the economy must be maintained. Exports must necessarily go to Germany, once the normal trade channels were blocked, in order to maintain imports vital to the daily existence of the population. Mass unemployment was a spectre to be held back. Many faced the option of closing down or accepting orders from the Wehrmacht. The setting up of the Administration Council on 15 April 1940 signalled an official policy of temporary co-operation with the Germans. As a result the line between proper and improper assistance to the enemy was necessarily blurred. The vacillating situation lasted until 25 September 1940 when the negotiations of a pro-German puppet government ended in failure, owing to the stubbornness of the Norwegian negotiators.

The climax of this policy of voluntary co-operation with Germany was the setting up of the German-Norwegian Chamber of Commerce in Oslo in the autumn 1940. Initiator of the organisation was the Reichskommissar. According to the statutes the chamber sought 'to promote the mutual commercial relations between Norway and Germany and the personal contacts between businessmen of both countries'. The formal opening was held at the Grand Hotel in Oslo. It was attended by Terboven, several Kommissariat ministers, the presidents of Norway's

Federations of Industry and of Arts and Crafts, the Mayor of Oslo, the Governor of Norges Bank, representatives of leading interest organisations and the largest industrial companies.[43] From this moment onwards the climate changed. Gradually the view prevailed that collaboration with the Wehrmacht beyond a certain point was unpatriotic. That line became more clear as time went on and the Home resistance succeeded in getting information and paroles through to those involved.

To turn to the quantitative evidence, what basis can be found for a general war profit bonanza? Table 8.4 offers excerpts of production figures for suspected industries.

Table 8.4: Production of Selected Commodities 1938-1945

	Cement Million kilo	Sawn timber 1000 m^3	Planed timber 1000 m^3	Mechanical Pulp 1000 tons	Cellulose 1000 tons	Paper board & cardboard 1000 tons
1938	332	870	526	444	455	41
1939	390	871	654	470	495	50
1940	338	1083	682	178	403	43
1941	313	1118	688	199	398	37
1942	374	965	525	168	326	30
1943	311	704	385	128	305	26
1944	320	621	284	76	244	24
1945	142	506	253	105	149	25

Source: *Historical Statistics 1978*, Table 140.

The volume figures in Table 8.4 serve to dispel any notions of a massive production upswing in either the cement industry, the wood industries or the pulp and paper industries. Since prices of both inputs and outputs, including wages and sales prices, were fixed by the price control authorities throughout the war and taxes were stiffened, the charge of a production bonanza reaped by industrial capital is not tenable unless one dismisses the existing statistical evidence. Admittedly some of the aggregate statistics for the war years, notably the industrial production index, are apt to understate the development in individual sectors.[44] Looking at the construction sector alone, for example, one is indeed struck by the dimensions of the German building projects and their role for boosting private and central government construction. Total manhours in mining and manufacturing thus declined in the war years, but they quadrupled in private construction and increased 35 per cent as far as central government construction is concerned. Overall, manhours in the secondary sector increased by 37 per cent, up from 418,000 in 1939 to 571,000 in the peak year 1941, (Table 8.5).

Table 8.5 Manhours in Mining, Manufacturing and Construction 1936-1945 (1000 manhours)

	Mining & manufacturing	Private construction	Central Government construction	Total manhours
1936	295	45	36	377
1937	319	47	37	403
1938	313	49	34	396
1939	322	59	37	418
1940	297	107	46	450
1941	316	205	50	571
1942	312	186	42	540
1943	309	150	41	500
1944	293	128	42	463
1945	274	62	39	375

Source: *Historical Statistics 1978*, Tables 131, 148.

Table 8.5 brings out that over the long haul, however, industry backslided during the war; after a brief surge in manhours 1941-1942, they declined to a lower level in 1945 compared with 1940. Additionally, air-raid destruction was considerable, stocks were used up, capital assets wore out, replacements were seldom made, so the general level of productivity no doubt declined for industry as a whole. One estimate is that productivity fell by 20-25 per cent by 1942.[45] Go-slow actions were tacitly staged, as was sabotage, though they were not too common, since apart from construction projects the Germans, represented by Org. Todt, I.G. Farben or Nordag, seldom acted directly as employers. It was one thing to place limpets on German war ships, it was something else to place a bomb in a neighbour's yard. On the basis of the foregoing, what of the imputed profit bonanza during the war in mining and manufacturing? Existing statistics on values added offer information for evaluating the charge (Table 8.6).

Table 8.6 offers information on total value added in mining and manufacturing and the share captured by the workers 1935-47. That share was 49 per cent in 1935. During the war years it fluctuated between 44 per cent and 45. The drop is marginal. Labour's share was down to 42 per cent by 1947, that is two years after the termination of

Table 8.6: Value Added and Total Wages in Mining and Manufacturing
1935-1947 (Million kroner)

	Total value	Total value added	Wages & salaries	(2) : (1)
		(1)	(2)	(3)
1935		761	376	0.49
1936		867	424	0.49
1937		1016	488	0.48
1938		1044	522	0.50
1939		1153	551	0.44
1940		1243	552	0.44
1941		1378	619	0.45
1942		1384	642	0.46
1943		1502	664	0.44
1944		1457	665	0.46
1945		1382	708	0.51
1946		2272	989	0.44
1947		2925	1241	0.42

Source: *Historical Statistics 1978*, Table 131.

the war, and at a time when Labour was in power. Fluctuations are
observed in the wages ratio. They show no special or systematic variations, however, during the years 1940-5. The observed variations most
likely are due to changes in prices, taxes and plant capacity utilisation, as
pointed out in 1945 by Gunnar Jahn, director at the time of the
Central Bureau of Statistics. The price effect mirrored the massive injection of paper money into the economy.

In addition there remains an element of black market production,
the size of which is not known. A good deal of clandestine production
for the home resistance organisation took place, notably the making of
shoes, boots and cloth for the resistance soldiers away in the backwoods. However, even adding a hypothetical 10 per cent to the figures
in column 1 in Table 8.6, to allow for unregistered German orders, this
would still leave a wage ratio in 1947 *below* any of the war-year ratios;
hence the charge of super profits reaped by capital during the war is not
backed up by the evidence. The fact that industry was unable to make
normal investments to maintain plant and stocks during the war, and for
that reason ran up accumulated reserves, does not alter the verdict. To
equate the postponement of normal investments in plant, stocks and
machinery with super profits, amounts to a misconception of the
nature of company profits and ordinary depreciation expenditures.

At bottom the attempts at indicting wholesale the leaders of Norwegian industry for large scale economic war crimes, merely echo the Communist charge that Norwegian workers wanted to fight the German invaders in 1940, but were prevented from doing so by representatives of the ruling bourgeois class. The charge does not stand up when examined, nor is it phrased in a form that allows its being tested along class lines. Suffice it to say that the observed willingness to fight the invading Germans bore no discernible class bias, though samples taken do suggest that middle class recruits had a share among resistance personnel higher than their share in the population. This is contrary to the phantasies of the extreme left. Behind these phantasies lingers their shame of the early war months, when the Communists, at a time when the Hitler-Stalin pact was in force, called for an immediate halt to Norwegian resistance and denounced 'the aggressive policies' of Great Britain.

The Costs of War

Loss of Real Capital

In 1943 the staff of the Central Bureau of Statistics was ordered by the Nazi government to work out an estimate of what the war had cost Norway, in order that the goverment later could present its damage claims against England! The request led to a thorough investigation of the economic costs, and with an eye on Germany rather than England estimates were published in 1945[46] and more fully in 1946.[47] The general idea was to compare the value of reproducible capital in 1939 with its assessed value in 1945, and on the basis of the difference, arrive at an estimate of the real capital reduction that had been caused by the war. The investigation was not a monetary exercise, pertaining to the German drawings on the central bank; rather this study dealt with the physical stock of capital and its reduction, including land, forests, buildings, machinery, transport systems, including ships, and stocks. A summary of the findings is given in Table 8.7.

On the basis of Table 8.7 one can say, with some confidence, that in real terms the overall capital stock of the country was reduced by 18.5 per cent or close to one fifth. Individual sectors suffered more than the average: in shipping the loss amounted to 56.7 per cent, in whaling 67.9 per cent, in industry 31.8 per cent against a mere 4.5 per cent in agriculture.

In evaluating the loss figures, however, it should be observed that they are gross figures, since the accumulated revenues in whaling and shipping are excluded. The Bureau made a point of this in its 1946

Table 8.7: Real Capital by Sector 1939 and its Reduction 1939-1945, in Million 1939-kroner and as %

Sector	Real capital 1939 Mill. kr	Reductions 1939-1945 Mill. kr	Reduction as % of 1939
Agriculture	4016	175	4.5
Forestry	1500	100	6.7
Fisheries	305	130	42.6
Whaling	81	55	67.9
Industry	4500	1430	31.8
Transport,	4743	1070	22.6
of which shipping	1500	850	56.7
automobiles	400	300	75.0
Commerce	1850	790	42.7
Buildings, incl. dwellings	10337	800	7.8
Stocks	240	50	20.8
Personal wealth	3800	1200	31.6
Total	31372	5800	18.5

Source: *Nasjonalinntekten i Norge 1935-1943*, Nos X, 102, Oslo, 1946, pp. 141-2.

study.[48] Again, moving from the national level to the individual company, the war years had generally meant full capacity utilisation. Earnings, whether below or above the national average for industry, were earned in war-inflated money. The revenue, moreover, tended to accumulate since as long as the war lasted, almost nothing could be had for the money, except art or antiques. Normal investments in stocks, plant or machinery had to be postponed. Hence, although the real capital of the country was reduced by 18.5 per cent, the country was not without the wherewithal to rebuild the capital stock when, or if, peace returned. The same can be said for the individual company or firm. Both the national economy and the firms had built up reserves, as represented by the shipping revenues from Nortraship, the maritime insurance claims and the accounts held by individuals and companies with the banks. If these reserves are brought to bear, the capital loss account would show quite another picture of the net capital loss suffered by the nation and the firms during the war.

Failure to distinguish between gross and net loss, and aggregate and disaggregate levels in discussing the issue of the costs of the war, goes a long way to explain the misunderstandings that still surround the subject.[49] In addition, as claimed by Johan Vogt, one suspects that the German projects expropriated as enemy property after the war, were assessed too low. Johan Vogt, however, adds no evidence in support of this charge.[50] It is also likely, again as noted by Vogt, that the capital depreciation figures overstated the real loss. They were based on information from management. They may have contained an element element of bargaining, pending future insurance settlements. All one can say is that some exaggeration of capital losses appears likely. It would tie in with the speed with which the economy recovered after the war. In all, gross real capital loss may have hovered around 6,000 million 1939 kroner.

The Occupation Burden

The costs of the war, moreover, included the current burdens of the German occupation. An estimate of the extent of the burden would be obtained by estimating national income for each war year and deducting from this the share expropriated by the Wehrmacht. The share would include net payments to the Wehrmacht through the occupation account at the Central bank, German requisitions and confiscations not paid for, minus import surplus − if any − on the German-Norwegian trade balance. The latter was accessible from the clearing account. From an estimate along these lines it appears that the direct German occupation costs averaged 35 per cent of the national income for the years 1940-5 with a low 30 per cent in 1940 and a high 39 per cent in 1944.[50]

Income Opportunities Foregone

Thirdly, the computation of the war costs should include an estimate of the extra hypothetical income in contrast to the actual income that Norway would have had in the absence of occupation. One recalls that the gross national product had shown a rate of growth of 4.1 per cent yearly between 1934-9. A hypothetical growth rate for the lost years 1940-5 of 2 per cent could hardly be considered excessive. Adding the above cost items, one arrives at a grand total of 17.5 billion kroner which represented the total material costs of the war.[51] By contrast the gross national product for 1938 was 5.8 billion kroner and 6.3 billion in 1939.[52]

However, looking back the economic aspects of the war appear trifling compared to the human costs. The war caused the death of 10,000 Norwegians. About 40,000 persons were imprisoned by the Germans or NS. Among them 363 men and 3 women were executed, in some cases after a formal trial and sentence, in others none. Another 1,600 were killed during encounters or during arrests or perished in prisons and concentration camps. As noted earlier, the 10,000 dead also included 4,000 seamen and 2,000 from the armed forces. In all 3 per mille of the population died. Admittedly the figure pales in comparison with the human losses suffered by Poland or Yugoslavia.

A special tragedy was the attempted German deportation of the entire civilian population of Finnmark and northern Troms, announced on 31 October 1944 by the Wehrmacht. The enforced deportation was part of the German retreat from the Northern front. The action meant that the German troops systematically destroyed all homes, piers, bridges, roads, and buildings over an area of 55,000 km², an area exceeding Denmark's 43,000 km². Apart from the reindeer herds on the inland mountain plateau, all cattle were slaughtered, all crops burned, 100 out of 160 saith nets and about 100 out of 170 herring nets were lost. The evacuation was effected by local passenger ships and local fishing vessels, requisitioned for the purpose, in part by German lorries and ships. By 4 January 1945 Tromsø reported that 44,000 evacuated persons had been registered in transit. The autumn weather proved uncommonly clement, which explains why the mass deportation – enforced at gun point – occurred almost without loss of human lives. About 30,000 people found temporary lodgings in Nordland and Troms, the rest were placed in various counties further south, often in humiliating circumstances. In all the deportation involved 50,000 people.[53] There were still a good many left in hiding from straying German patrols in the area. The patrols are reported to have shot civilians who failed to obey the deportation orders right up till capitulation day, 7 May 1945. By then the Soviet army was in control of the eastern parts of Finnmark, including Kirkenes. On 8 May Reichskommissar Terboven blew himself to pieces in his bunker at Skaugum, and the German army in Norway surrendered. One month later on 7 June, a symbolic day, King Haakon and members of the Royal Family returned to Norway, five years to the day after their departure in 1940.

Notes

1 An early broad survey is Sverre Steen, ed., *Norges krig*, vols. I-III, Oslo, 1947-1950. A recent general survey is Edvard Bull, *Klassekamp og fellesskap 1920-1945*, Oslo 1979, vol. 13, in the Cappelen series, chapter 'Under den annen verdenskrig'. pp. 392-454.

2 T. K. Derry, *The Campaign in Norway*, London 1952. Also by the same author, A *History of Modern Norway 1814-1972*, Oxford UP 1973. A brief introduction on the legal and constitutional aspects is Johs. Andenaes, Olav Riste & Magne Skodvin, *Norway and the Second World War*, Oslo, 1966. The latest re-

view is Johs. Andenaes, *Det vanskelige oppgjøret*, Oslo, 1980. Andenaes refutes Ralph Hewins, *Quisling. Prophet without Honour*, London, 1965. Hewins takes up the old Nazi claim that the military surrender, negotiated in Trondheim 10 June 1940, by Lieutenant Colonel Roscher Nielsen on behalf of the Norwegian army and Colonel Buschenhagen, representing the Wehrmacht, marked the end of the state of war existing between Germany and the Kingdom of Norway, pp. 97-105. If the war had been over in June 1940, of course, the Nazis would not have been traitors or guilty of later war crimes. Their old thesis does not stand up to the evidence.

3 Magne Skodvin, *Striden om okkupasjonsstyret*, Oslo, 1956, for a standard treatment of the period April-September 1940.

4 Hans-Dietrich Loock, *Quisling, Rosenberg und Terboven, Zur Vorgeschichte und Geschichte der nazionalsozialistischen Revolution in Norwegen*, Stuttgart 1970, Norwegian edition, Oslo, 1972. Summarises all important research results in the field.

5 Olav Riste & Berit Nøkleby, *Norway 1940-1945: The Resistance Movement*, Oslo, 1970; Sverre Kjeldstadli, *Hjemmestyrkene*, vol. I, Oslo, 1959.

6 Nils Ørvik, *Norge i brennpunktet*, Oslo, 1953; Jon Rustung Hegland, *Nortraships flåte*, 2 vols, Oslo, 1976, also John O. Egeland, *Gjennom brott og brann*, Oslo, 1968, p. 44 ff.

7 Per 9 April Nortraship had registered 1028 ships, per 8 June 1940 a total of 985 ships, 43 ships having been sunk in the meantime. J.R. Hegland, *Nortraships flåte*, pp. 35-6.

8 J.O. Egeland, *Gjennom brott og brann*, Oslo, 1968, pp. 153-4.

9 *Nasjonalinntekten i Norge 1935-1954*, Nos X, 102, Oslo, 1946, p. 141.

10 J.O. Egeland, *Vi skal videre. Norsk skipsfart etter Den annen verdenskrig. Perioden 1945-1970*, Oslo, 1971, pp. 49-50. St. meld. nr. 76 (1963-64), Final report on the Nortraship settlements.

11 J.O. Egeland, *Vi skal videre*, pp. 49-8; Bjørg Askelund, *Mellom nøytrale og allierte*, Oslo, 1968.

12 Knut Utstein Kloster, *Den norske stormakt. Vår skipsfart gjennom tusen år*, Oslo, 1945, p. 180, quoting an article in *New York Times*, July 1945.

13 *Historical Statistics 1968*, Table 84, 1 feed·unit = nutritional value of 1 kg barley.

14 *Statistical Survey 1948*, Nos X, 178, Oslo, 1949, Table 67.

15 *Historical Statistics 1968*, Table 95.

16 Ibid, Tables 97 and 98.

17 St.meld. nr. 37, 1945/6: *Report on the Activities of the Department of Supplies during the Occupation*, pp. 44, 49.

18 Gunnar Christie Wasberg & Arnljot Strømme Svendsen, *Industriens historie*, Oslo, 1969, p. 224.

19 E. Bull, *Klassekamp og felleskap*, pp. 418, 431, 438, 440.

20 *Historical Statistics 1968*, Table 120.

21 The Norwegian Fishery Directorate, where Professor Gerhardsen worked 1938-46, supplied the herring statistics to the Central Bureau of Statistics. Information obtained in interview with Professor Gerhardsen, Norwegian School of Economics and Statistics.

22 *Historical Statistics 1968*, Table 118.

23 Ibid, Table 132.

24 Alan Milward, *The Fascist Economy in Norway*, Oxford UP, 1972. Also by the same author: *War, Economy and Society 1939-1945*, London, 1977.

25 Johan Vogt, *Elektrisitetslandet Norge*, Oslo 1971. pp. 116-7.

26 A. Milward, *The Fascist Economy*, p. 173; *Metalstatistik*, Metallgesellschaft A.G., Frankfurt a.M., 24. and 29. Jahrgang.

27 A. Milward, *The Fascist Economy*, pp. 173-180.

28 A. Milward, *The Fascist Economy*, p. 178; *Historical Statistics 1968*, Table 148.

29 Ibid., Table 62.

30 *Statistisk-økonomisk oversikt over krigsårene*, CBS, Oslo, 1945, p. 191.

31 *Statistisk-økonomisk utsyn over krigsårene*, CBS, Oslo, 1945, pp. 237, 239 and Kjell Aukrust & Petter Jakob Bjerve, *Hva krigen kostet Norge*, Oslo, 1945, p. 79. The cost of living index was compiled by the Central Bureau of Statistics 1914-58. This index was superseded by the present consumer price index in 1960, worked ou at CBS on the basis of consumption expenditures for families and households from the whole population, rather than from merely urban working class households.

32 Aukrust & Bjerve, *Hva krigen kostet Norge*, p. 80.

33 Gunnar Jahn et al., *Norges Bank 150 år*, pp. 317 ff.

34 *Statistisk-økonomisk utsyn over krigsårene*, pp. 46-7.

35 *Statistisk-økonomisk utsyn over krigsårene*, pp. 96-7.

36 Aukrust & Bjerve, *Hva krigen kostet Norge*, p. 30.

37 Alan Milward, *The Fascist Economy*, p. 104.

38 Gunnar Jahn et al., *Norges Bank 150 år*, s. 320 ff; *Norges Bank. Virksomheten i hvert år årene 1940-1944*, Oslo, 1945, p. 10.

39 Ibid., p. 11.

40 Alan Milward, *The Fascist Economy*, p. 110.

41 Odd Aukrust og Petter Jakob Bjerve, *Hva krigen kostet Norge*, p. 52.

42 Terje Valen, *De tjente på krigen*, Oslo, 1974.

43 Johs. Andenaes, *Det vanskelige oppgjøret*, pp. 50-1.

44 T. Valen, *De tjente*, pp. 30, 34.

45 Aukrust & Bjerve, *Hva krigen kostet Norge*, p. 42.

46 Aukrust og Bjerve, *Hva krigen kostet Norge*, Oslo, 1945, pp. 21-50, 103-9.

47 *Nasjonalinntekten i Norge 1935-1943*, Nos X, 102, Oslo, 1946.

48 Ibid., p. 161.

49 Terje Valen, *De tjente på krigen*, passim; Johan Vogt, *Vår økonomiske stilling. En kritisk vurdering av gjenreisningsperioden*, Oslo, 1950, pp. 12-13; G. Chr. Wasberg & A. Strømme Svendsen, *Industriens historie*, p. 230, passim.

50 Johan Vogt, *Vår økonomiske stilling*, Oslo, 1950, p. 12.

51 Aukrust & Bjerve, *Hva krigen kostet Norge*, pp. 44-5.

52 *Nasjonalregnskap 1865-1960*, Table 49, p. 342.

53 *Norges Bank, Beretning om den økonomiske stilling i de forskjellige landsdeler for årene 1940-44*, Oslo, 1945, pp. 222, 278-81.

9 RECONSTRUCTION 1945-1947: FIRST PHASE

Transition Period 8 May — 8 October 1945

The day of liberation, 8 May 1945, was a day of jubilation and thanksgiving, tears and a new resolve. On the mundane level the responsibility for keeping the people warm, clothed and fed now devolved on the Norwegian authorities. The Home Front, with Chief Justice Paal Berg as head, took temporary command. On 13 May Crown Prince Olav returned to Norway, accompanied by a government delegation of five members of the London government, to run matters till the rest of the national government could resume its functions. This happened on 31 May when the Nygaardsvold cabinet and its entourage stepped ashore in Oslo, to be followed by the return of King Haakon on 7 June. On 22 June an all party coalition government was appointed to run the country until normal Storting elections could be held again. To authorise the government's decisions the old Storting, which had been dissolved unconstitutionally since 1940, now reconvened, also as a transitional body.

Apparently the country's constitutional machinery came away from the war without any damage. The spirit of occupied Norway, however, was not quite in tune with that of exiled Norway, above all the mood of 1945 differed sharply from the mood of 1940. The old men, parties and institutions were suspected of having failed their duties and responsibilities in the April days of 1940. A dominant wish, however, at a time when patriotism and a feeling of national unity ran high, was to cut the ties with the past and build a new future. The transitional government was headed by Einar Gerhardsen (b. 1897), a man who possessed just that combination of qualities which the emergency situation demanded. He stemmed from a working-class family in Oslo, grew up with the Labour Party and rose to become Vice Mayor of Oslo in 1940; during the war he spent 3½ years in concentration camps, at Grini, outside Oslo, and in Sachsenhausen in Germany. Now he had just been elected party Chairman of Labour and Mayor of Oslo. A man of ascetic appearance and devoid of social pretensions, he spoke simply and directly, and had friends in all social groups from all parts of occupied Norway, acquired not least during the years in German concentration camps. And he was untouched by the national debacle and

130

political failures of 1940. With such qualities and credentials the new prime minister had a moral alibi to call on his fellow countrymen for continued sacrifice and national unity to rebuild the economy and mend the wounds of war.

The Joint Programme 1945

The tasks crowded at the door. However, the government's goals were well defined. They had been worked out in a joint manifesto in the autumn of 1944 at the request of the Mil. org, and passed on to the London government. The text of the manifesto was reviewed by representatives from all the parties, including the communists, in June 1945, and formally published on 26 June with the endorsement of all parties. This document, called the Joint Programme, easily formed the basis for the Gerhardsen coalition government; indeed, when presenting itself to the Storting and the nation, once again tuned in to its radios, the new government read a brief declaration, which was largely a summary of the joint programme.[1] It is fair to say that the programme drew its inspiration mainly from Labour. Among the immediate tasks ahead were the need to

- secure continued basic supplies to the country and ensure a just distribution of all consumer goods.
- undertake special and strong measures to alleviate conditions in Finnmark, northern Troms and the northern parts.
- call upon the united strength of the people as well as all the means of production, to rebuild the economy in a spirit of confident cooperation between government, the private sector and workers' and functionaries' organisations.
- return to a normal situation at all levels of public administration and strengthen all democratic forms of government.
- rebuild and extend educational and cultural institutions and opportunities.
- ensure a swift and just trial of those who had failed in the national struggle. Those who had served the enemy for personal gain and speculated in the needs of their fellow country men would resign that gain.
- continue in the sphere of foreign policy the work started by the former government. In particular it would endeavour to take an active part in the United Nations' efforts to secure peace and it

would promote co-operation between our Allies and our Nordic neighbours.

The key words included democracy, reconstruction, supplies, work for all, a just distribution and a swift trial of war criminals. Einar Gerhardsen ran the coalition government until general elections were held on 8 October 1945. In the hectic transition period, the government dealt with demobilisation and the return of a German army of 366,000 men, 87,000 prisoners of war, mostly Russians, and 30-40,000 civilian workers brought to Norway to work for the Wehrmacht. Almost 500,000 men were sent back to their home countries in a relatively short time. Other pressing tasks were the organisation of a machinery for the trial of war criminals, among them Quisling, laying the foundations for rebuilding Finnmark, maintaining daily supplies, and dealing with the hosts of problems in the economic field. New jobs had to be found for 90,000 workers on former Wehrmacht projects. The longer term goals were kept in the background till the future Storting elections had cleared the parliamentary ground for normal party government.

Legislative authority for its decisions the government found in part in the provisional ordnance promulgated by the London government on 8 May 1945 (the Lex Thagaard), that granted the government almost dictatorial powers over the economy. An exception was wages, which for reasons of expediency, remained largely a matter of free bargaining between unions and the employers, LO and NAF. As mentioned earlier, wages for industrial workers had been frozen during the war. Since the cost of living had gone up by 56 per cent, some compensation to the wage earners appeared justified. Indeed, an agreement on wage increases had been reached between management and the unions, both in exile, in Stockholm in March 1944. According to this agreement wage earners were to get a pay raise of 30 øre per hour for men, 20 øre for women, effective from liberation day for three months, after which they were to be renegotiated. The compensations for other workers were scaled accordingly. They represented 40 per cent of the price increase during the war. New tariff negotiations were to settle the pay levels in the future. When the agreement lapsed in August 1945, the trade unions demanded more pay. The demands were granted on 12 September 1945 by the temporary Wage Board, set up on 3 July 1945 to decide pay questions in cases where wage disputes between LO and NAF reached deadlock. In historical perspective the Wage Board was a provisional replacement of the arbitration court in force in the years 1916-28. The awards were 20 øre for men and 14 øre per hour for women.[2] In percentage terms the two wage awards represented an average pay increase of 32.5 per cent. Not matched by productivity increases, the new pay levels added to the inflationary pressure, already dangerously high. In this field matters called for emergency measures.

The Spectre of Inflation

During the war the Wehrmacht, as noted, cashed with the Central Bank a total of 11,290 million kroner. This represented the equivalent of the amount of goods and services bought by the occupation authorities in Norway. The Central Bank was left with a corresponding massive claim on the occupation power, but alas, the claim was to remain largely a nominal balance in the future annual reports of the bank. The effect was a swollen money volume in circulation, at a time when the range and amounts of goods dwindled. Hence the threat of inflation.

The threat was contained by a severe system of war time controls, but the problem surfaced once the war was over. Circulating note issue was 3021 million by the end of April 1945, five times the amount at the outbreak of war in 1940. By contrast the consumer price index stood only 56 per cent higher than in 1939 and the wholesale price index only 83 per cent. What if all the demand deposits and all the paper money were unleashed in the economy? In percentage terms the monetary expansion was more serious in Norway than in the other German-occupied countries. This is revealed in the country figures for note issues (Table 9.1), wholesale prices and costs of living from 1939 till 7 May 1945.

Table 9.1: Increase in % of Note Issues, Wholesale Prices and Costs of Living, 1939 − 7 May 1945

	Norway	Denmark	Sweden	Britain	USA
Note issue Aug 1939 = 100	502	278	101	136	267
Wholesale prices 1939 = 100	83	99	79	72	38
Costs of living 1939 = 100	56	58	44	32	29

Source: *Norges Bank under okkupasjonen*, St. Forh. 1945/6, Document nr. 10.1, p. 132. The figures for wholesale prices and costs of living taken from Société des Nations: *Bulletin Mensuel de Statistique*.

While the notes in circulation more than doubled during the war in countries like the United States and Denmark, Table 9.1 brings out that the money volume quintupled in Norway. The Central Bank of Norway and its London office had contemplated various plans for a swift monetary reform. A set of proposals was presented to the government on 11 July 1945. It included four measures: a redemption of all circulating notes, a temporary freezing of all bank deposits, registration of all financial holdings, and a huge government loan to be taken up by the public. The withdrawal of all circulating notes meant their immediate registration. New notes were to be issued to the bearers only in limited amounts, the rest to be blocked for the time being. The government had its proposals passed by the Storting on 5 September.[3] They included only two immediate measures: registration of all note holdings, bank deposits and securities, and a freezing of part of the public's bank deposits and note holdings, the rest to be transferred to a 'national deposit account' at Norges Bank for an unspecified period of time. The first measure was expected to soak up 1.5 billion of a circulating issue of 3.2 billion kroner; the latter measure would bind 800 million out of 2.3 billion in bank deposits. The third measure of a single tax on wartime wealth appreciation had to await the results of the ordered registration. The final measure, a government 'liberty loan', was dropped, although the Storting gave its consent to a government bill for a loan of 1.5 billion kroner in July 1945.

Note Exchange 9 September 1945

The public got wind of the scheduled note-exchange operation.[4] As a result it rushed its cash reserves to the banks to prevent blocking. Circulating note issue dropped from 3,000 million in April 1945 to 1,400 million on conversion day 9 September 1945. Bank deposits increased correspondingly. Against two clippings in the rationing card each note bearer was allowed to exchange 100 kroner. Of amounts exceeding this 60 per cent was paid out in cash, while 40 per cent was credited the owner in the form of a deposit in a new national deposit account. It was blocked, pending future development in the liquidity situation. Since the circulating note issue came down from 1,400 to 1,018 million after the exchange operation, one may say that a little less than 400 million in notes was blocked.[5] Also bank deposits were registered.

Wealth Registration 1945

To obtain material for a wartime single tax, all bank deposits, bonds, shares and securities were registered during the period 9 September-15 November 1945. Anything not registered in this period passed on to the state as public property. A total of 16.7 billion was registered, of which 6.6 billion comprised bank deposits. A mere 800 million of this was blocked and transferred to the national deposit account. Taking into account the blocked paper notes, we see that a mere 1.1 billion in all was soaked up by the operation, less than half the amount originally expected by the Central Bank. War profiteering, hiding behind false accounts, was also overrated, as a mere 70 million failed to appear for exchange or registration.[6]

The Single Tax

The purpose of the registration in the autumn 1945 was to provide a basis for a single tax on wealth appreciation during the war. The bill, presented on 21 September 1945, was postponed in the Storting till a new ordinary Storting could be elected on 8 October 1945.[7] The Gerhardsen Labour government presented a revised bill in February 1946. In part its aim was to reduce liquidity but the overriding aim was to contribute to a more just distribution of the economic burdens of the war. At a time when the country as a whole had become poorer, it was only fair that those who had increased their wealth should resign part of that increase to the nation. So much for justification. The bill passed the Storting in February 1946 and emanated as law 19 July 1946. By now 15 months had passed since liberation. The law, when passed, could be effective only during 1947; hence it could not influence the liquidity situation in 1946. The delay meant that the single tax was largely argued out of considerations of justice. At the same time it became evident that the liquidity problem could be tackled by other means, among them continued import controls, rationing and price controls. Besides, it was argued that once the most basic replacements had been effected, companies and the general public would hold on to their reserves rather than activate them for spending purposes at a time when by so doing they merely succeeded in bidding up prices. The prevailing view in February 1946, nine months after the war, was that the liquidity reserves posed a smaller inflationary threat than originally thought. A far greater cause for inflation would be uncontrolled wage increases unmatched by corresponding increases in production.

The single tax was levied at strongly progressive rates. The first 5,000 kroner were exempt, but the tax took 30 per cent of the next

10,000 kroner, increasing to 90 per cent of amounts exceeding 40,000 kroner. The 90 per cent limit was later raised to 70,000. Still, when paid in, mostly in 1949, the tax brought in just under 500 million, which was somewhat less than expected. Of this one hundred million was credited to the 'occupation account', the rest deposited at a government 'regulation account' with the Central Bank.

The Low-interest Policy

So far we have reviewed measures to bring down liquidity and prevent inflation. Obviously, in a situation of too much money, high rates of interest would be natural and desirable. On closer inspection, however, contractive measures were seen to harbour the threat of deflation, that is, a return to the events of the 1920s. Clearly, there was a conflict between two goals: the expansionist economics, proposed by Labour's advisers, called for easy credits and low interest rates, but the steps to halt inflation made dear money imperative. The government, on the advice of the economists, decided to clamp down a policy of cheap money. Accordingly, on 9 January 1946 the Central Bank discount rate was set at 2½ per cent, the time deposit rate 2 per cent and the call deposit rate 0 per cent.[8] These interest rates were the lowest in the country's financial history. The discount rate had been 3 per cent since 1942.[9] They provide a testimony of the self confidence held by the new economists as to how far they could flaunt conventional experience of the behaviour of markets. The low-interest policy caused strong criticism from monetarists; its supporters in the Labour camp answered that the resulting pressure on prices could be tackled through price controls.The distributional aspect must also be kept in view; low interest rates minimised payments on the national debt, that is transfers to the creditor side of the economy.

The Legacy of Inflation

Compared to the plan originally presented by the central bank authorities, it is safe to say that the monetary policy actually implemented by the Labour government after 1945 was far more lenient. It was due in part to increased insight into the stabilisation problems acquired with the passage of time. Less obvious, the outcome was also due to new priorities. To Central Bank governor Nicolai Rygg, the value of the currency was instinctively the primary goal, but to the new generation of politicians, some of whom had been exposed to the teachings of Keynes, the overriding concern was to avoid mass unemployment. In two addresses shortly after liberation governor Rygg called for stern measures to cut down the money volume in order to restore the old value of currency. That call had been heard before. It cut no ice with the generation that had gone through the era of mass unemployment.

Rygg resigned as governor in January 1946. In 1949 the Central Bank was turned into a state-owned bank as the Storting voted to buy out the remaining private shareholders. France and Great Britain also nationalised their central banks in the first postwar years. Power over monetary policy at the same time passed from the bankers to the politicians. Inflation thereby presented itself as a social choice: Minister of Finance Erik Brofoss (1908-79) in February 1946 saw the choice this way: cutting down liquidity meant undermining the basis of reconstruction, above all the house building programme. He was not willing to sacrifice the latter for the sake of maintaining a stable value of the currency. The employment of men was more important than the prestige of the krone. The legacy was that inflation was not removed. Instead its effects were to be controlled by a huge machinery of price controls. Before reviewing the nature of the government regulations, we will briefly take a look at the trials of war profiteers. The section harks back to the earlier discussion of the subject in Chapter 8.

Economic War Crimes

As to the extent and nature of real as opposed to imagined economic war crimes, the published minutes of the court proceedings and the statistics compiled afterwards provide readily accessible information.[10] This category of war crimes involved cases charged under the criminal code of 1902, §§ 86 and 98, the military criminal code and a special war crimes ordinance issued in 1942 and later revised 15 December 1944. The latter carried the principle of retroactive justice. For that reason it was controversial. Besides it was superfluous, for the offences in question were covered by § 86 of the criminal code. It was above all article § 25, introducing the principle of collective responsibility upon all members of the Nazi Party, that caused concern. The article conflicted with the general principles of liability and damage. Article § 2 of the special war crimes ordnance pertained specifically to economic crimes. The article made it a criminal offence after 8 April 1940 for anyone to provide or take part in providing services for the enemy in a manner which under the circumstances must be deemed improper. The term improper was vague. In practice the judges and the courts therefore tended to weigh each case *ad hoc*, on its own merits, until experience and Supreme Court rulings had helped set reliable guidelines. The courts in evaluating a case, were to consider

- whether the work in question was more or less strategic,
- whether the defendant had undertaken the job more or less freely or acted under coercion,
- whether the firm was an old one, maintaining jobs for its workers, or a new company set up to reap advantages from the war situation,
- the time of the contract.

The decision handed down were often contested, notably by the Labour press, and many verdicts were given with dissenting votes. Nor is it easy to follow clear cut principles in the decisions. In general, tempers softened as time passed, and sentences were scaled down accordingly.

Under this legislation a total of 3,355 persons were charged for economic war crimes, of which, 1,857 were in towns and 1,498 in rural areas. The war crime register, kept at the National Archive, which excludes those who worked as 'German workers' only, gives the lower total of 3,262. Among the war profiteers charged, a total of 1,742 were convicted, and of these 161 received prison sentences, 1,305 were fined, and in 54 cases the charge was later dropped.[11] Up to 1 July 1952 the amounts of damages, fines and confiscations handed down, were as follows:[12]

Fines	51.7 million	of which paid	45.4 million kroner
Damages	71.7 "	"	57.7 " "
Confiscations	165.- "	"	75.1 " "
Total	288.4 million	of which paid	178.2 million kroner

The total of 178 million may be compared to the proceeds of the single tax of 500 million. Obviously, economic war crimes were of limited dimensions. Loss of civil rights, usually for 10 years, was applied in 358 cases under this heading. For a number of reasons, capacity problems among them, the settlement did not include those who merely worked on German war projects. This group as noted included from 100,000 to 150,000 men at one time or another.

Looking at the war crimes proceedings as a whole, a total of 98,694 cases was decided upon. But 44,878 cases were summarily dealt with in the police courts, as cases involving merely passive membership in

Nasjonal Samling, the Nazi party, at one time or another after 8 April 1940. Of the 46,000 persons actually charged, 9,800 were convicted for active membership in the 'Hirden', the paramilitary Nazi police, another 7,173 received sentences for active participation in other Nazi organisations, including front service in the Soviet Union, 5,330 were convicted for work for the Reichskommissar, Org. Todt and similar employment, and the rest were charged with a variety of less severe offences. As for the type of penalty imposed, prison terms were applied in 18,000 cases. A total of 30 death sentences were given, of which 25 were carried out. Among the rest 28,000 got away with a fine and loss of civil rights or one of the two.

Comparisons with the war crime proceedings and settlements in the Netherlands, France and Denmark, show that in view of the size of the respective populations, the Norwegian settlement was of average extent, but given the number of death sentences, prison terms, summary executions and pardons, the settlement in Norway was less severe than elsewhere. In France lynchings took the lives of thousands in the chaotic transitional period. Figures cited under this category range from 14,000 to 40,000. If one counts the liquidations of 'collaborateurs' just prior to liberation, the French historian Robert Aron estimated that 30,000 to 40,000 killings or summary executions occurred in France.[13] In the more comparable country., the Netherlands, the war crime settlement also included retroactive legislation, as in Denmark and Norway. A total of 31 deaths among former collaborators occurred, due to lynch justice. In all 48,000 sentences were given, involving loss of freedom. The death penalty was applied in 215 cases, of which 30 were carried out. In addition, 100,000 got away with a fine or conditional pardon.[14] In Denmark the settlement involved 13,000 sentences entailing loss of freedom (as against 18,000 in Norway). On the other hand, the death penalty was used in 78 cases (as against 30 in Norway). Of these 46 were executed (against 25 in Norway).[15] As for the 8-9,000 Norwegian women who had children by German soldiers, they were momentarily harassed, but quickly dropped out of sight, later to be reabsorbed in society, as were their children. No lasting rancour has been rumoured.

A general amnesty for all war criminals was declared in 1953. It remains to add that leftwing authors, among them Helge Krog, Øivind Bolstad and Arthur Omre, wrote books that helped to keep alive the idea that the biggest war profiteers had gone unscathed while only the small fry had been caught.[16]

Labour and the Planned Economy

In 1945 all parties, including the conservative party Høyre, agreed that
to cope with the immediate situation the government had to have
emergency powers. Disagreement was bound to arise, however, on the
extent of the emergency legislation, its nature and duration. Two conflicting views appeared, the one representing Labour and the socialists,
the other the conservatives and the non-socialist parties, viz. the
Farmers' Party, the Christian Popular Party and the Liberal Party.
Initially, the socialists, as will be shown, wanted to exploit the emergency to pave the way for a socialist order, hence they insisted on broad
and lasting discretionary powers for the government. The conservatives,
in order to avoid just such a development, demanded that the emergency legislation should be reduced to what was absolutely necessary at
the time and that it be dismantled as soon as the ongoing work with
reconstruction allowed, in order to return to a freely functioning
market economy. The ideological conflict was accompanied by con-
trasting foreign policy ideas, with Labour, at least originally, taking its
ideals from the east, from the Soviet planning system, and the conservatives taking as their model the American market economy.

There were thus from the outset two opposing themes and policy
ideals present in the debate on ends and means. Positions and recommendations were also very much influenced by international political
and military events. Forced to make choice, Norway in the postwar
period emerged as an active member in the Western military alliance,
committed to the defence of the Atlantic member countries in Nato in
1949, and to the restoration of the international market economy
within the Marshall programme from 1948.

The contours of the political landscape became clearer with the first
Storting election held on 8 October 1945. The outcome was a victory
for Labour. The party took 76 out of 150 representatives, and was able
to form a majority government. The new Prime Minister was Einar
Gerhardsen who took office 1 November 1945. In addition, the Communist Party won 11 representatives, thus giving a very substantial
socialist majority in the national assembly. With the exception of a four-
week non-socialist coalition government in the autumn of 1963, following the squabble over the Svalbard coal mine accident, Labour remained
in power till 1965. Till 1961 the party had a parliamentary majority in
the Storting. Moreover, for 16 out of 20 years Einar Gerhardsen was
Prime Minister. Whatever Labour chose to do, it could command a
majority, among voters and in the Storting. It was Labour's golden

moment.

The socialist programme of Labour was in line with the party's origin, its ideology and its following. True, with government responsibility from 1935, the purity of the socialist vision had faded somewhat, and had been blended with the surge of national patriotism called forth by the war. A good many leading members, among them Trygve Lie, Halvard Lange and Jens Chr. Hauge, acquired friends among Western European politicians and diplomats during the war and after, and saw the ideological conflict between capitalism and socialism in a new perspective. The older party chiefs had rather gone to Moscow. But the socialist key words remained in the party programme. The party, if wished, was now in a position to bring about legal socialisation, in the form of state ownership of the means of production.

Of far greater interest here are the practical efforts by Labour to implement the three cardinal policy goals: full employment, income equalisation and economic growth. These three related goals provided the justification for the party's bid for power during reconstruction and after. They also provided the justification for the system of controls introduced in 1945. The machinery of controls was identified as a pioneering experiment in a planned economy.[17] Its Norwegian version included

1) The corporative co-ordination bodies, with the national body the Economic Co-ordination Council on top, followed by Branch Councils for each industry and Production Committees for each company or firm.
2) A system of direct controls over prices, consumption and production.
3) The national budgets as part of a new system of national planning.
4) The building blocks of state capitalism, including government take-overs of former German firms, patents and construction projects left unfinished at the Wehrmacht's capitulation. The take-overs provided a stepping stone for state-owned industries in the postwar era.

We will briefly review the four aspects of the planning experiments. They will precede a discussion of what all the blue prints amounted to in the real world. This is taken up in Chapter 10.

The Corporative Pyramid

The Economic Co-ordination Council

At the apex of the planned corporative pyramid was the Economic Co-ordination Council, mentioned in the Joint Programme and established by royal decree as early as 4 May 1945.[18] Like its historic predecessors in Mussolini's Italy, the council complemented, in part replaced, the traditional legislative assembly, the Storting. The members were drawn from the government and the major interest organisations, among them shipowners, industrialists, banks, trade associations, farmers, fishermen, management and the unions. As a sounding board the council was to offer advice and consent on major policy issues. Its recommendations were consultative. The council functioned till 1950, when confrontation replaced co-operation. It was formally dissolved in 1954. Its demise, however, marked only a temporary retreat of the corporative principle, for while in existence, the council had boosted the self-esteem of the interest organisations and immensely fed their appetite for political influence, which proved lasting. The corporative channel became a permanent and complicating addition to the political decision process.

The Branch Councils

Below came the branch councils for each industry, created by special enabling legislation in 1947 when private business, notably Norway's Federation of Industry, proved unco-operative.[19] As joint bodies for each industry, the branch councils were to co-ordinate and help implement the government's industrial policies. Counting representatives from industry, workers and the Department of Industry, they were given undefined, but largely consultative powers to propose production schedules and allocate licences, quotas and production among participating firms in each industry; moreover, to advise on cutbacks or expansion, rescheduling or downright close-downs of firms, and to advise on 'technical and organisational rationalisation'. Productivity issues were central. Participating firms were ordered to provide the branch councils or its consultants with every sort of information deemed necessary for pursuing their tasks, including patented knowledge. In 1947-8 ten councils were organised. Another two came in 1954.[20] Unlike the umbrella body, the Economic Co-ordinating Council, the branch councils proved permanent advisory bodies. They affected about half of the industrial workforce. Much of their justification disappeared, however, when the direct quota allocations, maintained during the

reconstruction period, no longer proved necessary. New price legislation, in force from 1 January 1954, also voided the government's
right to intervene by enabling legislation in matters of shut-downs or
incorporation of new businesses.

The Production Committees

The third tier of the corporative ladder set up in 1945 was the production committees, to be organised within each company or firm with
members from workers and management. The production committees
were mentioned in the Joint Programme in 1945, and were set up after
negotiations between spokesmen for the trade unions (LO) and the
employers (NAF) in December 1945. They were backed by a private
agreement, not by legislation, and as the employers hesitated, the
functions of production committees were reduced to welfare and
productivity matters. Labour originally wanted the committees to
spearhead economic democracy with worker representatives on the
board in a position to control management decisions. Such pretensions
had to be scaled down; from 1950 the committees' main task was to
facilitate rationalisation and higher productivity.[21] The trade union
leadership, always with an eye to practical gains, endorsed the new
course.

All in all, as later admitted by former Labour Premier Einar Gerhardsen in his memoirs, Labour did intend the corporative structure as
'an important step in transforming society into a socialist order'.[22]
The opposition parties at the time interpreted the corporative system
in the same way. However, as time passed and the Labour party chiefs
grasped the nature of the political backlash they would run into if they
ignored the opposition's warnings, the whole idea of a socialist order
was quietly shelved, though state ownership was later aired for
rhetorical effect once in a while.

Direct Controls 1945-1952

A second element in the blueprint for a planned economy, intended
as a stepping stone to a socialist order, was the direct controls. On 8
May 1945 the London government, by a piece of enabling legislation,
passed the temporary price regulation ordinance, immediately named
Lex Thagaard. The ordinance lapsed in 1947, and was replaced by
another provisional price act of 30 June 1947. The new act was
renewed each year till it was replaced by the present price law of 26

June 1953. The Lex Thagaard was an instrument to help the central authorities direct reconstruction and economic recovery, but the enabling powers were so sweeping as to give the government authority to restructure the entire private sector of the economy.[23] Article 2 authorised the Price Directorate to maintain such regulations as it deemed necessary in the extraordinary situation, including direct command over prices, profits, rents and dividends of any description, and control of production, distribution and other business activity with a view to eliminating harmful competition and promoting a better organisation of business. To achieve these goals the Price Directorate was authorised, at its own discretion, to

a) forbid cutbacks or shut-downs of production, distribution or any other business activity,
b) to order firms to produce certain goods or undertake prescribed services,
c) to forbid new entries and expansion, order firms to share markets or activities, or order shut-downs or reductions among firms sharing such markets, and
d) order firms to pay duties as contributions to price regulations, including price equalisation duties.

The Act was a recipe, or could easily be used as such, for a state-controlled enforced cartellisation of industry. Its provisions for punishing transgressors by fines, jail or confiscations, and for delegating authority, could easily pave the way for arbitrary exercise of power by anonymous bureaucrats, acting supposedly in the interests of the common good. The Labour Party and the trade unions, however, recoiled from the wholesale expropriation of private industry. Socialisation was redefined in 1949: a socialist order had up to then been an end; in the revised party programme adopted in 1949, it became a means to the mixed economy. The *volte face* stretched over a twenty year period and for that reason was hardly noticed by the public at large. In practice therefore, the direct controls were used as instruments in speeding up reconstruction, husbanding scarce foreign currency reserves, and ensuring a fair share for wage earners, i.e. the majority that sustained Labour in office.

Rationing, a saga stretching from 1939 over 20 years, was dismantled gradually, Locally grown fruit was decontrolled in 1945, spirits in February 1946, tobacco in March 1946, potatotes in May, detergents in June, cocoa in September, and oranges in October the same year. Textiles, however, were not decontrolled till December 1951, meat not until July 1952 and coffee, sugar and syrup not till September 1952. Private motorcars remained under rationing until 1960, fifteen years after liberation.[24] The above hint at the nature and extent of the consumption controls maintained in the first postwar years.

The direct controls also encompassed foreign currency transactions. Clearing and currency licensing to control foreign trade was continued till well into the fifties. Indeed, the clearing agreement system was vastly extended in the three first postwar years. Norway had clearing agreements with five countries at the beginning of 1940, and ten countries at the end of that year. Later agreements were negotiated with other countries on a bilateral basis and this practice was continued in 1945 and 1946. As a result there were about 200 bilateral payments agreements in force in 1947 in Europe alone, and about 900 agreements in 1949, without counting the Soviet bloc countries.[25] Dividends, rents, interest rates, and all sorts of prices were also policed by the price police corps, organised in each municipality all over the country under the central direction of Wilhelm Thagaard, head of the Price Directorate. To producers and consumers it seemed as if the war went on as before.

In pursuance of World War I legislation, rationing of construction and building materials also continued after the war. Special legislation was enacted by an act of 11 July 1947, which enabled the government to maintain detailed supervision over the level as well as the composition of investments.

National Budgets

A third element in the build-up of government control of the economy after 1945 was the introduction in 1946, of annual national budgets and accounts, followed by long-term programmes in 1948 (for 1949-52), and perspective analyses in 1969 (for the period to 1990).

Since 1815 the nation had grown accustomed to the term 'the state budget' and 'government accounts', the former providing a plan of central government expenditures and revenues for the coming budget year, the latter, an *ex post* survey of how far the projections had proved correct. Now the term budget was widened to include a forecast or a plan for the future use of the entire private and public sector inputs, whether for consumption, investment, imports or exports. Similarly, the national account gave an *ex post* survey of how far the forecasts had been fulfilled. The development of macro planning depended on estimation and collection of more accurate data for macro economic variables. It also depended on progress in data techniques or data manipulation. Finally, it depended on the development of Keynesian economic theory and clarification of the structural and quantitative relationships between the key variables assumed in that theory, among them production, consumption, investments, savings, exports and imports.

The social urgency of the plans stemmed from the recent experience of mass unemployment and the confident conviction among the new economists that government had both the power and the duty to ensure full employment in the future. Economic growth was not originally the end of national planning, but gradually growth was seen as a solvent of both the unemployment problem and the imperative of fair income distribution.

Owing to the pioneering theoretical and empirical work by Ragnar Frisch (1895-1973), professor of economics at Oslo University 1931-65, the Norwegian government was in a position to draw on a corps of academically trained economists immediately after the war, among them Erik Brofoss, Kjell Aukrust and Petter Jacob Bjerve, who now started careers, eager to make the world fit their conception of it. For his work Ragnar Frisch in 1969, together with Jan Tinbergen of the Netherlands, was awarded the first Nobel Memorial Prize in economics.

Ragnar Frisch, in developing economics as an academic subject at Oslo University, sought to justify the discipline in drawing a distinction between political decision-making involving choices between various goals, and economic advice, which in Frisch's view, consisted in presenting the likely consequences of alternative policy instruments. The choice of goals belonged to the politicians, who in turn represented the voters. The devising of ways to monitor and estimate how far goals could be realised in the Keynesian world of economics, was the task of the economist. One of the means to ensure scientific rigour was mathematics, another was statistics. Combining the two, econometrics became the badge of a new breed of academic economists with special skills in planning. Placed close to the seat of power they not unnaturally looked upon their task mainly as one of economic dirigisme.[26]

The new expansionism associated with Keynesian economics was voiced in February 1946. In a lengthy speech in the Storting, Minister of Finance, Erik Brofoss, introducing the next year's budget, first demolished traditional myths then justified new ones. As for the old truths, he shocked his listeners by telling them that the market economy did not possess a self-regulating mechanism by which investments turned out be the difference between productive capacity and consumption at full employment. The balance could just as well be struck at a level far below full employnent. Who was to fill the investment gap? The government. How? By borrowing. But was it not wrong for the government to run an unbalanced budget? No, there was no parallel between the household budget and the government budget, for in certain situations the sum of individual rationality would add up to collective folly. He went on to point out that monetary instruments, among them changes in the Central Bank discount rate, would fail to regulate the level of activity. The economy was already swamped with liquidity. But would not government borrowing impose a burden on future generations? No, apart from the case of foreign borrowing, the truth was that current production always paid for itself. Thus, on the assumption that unemployment was imminent, the era of government deficit budgeting in postwar Norway was launched.

Brofoss also sketched the options. The sketch introduced the national budget in political debate.[27] It formed an addition to the ordinary state budget. Using the figures for total national production, provided by the planning office, Brofoss was able to present to the Storting numerical examples of alternative trade-offs between consumption and investment and how choices would affect the growth in real goods and services in the immediate years ahead.

The sketch also appraised the economic outlook. It dovetailed with informed assessments made before the war. Because of limited resources no substantial expansion could be expected in fishing, nor in agriculture, nor in whaling. Next, in forestry renewable resources were also limited upwards to about 8 mill. m^3 yearly, besides, existing plant capacity was sufficient to cope with the timber cut in normal years. In fact, imports of timber from Swedish forests were soon considerable There remained shipping, hydro-power development combined with metal refining and exploitation of the country's low grade mineral deposits. These promised to serve as bridgeheads to higher future income plateaus. The Storting, in deliberating strategies, considered the need to prevent a return of mass unemployment, the likely shortage of foreign reserves needed to cover vital imports, as well as the long term possibility of *per capita* economic growth. Priority was in the end given to long term goals. Jam was to be postponed. This meant that industrial development, electrification and shipping were selected as the favoured investment areas. The following year Brofoss, in presenting the second national budget, was more concrete.[28] Here the government declared its programme to be the development of large-scale export-industry, development of hydro-electric energy production, and the rebuilding of the merchant fleet with a view to earning foreign currency needed for rapid reconstruction and long term growth.

Peace in labour relations was a precondition for the success of the ambitious plans. Strikes would cripple reconstruction. The London government, foreseeing the need for compulsory arbitration in wage disputes, secured legislation for dealing with the emergency. Avoiding the old term 'compulsory arbitration', the new legislation provided for a temporary Wage Board, with a chairman and six other members, among them two representatives each of labour and management. Both sides accepted the need for the board which continued to pronounce binding verdicts in the years 1945-52, when labour and management regained full responsibility for settling wage and labour issues. In return the Labour government secured gains for labour: child allowances were introduced in 1946, in 1950 shift workers had their week reduced from 48 to 45½ hours and miners to 40 hours. In 1947 the Annual Holiday Act secured every employee a paid three week vacation. The length of the annual holiday was increased to four weeks in 1964.

State Capitalism

Of some importance for bringing the means of production under government control was the series of confiscations of enemy property after liberation. Among the industrial holdings that fell into the government hands in this manner were A/S Nordag's huge works in Årdal, Glomfjord, Sunndal and Tyssedal and the German-owned stock in Hydro (47 per cent) which gave the government control of the company; moreover, the German subsidiary companies of Siemens, AEG and Telefunken, and the German shares of A/S Syd Varanger, were now cancelled. These offered opportunities for broadening government interests in industry and mining. An unknown number of German patents was also simply taken over, in the sense that Norwegian entrepreneurs just started production of articles hitherto subject to patent licensing from German companies.

In recommendations for the state budget for 1946-7 Labour members proposed the socialisation of banks and insurance companies. There were also Labour proposals for nationalisation of the mining industry, large forest properties in private hands and A/S Nordisk Lettmetall at Herøya. These demands appeared also in the party's programme in 1945 and again in its revised programme of 1949. The communists for their part called for the socialisation of banks and key industries.

The government during the war had bought the British holdings in A/S Union Co, the huge paper mill at Skien. During the years 1946-59 the board and the government fought a drawn-out battle about these shares. The government, represented by the Department of Trade, proposed to make Union a state-owned company, but lacking sufficient votes, it held on to its stock till 1971. The Skien company remained a private company.[29]

Labour had traditionally championed state-owned operations for infrastructure, including telephones. By a letter of 13 May 1935 the Nygaardsvold government ordered the telegraph director to prepare a situation report and submit plans by which all or as many as possible of existing private telephone companies could come under the state.[30] At that time 45 per cent of the telephones were run by private companies. The take-over operation was speeded up after 1945, and by 1960 just about all private companies had been eliminated. In this field we note that the railways were run as state enterprises (from the 1890s) as were the post (18th century) and broadcasting (1925). The grain monopoly dates from 1928, the state liquor monopoly from 1927. The list swelled when the Norges Bank was nationalised by an act of 8 July 1949. In 1953 the Gerhardsen government set afoot a state monopoly for imports of fishing gear (Statens Fiskeredskapsmonopol), medicines (Statens Medisinaldepot), and even imports of feed concentrates (Statens Kraftfor-forretning). All were justified by the promise that by cutting out private profit interests, customers would obtain better and cheaper goods. Energy supply in gas and electricity had furthermore been handled by county and municipal governments from the start.

In most European countries the infrastructural tasks were similarly operated as public utilities. Public operations in these fields had nothing to do with a specific socialist ideology. Both from a technical, economic and administrative point of view, the infrastructure possessed attributes that made the services in question collective rather than private goods. When this is conceded, it is nonetheless true that with Labour's dominant position after the October elections 1945, the idea of socialisation and state ownership took on increased urgency. Nor was this unnatural. The unpropertied class received a symbolic compensation. 'When the state owned,' said Einar Gerhardsen at Labour's party Congress in 1945, 'all members of society gained an allodial right.'[31] Again in an address in Drammen in December 1945, he asked: 'The development of economic and industrial democracy, with a view to setting up a socialistic society without lapsing into dictatorship or reducing the living standard, has never yet been tried, but should not Norway be one of the countries to show the way?'[32]

Labour did not attack the private credit systems directly, but sought to counteract their power by setting up state banks and channelling funds to them. We mention two efforts.

The National Housing Bank of Norway, a government bank set up in 1946, was one of the new instruments designed to provide the unpropertied masses with government subsidised housing. In Finnmark special efforts were called for. Here 12,000 dwellings had recently been destroyed and up to 60,000 people uprooted. The area of 75,000 km² in all represented a fifth of the country's territory, and had been the home of 75,000 inhabitants before the war. In the summer of 1945 the refugees, against advice and expectations, returned to their burnt-out hamlets. As refugees many were shabbily treated in Oslo. To forestall another tragedy barracks were built with government money in the fall of 1945, a work supervised by Peder Holt (1899-1963), consultative minister, who put up his makeshift headquarters in Harstad. Here the Norwegian State Housing Bank provided long term mortgages at low interest, the private war risk insurance paid part of the costs, and to ease top financing, freight bounties were offered. A nationwide campaign to collect charity money for Finnmark was staged in the fall of 1945.

To roll back the traditional power held by the private banks in another field, Labour in 1950 secured legislation for a government Post Office Savings Bank. An innovation in Norway, though not in European history, the government bank was to use the country's 4,771 postal offices as branch offices. The idea was to provide easy and safe deposit opportunities for personal savers and other customers who so far had not set their foot in a bank. Labour spokesmen championed the new government deposit bank as a bridgehead to further socialisation. Non-socialist politicians condemned the plan for the same reason. In its first year of operation the bank attracted 93,000 new deposit accounts, in its first five years 500,000; indeed, it was the first bank in Norway with a really nationwide branch network. It soon had more personal savings accounts than any other bank, though its share of total deposit capital remained an insignificant 0.3 per cent by the end of 1950 and 5 per cent ten years later.[33]

State capitalism meant above all the emergence of government as employer in industry, construction and mining. The biggest industrial commitments were the construction of a huge state iron works in Mo, Nordland county, voted in 1946, the completion of the government-owned aluminium works in Årdal, also voted in 1946, the state-financed reconstruction of the Syd-Varanger mines, the Svalbard coal mines at Kings Bay, and the series of electrification projects. In the northern counties government money was also poured into fish processing, refrigeration, and development of fishing tackle. The motive varied, but in general government was seen by Labour as an instrument, if not an end, to further social control and socialisation. In a European context however, state capitalism in postwar Norway was a phenomenon of the early postwar years and was of average proportions (Table 9.2).

Table 9.2: State-owned Industries* in West European Countries 1960 — Their Share of the Labour Force, Gross National Product, Share Capital and Gross Capital Formation

	Labour force	Gross national product	Share capital	Gross capital formation
	%	%	%	%
UK	10.0	17.0	—	18.8
France	5.5	10.0-15.0	—	24.7
Italy	3.0	12.0	—	—
West Germany	6.0	—	20.3	16.0
Austria	9.0	15.5+	—	—
Norway	5.5	13.0	15.0	15.0
Sweden	5.9	13.0	—	11.0

Source: Christian Smekal, *Das verstaatlichte Industrie in der Marktwirtschaft — Das österreischische Beispiel*, Carl Heymanns Verlag KG, 1963, cited from Sverre Thon, *Statsdrift i Norge og andre land, Omfang, former, resultater, problemer*, Oslo, 1965, p. 25.
*includes public utilities, energy, transports, communications and industrial establishments, but not the military services.
†only industrial establishments.

With 5.5 per cent of the labour force producing 13 per cent of the gross national product, the state industries sector in Norway comes in the middle range when compared with other West European countries. The state sector in the United Kingdom was larger, when labour is taken as yardstick. As far as capital formation is concerned, we see in Table 9.2 that Norway's state industries ranked behind those of France, Great Britain and West Germany.

In the preceding sections we have been concerned to describe how the postwar era offered Labour a golden opportunity to create a socialist society backed by majority opinion. We have described some of the salient, ideas, tasks, plans and institutions by which the high ideals were to be transformed into reality. How far did Labour succeed?

Notes

1 Einar Gerhardsen, *Fellesskap i krig og fred. Erindringer 1940-45*, Oslo 1970, pp. 150-60.

2 A. Strømme Svendsen & G. Chr. Wasberg, *Industriens historie*, p. 244.

3 Ot. prp. nr 11, 1945; Preben Munthe, 'Tiden etter Den annen verdenskrig', in G. Jahn *et al.*, *Norges Bank gjennom 150 år*, Oslo, 1966, pp. 352-5; St. meld. nr. 8, 1945-6, Om sanering av pengevesenet.

4 St. meld. nr. 8, 1947, Om registrering av verdipapirer og bankinnskudd og om ligningskontrollen.

5 *Statistisk-økonomisk oversikt over året 1946*, CBS, Oslo, 1947, p. 16.

6 Preben Munthe, 'Tiden etter Den annen verdenskrig', *Norges Bank gjennom 150 år*, p. 355.

7 St. prp. nr. 18, 1945-6.

8 *Statistisk-økonomisk oversikt over året 1946*, CBS, Oslo, 1947, p. 18.

9 Ibid., p. 79.

10 *Om landssvikoppgjøret*, Report from a seleect committee of 22 December 1955 to prepare information on the war crimes settlement for a final government paper to the Storting, presented 11 January 1962, Gjøvik, 1962, pp. 239, 276 ff. Full bibliography appendix 2; Johs. B. Andenaes, *Det vanskelige oppgjøret. Rettsoppgjøret etter okkupasjonen*, Oslo, 1980. A full balanced possibly final account of all aspects. Full bibliography pp. 282-95.

11 Ibid., p. 239.

12 Johs. Andenaes, *Det vanskelige oppgjøret*, p. 168.

13 Robert Aron, *Histoire de la libération de la France*, Paris, 1959, pp. pp. 638-55, 423.

14 Henry L. Mason, *The Purge of Dutch Quislings. Emergency Justice in the Netherlands* (1952); A.D. Belinfante, *In plaats von biljtjesday* (1978) gives 135 death sentences of which 40 were executed.

15. E.W. v. Eyben, *Thi kendes for ret. Retsopgjøret efter besaettelsen*, København 1968, all cited from Johs. Andenaes, *Det vanskelige oppgjøret*, pp. 170, 290.

16 Helge Krog, *'6. kolonne'*, (1946), Øivind Bolstad, *Profitøren* (1947), Arthur Omre, *Linedansere* (1946).

17 Alice Bourneuf, *Norway, the planned revival*, Cambridge, Mass. 1958.

18 Trond Bergh, 'Norsk økonomisk politikk 1945-1965', i *Vekst og velstand*, ed. Trond Bergh, Helge Pharo *et al.*, Oslo 1977, pp. 11-99.

19 Trond Bergh, *Opprettelsen og utviklingen av bransjerådene*, History thesis, University of Oslo, 1973; Ot. prp. nr. 153, 1945/6, Utkast til lov om Bransjeråd.

20 St. meld. nr. 18, 1979/80.

21 Tore Grønlie, 'Norsk industripolitikk 1945-65', in *Vekst og velstand*, pp. 99-165; Trond Bergh, 'Norsk økonomisk politikk 1945-65', p. 47.

22 Einar Gerhardsen, *Samarbeid og strid. Erindringer 1945-55*, Oslo, 1971, p. 256.

23 The text printed in *Norsk Lovtidend, London-utgaven 1940-45*, pp. pp. 493-507.

24 G. Chr. Wasberg & A. Strømme Svendsen, *Industriens historie*, pp. 244-5.

25 Leland B. Yeager, *International Monetary Relations. Theory, History and*

Policy, New York 1969, p. 359.
    26 Petter Jakob Bjerve, *Planning in Norway 1947-1956*, Amsterdam 1959
(Doctoral thesis); ——, Utviklingstendenser i den kvantitative økonomiske plan-
legginga i Norge, *Sosialøkonomen 1965*, pp. 11-22; ——, *Trends in Norwegian
Planning 1945-1975*, Art. from Central Bureau of Statistics, Oslo, 1976. General
description is given by Trond Bergh, 'Norsk økonomisk politikk 1945-65', Øyvind
Østerud, *Samfunnsplanlegging og politisk system*, Oslo, 1972 and Øyvind
Østerud's more recent, *Det planlagte samfunn. Om sentralplanleggingens,
fremvekst og grenser*, Oslo, 1979. European in scope is Andrew Schonfield,
Modern Capitalism, London, 1965. Donald Winch, *Economics and Policy. A
Historical Study*, 1969, new ed. 1972, covers the Anglo-American field in particu-
lar.
    27 St. prp. nr. 1, 1945-6, 'Om nasjonalregnskapet og nasjonalbudsjettet'.
    28 St. meld. nr. 10, 1947 (Parliamentary Report no 10, 1947).
    29 A. Strømme Svendsen, *Union 1873-1973*, Oslo 1973; Tore Grønlie,
'Kampen om Union 1946-9', *Hist. Tidsskrift*, 1978, pp. 1-52.
    30 Ingolf Lenaes *Privattelefonen i Norge*, Oslo, 1966, p. 124.
    31 Cited from Åse Reikvam, 'Synet på sosialisering i DNA 1945-53', *Etter-
krigshistorie*, I, Universitetsforlaget Oslo, 1970, p. 99.
    32 Sverre Thon, *Økonomisk politikk i Norge 1945-1965*, Oslo, 1968, p. 20.
    33 Trond Bergh. *Fra Faedrelandssag til Storbank. Norges Postsparebank
1950-1975*, Oslo, 1975, pp. 65, 67, *Historical Statistics 1978*, Table 226.

10 RECONSTRUCTION COMPLETED 1947-1952

The Stabilisation Policy 1945-1950

Reconstruction, full employment and income equalisation served as rallying points in the first peace years. The 90,000 men who worked on Wehrmacht projects easily switched to new civilian jobs. Another 50,000 men from the military forces joined their ranks. Unemployment dropped out of sight. Unlike Finland and West Germany, Norway received no flood of refugees from territories lost to the Soviet Union during the war. The labour force and the population at large logged a modest yearly rate of growth of 0.4 and 0.7 per cent in the years after the war. Soon shortages of manpower were reported in several sectors, all in contrast to the sombre forecasts made beforehand. Total production rallied sooner than expected. While forecasts assumed that production and real capital would not reach prewar levels till 1950-1, production, measured by GNP figures, already exceeded that level in 1947, though private consumption did not match prewar levels till 1952. High liquidity ensured a strong overall demand pull, which was reflected in record high levels of investment: 31.1 per cent of GNP in 1946, 37.2 and 36.5 per cent in the following two years.[1]

Deficit Financing

The new Keynesian paradigm urged that budget deficits were to be created when aggregate demand threatened to fall short of that level required to maintain full employment. The command was heeded. The central government deficits for 1945/6 ran up to 565 million, corresponding to 30 per cent of a total expenditure of 1,897 million kroner.[2] Indeed, the deficits of the central government for 1945/6 equalled the entire state budget of the last peace year of 1938/9. Ships were the biggest investment item, taking 22.9 per cent of total capital formation for 1946, 25.1 and 24.0 per cent the two following years.[3] Trailing second came dwellings and third industry, both taking 16-17 per cent of total gross investments.

Production targets, especially for new flats and dwellings, were set too high. More important, the more performance matched ambition, the quicker the country emptied its stored-up currency reserves. These, as will be recalled, totalled just under 4 billion kroner, and represented

154

mostly Nortraship money and insurance claims for ships sunk during the war. The foreign balance 1946-50 reveals record high deficits on current account (Table 10.1):

Table 10.1: Foreign Trade 1946-1950. Million Kroner

	Exports	Imports	Deficits	In % of Exports
1946	2651	3245	− 594	22.4
1947	3847	5050	− 1212	31.5
1948	4485	5179	− 694	15.4
1949	4674	5848	− 1174	25.1
1950	6035	6826	− 791	13.1

Source, NOS, *National Accounts 1865-1960*, Table 1, p. 65.

Table 10.1 indicates that the country dipped into its sterling and dollar reserves with reckless abandon. Imports exceeded exports by 594 million kroner in 1946, and a record of 1,212 million in 1947, which corresponded to 31.5 per cent of total exports. By 1950 the country had run up a deficit of 4.4 billion kroner on its current account dealings with the external world. The shipping insurance money was spent before the end of 1947. The additional deficits were covered by sales of foreign government bonds purchased during the war, by borrowing from the US Export-Import Bank, and after 1948, through grants received under the European Recovery Programme, better known as the Marshall Plan.[4]

In 1947 the reconstruction effort seemed to lose momentum, as too much was tried simultaneously. Also the conflict between ends and means surfaced more strongly. The most glaring discrepancy between the diverse policy objectives was the impossibility of reconciling full employment with stable prices. Another conflict was how to combine wage equalisation with increased productivity, a third how to combine high investment levels with low interest rates and a fourth concerned the promise of reconciling more material comforts with more socialism. The latter ideal looked inward to a collective, non-competitive society, but increased material comforts called for an outward-going economy, geared to competitive exchange in international markets with payments in currencies acceptable abroad. Clearly, all the policy objectives could not be achieved at the same time, but perhaps the symptoms of the built-in discrepancies could be held in check? On that assumption the entire structure of wartime controls was maintained, and a policy of subsidies was initiated by the Coalition government in September 1945. Together they formed the guidelines for the stabilisation policy of the first five years.

Subsidies Introduced 1945

Harking back to World War I, experts thought the past would repeat itself. After the war there would come a brief boom, prices would rise until stocks had been replenished, after which the capitalist world would drift into depression with an inevitable fall in all prices.[5] Why not try to cut through that postwar price peak? It could be done by shielding the home economy from the world market by a combination of quota controls and subsidies.[6] Added urgency derived from the belief that inflation would hurt the workers, stable prices would benefit them. Economic democracy had been proposed by the exiled LO-secretariat in 1944.[7] In order to co-operate, Labour must have a guarantee of a fair share of gains. The Joint Programme issued in June 1945 contained a promise that farmers also were to have an equal share of future gains. Equal returns to labour, regardless of demand, were thus a commitment from the start. The first round of joint price increases on farm products and subsidies to farmers came as early as 1 September 1945.[8] Their magnitude soon reached unbearable proportions. Depending on definitions and the number of items included, subsidies for price stabilisation purposes on food and to farmers went on increasing through to 1949. Table 10.2 offers information for the years 1946-53.

The subsidies for agriculture in Table 10.2 included grain subsidies and a host of minor investment supports, some of which originated in the 1930s. Food subsidies comprised the new price stabilisation subsidies on eggs, milk, milk products and margarine. Subsidies listed under 'Trade' line 3 in Table 10.2, included price stabilisation supports for grain and flour and subsidies to the cod fisheries. Their size is indicated when compared with the total expenditures of the central government: 18 per cent in 1946, increasing to 24 per cent in 1948. In the culminating year total subsidies, as seen, exceeded 1,100 million, which represented 10-12 per cent of total private consumption. Not much need be said about the war damage compensations; they represented a temporary tax levied nationally up to 1953 to help finance reconstruction in the north.

The stabilisation policy, though maintained against increasing odds till the summer of 1950, turned out to be built on the wrong assumptions. Unemployment did not materialise. International prices failed to come

Table 10.2: Subsidies by Industry 1946-1953. Million Kroner. Current Prices

	1946	1947	1948	1949	1950	1951	1952	1953
Agriculture, forestry, fishing	66	95	111	104	96	126	125	151
Food	190	260	427	433	329	337	380	430
Trade	213	367	418	443	421	385	419	265
War damage compensations	87	122	119	78	56	32	20	
Others	17	29	64	103	136	158	115	269
Total subsidies	573	873	1139	1161	1038	1059	1180	1115
Of which Food & Trade	403	627	845	876	750	722	799	675
Central Government Expenditure	2275	2950	3486	4002	4739	4597	5022	4890
Food & Trade subsidies in % of Central Government expenditure	18	21	24	22	16	16	16	14

Source: *National Accounts 1865-1960*, NOS XII, 163, Table 18, 17 A.

down. They inched upwards all the time. Imports consequently tended to push subsidies beyond acceptable limits. Besides, accidents and war intervened. A review of the events that were decisive in leading to the eventual cancelling of the stabilisation policy is given below.

An early setback for the price freeze policy came in 1947 when imports and import licences already granted threatened to empty all the remaining hard currency reserves. To save the situation the authorities first annulled all currency licences granted so far. In September 1947 all outstanding licences were registered, and on the basis of this list the Ministry of Finance began a strict rationing of import licences in hard currency, above all dollars and to a lesser degree the pound sterling and Belgian francs. Other Western countries were in difficulties. Some talked of imminent danger of hunger, others of economic collapse. Moderate estimates foresaw that a major economic setback loomed ahead, primarily because West European governments could not earn enough dollars with which to maintain the reconstruction and full employment policies which they had promised their voters.

Norway accepts the Marshall Plan

The situation was saved by the Marshall Plan, announced in June 1947 by the US Foreign Secretary George Marshall, and put into effect in April 1948 for 16 Western countries, among them Norway. The American aid program aimed at reconstruction and recovery in Europe by means of a vast transfer of American raw materials, machinery and technology in the next four years. In addition, the plan foresaw a removal of existing customs tariffs and quota regulations in Europe, and the revival of sensible payments transactions for inter-European trade. Trade was obviously the key to lasting recovery on the European continent. The European participating states were expected to maintain discriminatory tariffs and quotas for US goods till 1956 in order to achieve a lasting balance in their foreign trade. The aid programme was to be voted by the United States Congress, and financed mostly by American taxpayers, in part also by credits from the International Bank for Reconstruction and Development (IBRD), organised in Washington DC in 1947, better known as the World Bank.

Both by its astronomic size and its magnanimous terms the Marshall Plan represented a watershed in international relations. For this reason it was from the start maligned by the communist countries as a disguised crusade of American dollar imperialism in search of new markets. The charge rested on the debatable proposition that motives rather than results provide a sufficient basis for appraising human action. It also rested on the false assumption that foreign trade was an important element in the US-economy. With an export ratio of 3 per cent to GNP (as against 35-40 per cent for Norway) foreign trade could hardly be said to be vital to the US economy. Finally, the charge of dollar imperialism is contradicted by the provision, noted above, that the participating states were to uphold discriminatory tariffs and quotas to keep out American goods till 1956. So much for the relevancy of motives rather than results.

To implement the programme European countries were enjoined to set up international organs to co-ordinate their reconstruction plans and mutual efforts to restore international trade and multilateral payments. For this purpose the participating countries in 1948 established the Organisation for European Economic Co-operation in Paris to coordinate the work. As a member, Norway was asked to present an estimate of the dollar deficits it expected to accumulate in its programme for production, investments and trade over the next four years with the American dollar area.[9] A similar request went out to the other countries. In this way the Marshall Plan inadvertently made central government long-term planning part of the reconstruction era in all 16 participating countries. In his memoirs Einar Gerhardsen recalls the four year-programme that his government submitted to the OEEC in the late fall of 1948 as Norway's first long-term plan.[10] The goal of the plan was to rebuild the country's economy and for this purpose to develop industries with the best dollar-earning prospects, above all electro-metal industries and shipping.

Plans for restoring international trade and payments systems had in fact begun earlier, and resulted in 1944 in the signing of the Bretton-Woods agreement. This treaty, ratified by 44 states, among them Norway, established fixed exchange rates between the currencies of the treaty states, all convertible to dollars, hence gold, and set up the International Monetary Fund. The Fund, which began operations in 1947, controlled a currency pool in gold or dollars, based on contributions from treaty members, from which within limits member countries could buy the currencies they needed in return for their own currency and thus extricate themselves from temporary difficulties with their balance of payments. In the case of chronic deficits on the part of a member country, the Fund's rules foresaw an ordered reduction of the exchange value of its currency, rather than the drastic devaluations of the interwar years. The Fund was to help restore the traditional system of multilateral trade, foreign investments and payments that had rested on the gold exchange standard, but which depression and war had destroyed out of recognition.

However, despite the good intentions of Bretton-Woods, the World Bank and the International Monetary Found, events showed that by 1947 the international economy was back to war standards with its bilateral trading arrangements. The need for dollars exceeded forecasts by a wide margin, and since the dollar was the only universally acceptable currency by 1947, every country, in attempts to husband its dollar reserves, was hampered both in its ability to buy and in developing its ability to sell, with the result that the system of bilateral trade in non-convertible currencies became more and more entrenched. Instead of international co-operation, the postwar period saw the world divided into two antagonistic spheres of influence, controlled by the Soviet Union and the United States.

In line with the country's tradition of neutrality, the Norwegian Labour government in the first two postwar years had pursued a policy of bridgebuilding between east and west. By 1947 it was pretty clear that neutrality was a lost game. But the choice of taking sides was difficult for a government that built its programme on a socialist ideology. 'We wanted no crusade against communism,' said Minister of Finance, Erik Brofoss in retrospect. While the Marshall Plan was announced on 5 June 1947, the headquarters of the Oslo Labour Party, of which Premier Einar Gerhardsen was chairman, hesitated till 3 February 1948 before commenting on the plan, in a tone at best non-committal.[11] Probably, the government feared that the conditions would erode the existing system of planning and controls, though Brofoss has later denied this.[12] The political implications were obvious. A new era in the country's foreign policy was at hand.[13] At all events, the communist coup in Czechoslovakia (25 February 1948) made the political choice easier. The Norwegian communists were soon branded potential traitors. Majority opinion now actively swung behind the Marshall Plan and the idea of Western co-operation under American leadership. Still, Norway initially asked for a mere 60 million dollars, later raised to 100 million. The latter included earlier unused American credits. Sweden, which had not been at war, set its need at 300 million dollars. The final Norwegian estimate was raised to 170 million during the Paris talks on the Marshall programme later in summer 1948. The Norwegian delegates contrived to draw such an optimistic picture of their country's prospects, that Norway was the only country committed to paying back in full any aid received under the Marshall programme.

Both regarding size and condition, the aid that was eventually granted Norway, turned out quite differently. Up to 1952 the country received a total of 400 million dollars or 2.8 billion kroner, of which about 49 million dollars were credits, the rest, about 350 million, gifts.[14] The total ran to 425 million dollars up to 1955.[15] There was initially a good deal of uncertainty about the conditions. In the text of the original treaty, whereby Norway acceded to the European Recovery Programme, no mention was made of rates of interest, amortisation payments, nor anything about loans or gifts.[16] Even the business weekly *Farmand*, conservative and pro-American, voiced concern at the lack of formality of the treaty text.[17] The aid was given to the country's government, which in turn issued dollar licences to individual firms and companies to cover their import orders from America. The Norwegian companies paid the counter values in local currency and the amounts were credited to a separate account at the Norges Bank. By later waiving repayments, the United States in effect granted about 350 million dollars as aid, 50 million as credits. The counter value of this was later used to write down the German occupation account by about 2,000 million kroner.[18]

The Significance of Marshall Aid

The significance of Marshall aid for reconstruction varies with the yard-stick used. For one thing the OEEC countries pledged themselves to a time schedule during which existing barriers to inter-European trade were to be dismantled. From 15 December 1949 they were to place 50 per cent of aggregate private imports on a free list. Free listing comprised food, raw materials and processed goods, the percentage varying for each group. State monopolies in foreign trade were not included, which meant that those who wanted to could still cheat. The list was extended to services in 1950, but the dollar area was kept out, as will be recalled, till 1956. According to the timetable, the free-listed goods were to comprise 75 per cent of the imports of the OEEC countries by 1 February 1951, a target Norway reached only in May the following year. For Norway it was of importance that dry cargo ships were placed on the free lists from 12 May 1951, for during the dollar shortage in the previous two years the Norwegian government had refused all import licences for ships. Direct quota regulations thus had to be given up. The co-operation in the OEEC forced the Norwegian government into mental and practical adjustments. Clearly, the government had under-estimated how far reconstruction depended on dollar earnings. Equally, by joining the ERP, the government was forced to reciprocate, in part by lowering tariffs, in part by co-operating in the efforts to restore convertible currencies, which proceeded formally in the European Payments Union set up in 1950. The steps to a more open economy undercut the stabilisation policy; indeed, imports of free-listed OEEC goods made it only a matter of time before the price stabilisation policy had to be scrapped.

Second, when Britain devalued the pound in 1949, Norway along with most West European countries automatically did the same. The dollar had exchanged for 4.97 kroner since December 1945. After devaluation (18 September 1949) it exchanged for 7.15. One wonders what devaluations there might have been without Marshall Aid. The point here is that in the absence of American technology transfers, reconstruction probably would have taken somewhat longer. It is beside the point to say that it was Norwegian workers that rebuilt Norway, as former Premier Einar Gerhardsen did in a radio broadcast in June 1977, for labour is but one of the necessary production inputs. The inflow of American tractors, lorries, machinery and technological knowledge allowed Norwegian workers to be more productively employed than they otherwise would have been, hence the speed-up of reconstruction.

Third, one should consider the dimensions of Marshall Aid. Using this standard, Odd Aukrust plays down its importance, but he achieves this by comparing the 2.5 billion kroner *net* received with total net investments over the ten year period 1946-55, amounting to 32 billion kroner.[19] From such a comparison the American aid is reduced to a mere 7.8 per cent of the capital formation that put the country back on its feet. A more valid comparison would be to compare the aid with total net investments in the four years 1949-52 when the aid came in. Total net investments for the period amounted to 13.5 billion kroner.[20] Against this figure, Marshall Aid represented 18.5 per cent of the total, close to a fifth. In relation to total imports, including ships, Marshall Aid represented 15 per cent of all imports in those four years.[21]

Fourth, there is the time dimension according to which the above quantification is question-begging as long as it fails to show why the quantitative dimension offers the valid yardstick for assessing the significance of the aid. A person about to drown does not need a company in order to be saved. One soldier is enough. Nor is a company of much help if it arrives a quarter of an hour too late. Occasionally, time rather than magnitude is the crucial aspect in appraising the causality of an event. Undoubtedly the Marshall Plan illustrates the distinction. In a time perspective ERP simply reversed the general European backslide, from its course towards stagnation to one of continued reconstruction, to freer trade, markets and multilateral payments. In this causal chain the dollar injection was decisive, even assuming it had been a mere fraction of the actual amount. The aggregate transfers to Europe under ERP 1948-52 was 12.6 billion dollars.[22] Between 1945 and 1955 Western Europe received a total of 24.8 billion dollars in American aid.[23]

Trygve Lie, Foreign Minister 1941-6 and UN Secretary General 1946-53, wrote in retrospect: 'Afterwards I have too often the feeling that too many have already forgotten what America, "the arsenal of the democracies", meant for the liberation of our country.'[24] To which one adds, also for its reconstruction. George Marshall was awarded the Nobel Peace Prize for his achievements in 1953. Summing up, the decision on the part of the Labour government of Norway to participate in the Marshall Aid programme in 1948 meant in effect a trade-in of socialism in return for economic growth.

Promise and Performance 1947-1952

Prices

Since the Norwegian Labour government in the postwar era subjected the economy to controls more stringent than in other democratic countries, any survey of the reconstruction period 1945-52 will at the same time become a critique and an assessment of the government's policies. Coming back to the price freeze policy, we see that with imports of free-listed goods from the OEEC countries in 1950, subsidies to shield home prices from higher import prices were bound to increase. The devaluation in the fall of 1949 added to the pressure. Imports from the dollar area were suddenly 30.5 per cent more expensive. The outbreak of the Korean War, 25 June 1950, coming on top of it all, sent prices sky high, and led to the final, albeit tacit, discontinuance of the stabilisation policy. In April 1950 the price subsidies were cut. As a result food prices shot up. To illustrate, one kilo of beef cost a housewife kr. 3.02 in March 1950, but kr. 4.67 in October that year. Subsidies for beef at the same time had dropped from kr.1.64 to 0.18 per kilo. Similar price hikes were registered for meat, pork, coffee, bread, sugar and butter, though not for milk: one litre of milk remained fixed at 0.49 kroner throughout the year.[25] The index for import prices (ships not included) stood at 271 in August 1949 (100 = 1938), but at 344 in October 1950.[26] The difference suggests an increase of import prices of 27 per cent which just about matched the 1949 devaluation of 30 per cent. More important, the cost of living, measured by the consumer price index, was 100 in 1949, but 132.9 for 1952, up 33 per cent in three years. According to this yardstick, Norway thus had an annual rate of inflation of 9.9 per cent between 1949-52.[27] That figure alone documents the failure of the stabilisation policy 1945-50.

The system of detailed and direct price control was not dismantled overnight in 1950. For the majority of goods and services prices were still fixed as maximum prices and maximum margins till the present Price Law of 26 June 1953 took effect at the beginning of January 1954. What happened in 1950 was that some concessions and exceptions were granted for certain branches and products in that firms henceforth set their sales prices on their own, without prior permission from the Price Directorate, as long as the price setting observed the general commands of 'reasonableness' set out in special directives by the directorate. The liberalisation included oddities such as artificial flowers, combs, plaster figures, musical instruments and beekeepers' equipment, which suggests the extent of the price control system still intact in 1950.[28]

The gist of this is simply that once the lid was off, prices in Norway quickly realigned themselves to the price movements of the other OEEC countries. Inflation, in fact, had merely been held temporarily at bay. Judged by result, the draconian dirigisme of prices cannot be said to have been justified. Norway's commitments within IMF, OEEC and the European Payments Union gradually robbed the government of direct regulatory instruments. The original planning euphoria also abated.

At any rate, a certain resignation was shown in 1952 when the government tried to replace the provisional price legislation with a permanent price and rationalisation act. The new proposal, backed by omnipresent Thagaard, leaned heavily on the principle of enabling powers. The implementation of the Price Act was to be delegated to the Price Directorate which was to issue its own binding precepts in a manner reminiscent of eighteenth century enlightened despotism. The danger was that too much arbitrary power would be delegated to bureaucrats. Notably, the articles dealing with rationalisation were seen as going beyond constitutional tradition, in that the authorities, if firms in an industry failed to act in their own best interest, were empowered to order them to unite in cartels. Even voters normally in sympathy with Labour recoiled at the prospect. The interest organisations for commerce, banking and industry staged a nationwide protest campaign. Faced with opposition of such magnitude, the government backed down. The present price law of 26 June 1953, which took effect the following year, has no mention of compulsory cartellisation and rationalisation. The episode taught the government a lesson about the limits to the governmental power in a constitutional state based on the idea of private property. If it wanted to stay in power, it should avoid an open confrontation with the most powerful interest organisations. Henceforth a new balance was struck. When this is said, it must be added that Norwegian price regulation continued to rely excessively on bureaucratic command and very little, if at all, on competition. In this respect Norway was in a class by itself in the OEEC league.

Wages

As part of the chain reaction in 1950 wages, following normal pay talks on new tariffs, were raised to compensate for higher prices. In October 1950 and in April and October 1951 average pay rates for most industrial workers shot up by 34.5 per cent. The figure is taken from official statistics, which show that hourly earnings for men in mining and manufacturing stood at kr 3.04 in 1949 and kr 4.09 in 1952.[29] The tendency was similar for women and for other groups. Once inflation creeps into statistical figures, every one knows that one must pay a visit to the consumer price index in order to arrive at real wages. Table 10.3 does just that. The result may come as a surprise.

Table 10.3: Development of Wages 1939-1952 for Workers in Mining and Manufacturing. Hourly Average Earnings in Current and Fixed Prices, and Index Figures

	Hourly earnings, total kroner	Consumer price index 1949=100	Real wages per hour, kroner	Index of wages 1939=100
	(1)	(2)	(3)	(4)
1939	1.61	63.8	2.52	100
1940	1.71	74.4	2.16	86
1945	2.18	97.6	2.23	89
1946	2.51	100.1	2.51	99
1947	2.75	100.6	2.73	108
1948	2.91	99.9	2.91	116
1949	3.04	100.0	3.04	121
1950	3.22	105.3	3.06	121
1951	3.67	121.9	3.01	119
1952	4.09	132.9	3.08	122

Source: *Historical Statistics 1968*, Tables 285, 293.

The surprise in column (4) of Table 10.3 is that real wages remained unchanged between 1949 and 1952, at least for workers in industry, the index figures being 121 and 122 respectively. Note also that real wages dropped in the war years. The result documents the surprising support given the Labour government by the trade union chiefs. The centralised trade union structure of Norway in this context was an advantage, for it ensured that inflation, due to excessive wage claims, did not get out of hand, a point noted by foreign observers.[30] Instead we see that until the completion of the reconstruction period in 1952, wages just about kept pace with inflation. In this field the government was as good as its word. Austerity was proclaimed, austerity was accepted by the spokesmen for the unions. The promise was that higher investments would maintain full employment and by degrees offer higher consumption plateaux in the future.

The level of wages was one thing, their distribution another. Regarding distribution, we note that wage restraint was indeed accompanied by wages equalisation. The evidence is unmistakable as far as the years 1945-52 are concerned. Table 10.4 provides the relevant figures, taken from Odd Aukrust's survey of the Norwegian postwar economy. As Aukrust also uses the consumer price index and the standard figures for manufacturing,he arrives at index figures for wages in manufacturing in Table 10.4 that are indentical to those in Table 10.3.

Table 10.4: Development in Real Wages for Selected Groups of Workers. Relative figures. 1939 = 100

	1945	1946	1948	1949	1950	1952	1954
Men							
Agriculture, summer	164	198	261	280	287	273	281
Forestry, winter	147	170	208	213	221	218	223
Manufacturing, adult workers	89	99	116	120	121	122	126
Private construction	72	88	107	114	112	112	116
Private land transport	—	90	110	112	113	111	116
Women							
Agriculture, summer	152	180	239	262	276	263	280
Manufacturing, adult workers	89	101	125	132	134	141	144

Source: Odd Aukrust, *Norges økonomi etter krigen*, Oslo, 1965, p. 233.

In the interwar years wages for workers in agriculture and forestry had been less than half of industrial wages. After the war these groups benefited from the wages policy proclaimed by the government and practised by their trade union colleagues. Table 10.4 shows that workers in agriculture had their wages increased by 66 per cent, from 164 to 281 between 1945 and 1952. Forestry workers gained 48 per cent, industrial workers by contrast only 37 per cent. The tendency to wage equalisation was more pronounced for women in agriculture who increased their wages by 73 per cent in the reconstruction years to 1952. The effect of wage restraint was to make it easier to maintain high investment ratios. Burdens were increased for other social groups, matching the wage restraint of the unions. Taxes were substantially increased for high-salaried groups in 1950. The export industries, moreover, paid in special equalisation duties. The legal basis for the levy, not voted by the Storting, was the provisional price legislation in effect from 1945-53. The export duties, amounting to 265 million kroner 1951-2, creamed off the higher earnings reaped by the export companies during the Korean War.[31]

Investments

The most obvious feature of social planning after World War II was the high level of capital formation. This must be judged favourably, at least when the record of the 1920s is used as comparison. On the loss side came the steady erosion of the krone's value. This loss should be compared to 'the social loss' accompanying widespread unemployment. The alternatives, requiring the breaking of mental barriers, may have been fictitious in the heyday of reconstruction. The fact remains that the decision makers did think in terms of the two choices outlined above and acted on the conviction that those were the options.

As for volume of investments, the government must be credited with substantial success. As for returns on all those investments, the verdict is less favourable. In the plan submitted to the OEEC in fall 1948, the Norwegian government outlined what it intended to do under the European Recovery Programme. The main figures are listed in Table 10.5, which also includes the *ex post* investments realised 1949-52:

Table 10.5: Planned Investments under ERP 1949-1952 and Gross Investments in Fixed Assets by Industry 1949-1952. Current Kroner in Millions

	Planned investments *ex ante*		Realised investments *ex post*	
	Mill. kroner	In %	Mill. kroner	In %
Agriculture	1,200	6.6	1,520	6.3
Forestry	108	0.6	146	0.6
Fisheries	585	3.5	479	2.0
Whaling	240	1.4	363	1.5
Industry	3,000	17.8	4,721	19.5
Electrification	684	4.1	1,697	7.0
Shipping	3,700	22.0	5,070	20.9
Other transports & communications	2,689	16.0	1,977	8.2
Stocks	500	3.0	–	–
Dwellings	2,250	13.4	4,429	18.3
Miscellaneous	1,860	11.1	3,801	15.7
	16,816	100.0	24,203	100.0

Source: St. meld. nr. 54, 1948. Appendix, p. 36; *Økonomisk utsyn over året 1953*, NOS XI, 152, Oslo 1954, p. 74.

The *ex ante* estimate for the four-year period was 16.8 billion kroner, the real outlay 24.2 billion. Even allowing for price changes there is no doubt that performance supassed the planned estimates by a good margin; notably shipping, dwellings and industry experienced bonanza investments in the four years. In relative figures, however, the correspondence between projections and results is quite remarkable, with two exceptions: electricity and transport and communications. We will briefly review developments in four key areas of investments – shipping, housebuilding, hydro electricity and the state investments in industry launched in the reconstruction period. Their story bears on the nature of direct controls, the merits of state planning versus market allocation and the limits to the central government's power over the economy.

The Merchant Fleet. The merchant fleet had contributed to the Allied cause more than any other sector. Both the sailors and the shipowners felt this, and so did the nation. What of the rewards? The sailors ran into legal barriers when they demanded payments from the secret Nortraship Fund. The shipowners wanted to recapture the free use of their ships and gain access immediately to the Nortraship war earnings in order to place new contracts and recoup war losses. In both they were only partially successful. The government with an eye on the reconstruction problem, at first favoured shipping. No other activity promised to earn dollars more quickly or more effectively. The plan presented to the OEEC in 1948, as will be recalled, set aside 22 per cent of total investments for ships in the four years 1949-52. The final percentage settled at 20.9, not far off the mark.

The shipping community, despite this generous concession, still rankled under what it felt as unjustified taxes, controls and regulations imposed by uninformed landlubbers. In view of the rebuilding statistics the complaints on the face of it do not appear justified. Ignoring the pessimism for the future, the Norwegian shipowners in 1945 and 1946 ordered a total of 346 ships, in the next year 117 ships and 83 in 1948.[32] UK yards ranked first, followed by Swedish and soon also by Norwegian yards. Sigval Bergesen d.y. of Stavanger pioneered a constructive trend here. The results of all this contracting show up in statistics for shipping tonnage. On 8 May 1945 the merchant fleet stood at 3 million gross tons, down from 4.3 million at the outbreak of war in 1940. A total of 2.3 million tons had been lost. By the end of 1948 the war losses had just about been overcome. The tonnage at the year's end stood at 4.7 million gross tons. Reconstruction of the merchant fleet was thus completed in three years.

But the shipowners had their eyes on a wider horizon. They wanted to continue contracting at high levels. Instead the government enforced a ban on all shipbuilding contracts at foreign yards for two full years 1949-50. The background was the panic felt by the government that the country was about to exhaust its foreign currency reserves. In 1948 the reserves dropped from 1,600 million to 800 million kroner. Cutbacks on investments and imports were necessary. Such cutbacks in the government's view could best be borne by the shipping community. So, from late 1948 the government refused to issue any licences to shipowners, first for UK yards, next for Swedish yards. The foreign currency earnings from the merchant fleet were instead controlled by the government and spent on other imports deemed more necessary by the planners. On the other hand, the contract stop 1949-50 also prevented the kind of contract stampede that occurred in shipping later, during the Korean War boom in 1950, then in the 1960s and in 1973. As will be recalled, dry cargo ships were free-listed in May 1951 in the OEEC area, but for tankers and 'special types' of ships the Norwegian government maintained restrictions on imports till the end of the 1960s.[33]

Housebuilding. During the war about 20,000 dwellings were destroyed, of which about 12,000 were located in the North Troms and Finnmark. Housebuilding for civilians was discontinued for five years. Repairs and maintenance were neglected or postponed. The country's population was 2.97 million in 1940 but 3.09 million in 1945. The need for dwellings was higher for this demographic reason as well. From liberation through to 1948 a total of 38,500 flats were built, of which 4,500 were in the two northern counties Finnmark and Troms. Building and construction had high priority everywhere in Europe. In the plan for the four years 1949-51 which Norway submitted to the OEEC in 1948, the planning figures for dwellings were as listed in Table 10.6. They are placed beside the *ex post* figures for flats actually completed in those years.

Again, performance exceeded targets. The Labour government planned to complete 66,000 flats 1949-52. It achieved 93,628, which was 42 per cent higher than the initial target. To evaluate the figure, we note that there was a total of 787,000 dwellings in the country according to the 1946 census.[34] The building effort was maintained in the 1950s at around 28,000 new flats annually. The socialist government, despite the outcries against bureaucratic pettiness and insolence, helped to raise average standards and expectations of housing in town and country above the wildest forecasts. In international comparisons

Table 10.6: Dwellings Planned and Completed 1946-1952

| | Planned dwellings under the ERP 1949-1952 | Flats actually completed 1946-52 | |
		Flats	1000 m^2
1946	–	6,649	518
1947	–	14,922	1,307
1948	–	16,411	1,408
1949	15,000	17,658	1,534
1950	16,000	22,395	1,922
1951	17,000	20,875	1,634
1952	18,000	32,700	2,329
Total 1949-52	66,000	93,628	1,419
Total 1946-52		131,610	10,652

Sources: St. meld. nr. 54, 1948, Appendix p. 35; *NOS. Statistical Yearbook,* 1946-53.

Norwegian housing standards soon ranked near the top and way beyond what the rigours of the climate demanded. In an international ranking of 26 industrial countries according to housing standards a Hungarian study shows that Norway ranked fourth in 1960, second in 1968 and second in 1974, trailing the United States, and ahead of the UK, Sweden, Denmark and the rest of the OEEC and Comecon countries.[35]

The negative aspect of state subsidised building was that the country was saddled with the highest capital coefficient among the OEEC countries (see Figure 10.1). No doubt one of the main reasons for the low return on capital in Norway was housebuilding, which yielded creature comforts rather than marketable products. The matter was soon well documented and attracted international comment throughout the 1950s. The capital coefficient 1949-62 was 9.5 in Norway, against 5.5 in Denmark, 6.3 in Sweden, 3.3 in West Germany and 4.6 in France.[36] If one dislikes saying that money was wasted, at least one may observe that growth cost much more in Norway than elsewhere. One reason was the generous nature of the financing conditions. The State Housing Bank offered mortgages of 2½ per cent for up to 100 per cent of assessed value, with postponement if need be, of payments, and extra allowances for families with children. Originally based on means tests, housing subsidies were soon available to just about everybody, which ensured that queues never disappeared.

At first the state banks obtained funds for their loans by selling their long term bonds on the ordinary credit market. By 1950 the bonds, offering a mere 2½, proved unsaleable. Beginning in 1950, the government offered the state banks loans directly from the state budget. It

Figure 10.1 Growth of Output and Investment Ratio 1953-1969

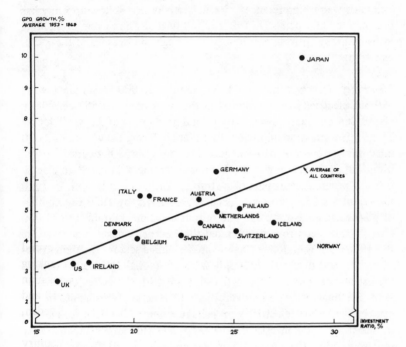

Note: Investment ratio is calculated as gross fixed asset formation in relation to GDP.
Growth rates for GDP in this table are calculated as compound rate of change between the end years
Source: OECD Economic Surveys, Norway 1972, p. 9.

obtained funds by drawing on its demand deposit account with the Central Bank, in effect by a method identical to the one used by the Wehrmacht during the occupation years.[37] In contrast to the earlier method, the new form of state bank financing meant a net liquidity injection into the economy. For 1951 alone these government loans to state banks totalled almost 500 million kroner. The injection fuelled inflation.

The combination of state banks and state financing in the field of housing offered the Labour government an opportunity to generate political election cycles with a view to winning the Storting elections. Petter Jacob Bjerve, Labour's planning chief, admits in retrospect that building licences tended to overstep preset targets in all postwar election years with the exception of 1955. In Bjerve's disarming words, the indulgence shown in election years reflected *inter alia* ' a shift in the Cabinet's welfare preferences'.[38] Ole Gjølberg in a follow-up study has documented the persistence of the political election cycle in building investment and private consumption through the decades of the 1960s and 1970s.[39]

Electricity Development. In 1937 about 650,000 inhabitants went without electricity. The country in that year operated 552 electricity plants, run by water power, with a total production of 9,000 GWh or 9 TWh.[40] The situation improved little if at all during the war, as 640,000 inhabitants were still without access to any electric network in 1946. Immediately after the war the Labour government initiated an electrification programme as part of a strategy for industrialisation. In 1950 the country's 671 plants produced 17,000 GWh; by 1960 the number of plants had gone up to 827 and output had almost doubled to 31,000 GWh.[41] Little controversy attended the electricity development before the 1970s. All the money came from the public sector. The dimensions of investments in electricity supply were substantial, ranking as the sixth biggest investment item through 1949, and fifth thereafter, trailing behind dwellings, ships, manufacturing and general government. In percentage figures new electricity projects represented between 7,2 and 9.0 per cent of total investment 1950-70. Electric power plants today represent more than a tenth of the country's total fixed capital.[42]

In a world context Norway's exploitable water power potential was set at 125 TWh in the 1950s. Later estimates raised the figure to 172 TWh.[43] By comparison the Soviet Union heads the world list with a potential of 2,000 TWh, followed by North America's 1,500 TWh.[44] The world's total is about 5,000 TWh. Clearly, Norway had a comparative advantage in power intensive industries.

Large-Scale State Industries. An innovation in economic planning after the war was Labour's decision to turn the state into an industrial entrepreneur in metal production. The first project, A/S Norsk Jernverk, the state ironworks, was voted in the Storting on 10 July 1946.[45] The 'need' for a national steel mill was an old idea, but voiced more strongly when the Nygaardsvold ministry took office in 1935. After the war the 'need' was taken for granted by all parties, above all by Labour. The Joint Programme 1945 even pledged all parties to support the plan. No economic bonanza was expected, nor any financial disaster. Self sufficiency was the decisive motive. To this came the idea of saving hard currency and the regional rivalry between Trøndelag and Nordland counties. The latter won since its need for new jobs was highest. Here the private alternative was out of the question. Minimum size dictated state ownership. The project was completed by 1955 at a cost of 550 million kroner, including the construction of Rössåga water power station. The Mo ironworks used thermo-electric smelting, not coal. All the capital was state capital. When the proposal to build the steel mill, with iron ore to come from the Dunderlandsdalen iron mines 18 miles to the north, was up for debate, no representative voted against, but Conservative Bent Ingvaldsen asked for a postponement to give the Storting time for a critical debate on the proposal. He was voted down by a majority of 40. Thus it may be said that in the case of the biggest industrial project in the postwar era, there was no vote-taking on whether the project should be realised, only a vote on the question where, i.e. whether at Mo or at Glomfjord.[46]

The prediction that the national steel works would become a substitute for imports of iron and steel proved wrong. In 1970 the state iron works had most of its customers abroad. Of total sales of 500 million, 335 million was exported, 67 per cent.[47] By contrast the country in 1970 imported iron and steel products valued at 1.5 billion kroner.[48] Thus the steel mill did not by any stretch of the imagination 'save' hard currency, though the national sufficiency motive is repeated as justification by former Premier Einar Gerhardsen in his memoirs in 1971. In the fifteen years 1955-70 he claims the Mo ironworks 'saved' currency amounting to 2,827 million kroner. But in two years alone, 1970-1, imports of iron and steel were valued at 3,125 million kroner.[49]

Next, the works turned into a white elephant, profits failed to materialise, and the return on capital was negative in normal years, which necessitated repeated requests in the Storting to provide fresh capital. The taxpayers were left with a loss-producing project, but for the northern regions the works provided distributional benefits: Mo had 2,500 inhabitants in 1946 against 20,000 in 1970, of whom about 4,000 were employed at the iron works. In 1909 the northern counties had 1.4 per cent of the jobs in manufacturing, in 1960 they had 11.5 per cent.[50]

The other major venture was aluminium. The German industrial complex at Årdal in Sogn was half finished in May 1945. In 1946 the Labour government obtained a majority for its plan to finish the Årdal aluminium plant and the Tyin power plant there. Production began in February 1948. The justification for state operation was traditional and ideological: Labour was to demonstrate that a government-owned enterprise could do better than private industry in terms of profits, labour management and welfare. Other arguments advanced included the saving of hard currency, the maintenance of military preparedness and regional development. The non-socialist parties accepted these motives and ends but asked why state operation? Here the private alternative was possible. During the roll-call all the non-socialists voted no.[51]

Labour in 1951 went on to propose a second huge aluminium smelter at Sunndal, located at the bottom of a narrow fjord on the Møre coast, ice free and deep watered like Årdal. The plan was backed by the same arguments as used for Årdal. All the non-socialist parties − except the local representatives − voted against. The negative attitude was mainly derived from ideology; the government was to stay away from business ventures which could adequately be left to private risk taking.[52] The Årdal-Sunndal smelters gave rise to a new government-owned company, A/S Årdal & Sunndal Verk, which soon loomed as a giant among national manufacturing companies. Among the top 500 companies in 1970 it ranked seventh in total sales, seventh in employment (3,700 employees), second in export sales and number one in terms of profits before taxes.[53] The company had no difficulty in running its operations as a normal profit maximising company. After Sunndal was voted in 1951 no new government industry was on the agenda until the 1960s.

The iron mines at Kirkenes were rebuilt after the war with government guarantees, priority loans and capital participation 1948-52. Government assistance was essential. Production and exports soon exceeded prewar figures.[54]

Taking into consideration the electricty programme and the launching of state-owned industries, we see again why Norway showed such an extraordinarily high capital coefficient among the OEEC countries in the 1950s. Power plants required a long period before a return on capital could be expected, if any, and so did the aluminium smelters, the iron mine and the iron works.

Summing up the Reconstruction Period 1945-1952

In all occupied countries the reconstruction era 1945-52 was dominated by the problem of investments and maintaining high investment levels. The Labour government of Norway profited from the expertise of academic economists and was able to formulate a coherent programme for the entire reconstruction task. Economic planning helped to maintain high investment levels in fields presumed by Labour's voters to bring the highest social and private benefits in the longer run, viz. in housebuilding, shipping, water power development and power intensive industries. In these fields reconstruction, defined as overtaking prewar levels, was achieved in shipping in 1948. By 1952 the number of new dwellings exceeded the number destroyed by the Gemans and bombed by the Russians. The production index with 1938 = 100, suggests that the home market industries reached prewar levels in 1946 while export industries lagged behind till 1949. The index figures were 109 and 102 in the respective years. Total industry scored 109 in 1947.[55] The index is open to criticism. The same holds for the consumption index. According to the latter, private consumption reached prewar levels in 1946, both in the aggregate and *per capita*. According to the long term programme presented to the OEEC in 1948, this was expected both in 1950 and 1952. If one widens the concept to embrace the notion of living standard, certainly 1952 would be nearer the truth. In that year the remaining wartime rationing of consumption goods was lifted. The difficulty here, of course is that the yardstick itself tends to change. The average *summum bonum* in 1938 was no longer the same in 1948 or 1950.

The reconstructon years also logged the biggest increases in total wealth creation. Using the gross national product as a yardstick the development is suggested by the following figures in constant 1955 kroner.[56]

1946:	16,533 mill. kr	. . . . .	—	
1947:	18,797 " "	. . . . .	13.7 per cent increase	
1948:	20,115 " "	. . . . .	7.0 " "	
1949:	20,625 " "	. . . . .	2.5 " "	
1950:	21,646 " "	. . . . .	4.9 " "	
1951:	22,813 " "	. . . . .	5.4 " "	
1952:	23,626 " "	. . . . .	3.7 " "	

In 1955 prices the national product jumped from 16,533 million kroner in 1946 to 23,626 million in 1952, up 43 per cent in six years, which implies an annual rate of growth of 6.1 per cent. By comparison the average growth rate 1920-39 is estimated to have been 3.2 per cent per year, and 4.4 per cent in the period 1946-74. Clearly, the increase was highest in the immediate postwar years. Table 10.7 sets these years in a longer Norwegian perspective.

Table 10.7: Average Annual Rate of Growth of Gross National Product at Constant Prices, Working Population and Real Capital. Selected Periods 1865-1980

	Gross national product	Labour force	Fixed real capital
1865-1890	1.8	0.7	1.7
1890-1915	2.6	1.3	2.3
1920-39	3.2	1.1	3.1
1946-74	4.4	0.3	4.0
1975-80	4.6	1.5	4.0
1865-1974	2.8	0.8	2.4

Source: Preben Munthe, *Sirkulasjon, inntekt og økonomisk vekst*, Oslo, 1981, 2nd ed., p. 262.

In a European context the figures, however, are not extraordinary. A general impression from observing international figures is that Norway came close to the average for the OEEC countries as a whole in the period to 1952 and in the following decades till 1970. The observation holds for such key indexes as unemployment, inflation and production, but not for investment, a field where Norway ranged 80-100 per cent higher than its neighbours in the OEEC. The result, already noted, brings into relief the low return on investments in Norway.

Next, the wages policy in the reconstruction period was a remarkable achievement, though the praise here belongs to the trade unions rather than the government. Evidence suggests that the real wages in manufacturing remained at a standstill from 1949 through to 1952, while wages in agriculture increased. This may be interpreted as an indication both of wage restraint and wage equalisation. The absence of wage pressures, in turn, permitted the nation to maintain record high investment levels. When the investment programme in 1947 threatened the foreign balance, the USA stepped in at the right moment. The Marshall Plan made it possible for Norway as an OEEC member to continue reconstruction policies without loss of momentum. The dimension of the Marshall Aid, 18.5 per cent of net investments 1949-52, provides at the same time a measure of Norway's dependence on foreign assistance in these years, and a measure of the calibre of the plans which underlay the reconstruction programme.

Much of the above was common experience in both Western and Eastern Europe in these years. It was common to all the countries in

Western Europe who sought to rebuild their economies without social-
ising the means of production or dictating wages. In the circumstances
they scored poorly in the management of prices.

The situation in Norway was that the authorities decided not to
curtail drastically the money volume after the war, but gambled instead
that high demand would boost production so that the latter, like creeping into a glove, would eventually match the liquidity volume, at which
point price stability would follow automatically. Meanwhile the authorities tried to freeze prices by means of direct controls, including ceilings
for prices, rents, interest rates, dividends, imports and currency
licences. But inflation was at best postponed, as the price jump 1950-2
was to show. Applying the term 'price policy' to this tends to smoke-•
screen what was at stake. More to the point is to conclude that, faced
with its own incompatible policy objectives, the Labour government
sided with the implicit interest of its unpropertied voters. Possessing no
capital itself, that majority could more easily tolerate its depreciation
through inflation.

Notes

1 *NOS. National Accounts 1865-1960*, Table 1, p. 64.

2 *Historical Statistics 1968*, Table 243.

3 *National Accounts 1865-1960*, Table 7, pp. 106-7.

4 Hermod Skånland, *Det norske kredittmarked siden 1900*, Oslo, 1967,
p. 192. Skånland presents figures for the deficits in these years that differ
considerably from those given in Table 10.1 above, Skånland p. 191.

5 Gunnar Myrdal, *Varning för fredsoptimism*, Stockholm 1944. Ragnar
Frisch: 'I will refrain from predicting when the depression will come in the
United States, but I do not hesitate to predict that the development will offer a
classic example of the most violent economic paroxysm which any modern
capitalist society is bound to experience when left to develop under far-reaching
freedom.' Art. 'Ends and Means in Economic Policies in the Postwar Period',
Samtiden, January 1947, p. 28.

6 Aukrust & Bjerve, *Hva krigen kostet Norge*, p. 136.

7 Øivind Stenersen, 'Framtidens Norge − et ledd i planlegningsvirksomheten
innenfor eksil-LO 1942-5', *Etterkrigshistorie 4*, Universitetsforlaget 1973,
pp. 73-96.

8 Sources of general and specific information include Odd Aukrust, *Norges
økonomi etter krigen*, CBS, Oslo, 1965, Gerhard Stoltz, *Økonomisk utsyn
1900-1950*, CBS, Oslo, 1955; CBS, *Økonomisk utsyn*, yearly economic survey
published since 1936; CBS, *Statistical Yearbook*, annual publication since
1881, *Stortingets Fordhandlinger*, (St. Forh.) multivolume parliamentary
records since 1815.

9 St. meld. nr. 54, 1948: Parliamentary Report on a long-term programme
submitted to the OEEC.

10 Einar Gerhardsen, *Samarbeid og strid. Erindringer 1945-1955*, Oslo, 1971,

pp. 121-2.

11 *Arbeiderbladet*, 3. February 1948. *Farmand*, no. 6, 1948, p. 12.

12 Nils Morten Udgaard, *Great Power Politics and Norwegian Foreign Policy*, Oslo, 1973, pp. 218-19 and *passim*; Helge Pharo, *Bridgebuilding and Reconstruction: Norway faces the Marshall Plan*, Norsk Utenrikspolitisk Institutt. Report no. 27, 1976, also in *Scandinavian Journal of History*, 1976. Erik Brofoss, 'The Marshall Plan and Norway's Hesitation', *Scandinavian Journal of History*, 1977.

13 Knut E. Eriksen, 'Norge i det vestlige samarbeid', i *Vekst og velstand'*, pp. pp. 176-7.

14 Preben Munthe, *Sirkulasjon, inntekt og økonomisk vekst*, Oslo, pp. 373-8; Odd Aukrust, *Norges økonomi etter krigen*, SØS nr. 12, Oslo, 1965, p. 189; Alice Bourneuf, *Norway, the planned Revival*, p. 145; Arnljot Strømme Svendsen & Gunnar Chr. Wasberg, *Industriens historie i Norge*, p. 248.

15 Knut Getz Wold, 'Marshallhjelpen 30 år etter', *Militaert Tidsskrift*, 1977, pp. 531-44.

16 St. prp. nr. 78, 1948, Ratification of an Agreement on European Economic Co-operation signed in Paris 16 April 1948.

17 *Farmand* nr. 27, 1948.

18 Preben Munthe, *Sirkulasjon*, p. 392.

19 Odd Aukrust, *Norges økonomi etter krigen*, p. 382.

20 *NOS. National Accounts 1865-1960*, Table 39.

21 Knut Getz Wold, 'Marshallhjelpen 30 år etter', *Militaert Tidsskrift* 1977, p. 543.

22 *Statistical Abstract of the United States 1954*, Table 1075, p. 899.

23 *Do. 1972*, p. 771.

24 Trygve Lie, *Hjemover*, Oslo, 1958, p. 205.

25 *Økonomisk utsyn over året 1950*, CBS, Oslo, 1951, p. 125.

26 Ibid., p. 127.

27 *Historical Statistics 1968*, Tables 276, 285.

28 L.B. Bachke & Kåre Willoch, *Prispolitikken i Norge*, Oslo, 1959, p. 40.

29 *Historical Statistics 1968*, Table 293.

30 Mark W. Leiserson, *Wages and Economic Control in Norway 1945-1957*, Cambridge, Mass., 1959, p. VIII and *passim*.

31 Odd Aukrust, *Norges økonomi etter krigen*, p. 388.

32 *Norwegian Shipping News*, no. 15, 1950, p. 771.

33 *Norwegian Shipping News*, 'Kontraheringsstoppen', no. 11, 1950, p. 540; John O. Egeland, *Vi skal videre. Norsk skipsfart etter Den annen verdenskrig*, Oslo, 1971, p. 117. A detailed review is Arnljot Strømme Svendsen, *Skipsfartspolitikken i Norge etter krigen,* Norw. School of Economics, Bergen, 1957.

34 *Historical Statistics 1968*, Table 317.

35 E. Ehrlich & Gy Szilâgyi, 'International Comparison of the Hungarian Infrastructure', *Acta Oeconomica*, vol. 24 (1-2), pp. 57-80 (1980).

36 M.M. Postan, *An economic History of Western Europe 1945-1964*, London, 1967, p. 114.

37 Per Meinich, 'Sparebankene etter 1945', i *Studier i sparing og sparebank-vesen i Norge 1822-1972*, Oslo, 1972, p. 219.

38 Petter Jakob Bjerve, *Planning in Norway 1947-1956*, Amsterdam, 1959, p. 292.

39 Ole Gjølberg, 'Høyrebølgen − et konjunkturfenomen', *Høyrebølgen − Epokeskifte i norsk politikk?* ed., Tor Bjørklund & Bernt Hagtvedt, Oslo, 1981, pp. 221-35.

40 *Historisk Statistikk 1978*, Table 146.

Units for electric energy and effect:

kWh	=	kilowatt hour	(energy)	
MWh	=	megawatt hour	=	1000 kWh
GWh	=	gigawatt hour	=	1 million kWh
TWh	=	terawatt hour	=	1 billion kWh
kW=	=	kilowatt	(effect)	
MW	=	megawatt	= =	1000 kW

41 *National Accounts 1865-1960*, Table 7, p. 102, *Historical Statistics 1968*, Table 65.

42 *Historical Statistics 1978*, Table 76.

43 *Vår virksomhet 1981*, p. 14. Annual report from the Norwegian Water Resources and Electricity Board (NVE).

44 Einar Hope, 'Norges energiforsyning', *Naeringsøkonomiske oversikter*, II, p. 329.

45 Tore Grønlie, *Jern og politikk 1945-1955. A/S Norsk Jernverk*, Oslo, 1973.

46 Letter to *Farmand*, 3 July 1982, p. 3.

47 *The 500 Largest Companies in Norway*, Oslo, 1971, pp. 32, 113, 117, 119.

48 *Statistical Yearbook for 1972*, Table 188, p. 153.

49 Einar Gerhardsen, *Samarbeid og strid. Erindringer 1945-1955*, Oslo, 1971, p. 99; *Stat. Yearbook 1972*, Table 188.

50 Einar Hope, 'Norges Industri', in *Naeringsøkonomiske oversikter*, Oslo, 1972, II. p. 262.

51 Tore Grønlie, 'Norsk industripolitikk 1945-1965', *Vekst og velstand*, pp. 123-5.

52 Ibid. p. 126.

53 *The 500 Largest Companies in Norway 1971*, pp. 32, 113-19.

54 Kåre Fasting, *Aktieselskabet Sydvaranger 1906-1956*, Oslo, 1956, pp. 84-7.

55 St. meld. nr. 54, 1948, Appendix p. 8; *Økonomisk Utsyn 1949*, CBS, Oslo, 1950, p. 127, gives the figure 115.

56 *National Accounts 1965-1970*, Table 51, p. 351.

11 GROWTH IN AN OPEN ECONOMY 1950-1980

Main Facts and some Opinions

Looking back on the recent period 1950-70 one easily falls prey to myopia; the facts are too close for a balanced assessment. What follows is an attempt to identify some salient trends in Norway's recent economic development, and to offer comments on possible causal connections that account for the outcome, both in the light of what happened before World War II and what occurred in the most recent decade since 1973. This chapter covers mainly the years till 1970.

The statistics on economic performance 1950-70 give the impression of a single protracted boom. Total output increased by a yearly rate of growth of 4.2 per cent, against 3.2 per cent for the interwar period. Absolute reduction of output did not occur in any year. In an OECD context the Norwegian performance was in the middle range. The level of activity was high, with unemployment hovering around an average of 1 per cent for the twenty year period. That was better than the OECD average of 2.9 per cent for the decade 1950-60 and 1.5 per cent for the following decade.[1] Inflation in Norway, a third key indicator, was 4.3 per cent per year against 3.6 per cent for the average OECD country. Total gross investment exceeded 30 per cent of GNP in most of the twenty years. Textbooks in economics, good barometers of the intellectual climate, ignored economic fluctuations for two decades. Encouraged by events, economists asserted that their new insights in macro planning had abolished for good business cycles and economic slumps, in the same way that modern medicine had ended such scourges as polio and smallpox. The setbacks after the Korean War 1952, and the Suez Crisis 1958, seemed innocuous, lasting at most a year, and could safely be written off as minor punctuations in the process of sustained growth.

International trade increased in value around 10 per cent almost every year, helped by such benign factors as world-wide trade liberalisation, restoration of convertible currencies and buoyant demand in war-ridden Europe and Japan. In the twenty four years 1946-70 Norwegian exports, in value figures, increased by 9 per cent, imports by 7.2 per cent per year.[2] Openness was a key word in the period. By accepting the Marshall Plan in 1948, Norway joined the Organisation for European

180

Economic Cooperation (OEEC), and participated as a member in the gradual trade liberalisation of the fifties. When the OEEC was replaced by the Organisation for Economic Co-operation and Development (OECD) in December 1960, Norway took up membership at once. After 'the inner six' had joined hands in the European Economic Community in 1958, Norway joined with 'the outer seven' countries in setting up the European Free Trade Association (EFTA) in 1960, with the mutual commitment to remove all tariffs and quantitative restrictions on industrial goods by 1969.

The outcome, in other words, was to some extent designed, not the result of the free play of market forces; nor for that matter, was free trade in the nineteenth century. Yet if the achievements did not stem from textbook economic liberalism, neither were they due to socialism. Rather they were the achievements of a genus of reformed capitalism, which may be called the mixed economy. In this economic system, plan and market are supposed to have married, in such a way that the private sector continues to obey the rules of the market, while being subject to government regulations designed to realize overriding macro economic goals. Clearly, the term 'the mixed economy' is a loose one; it is to be understood as a political euphemism rather than as a precise description.

Except for the four week Lyng coalition ministry in the fall of 1963, the nation kept Labour in power for twenty years from 1945-65. Labour dominated politics as it dominated the media and the public debate. In an environment of monolithic stability Labour, whose class basis, ideology and justification favoured material comforts, now set about realizing its programme, solidly backed by majority opinion. Policy instruments were devised to achieve full employment, rising living standards, social equality, balanced regional and sectoral development, external balance and reasonable cost/price stability. Echoing similar objectives of economic policy in the other OECD countries, these general goals were supplemented in Norway by specific policy aims. An outstanding feature was the desire to maintain super high investment levels, the implication being that capital formation was the decisive factor in economic development. To this end water power development and power-intensive industries, financed by public money, were given high priority. Another high-priority investment area was shipping, but the incentives offered to the shipowners were felt to be too small and too late to compensate for the contracting stoppage 1949-50.

A third group of priority considerations in Norway may be deemed non-economic, in that it was designed to placate regional political pressures to preserve population in outlying areas in the north and in rural areas, and to conserve a high degree of self-sufficiency in agricultural products. These considerations led to the adoption of various regional support and development programmes, including the North Norway Plan of 1952, and the Regional Development Fund (RDF) of 1961, which aimed at conserving the fishing communities and agricultural regions by means of direct and indirect credit, transport, tariff and taxation support schemes.

A fourth feature of the policy instruments was the maintenance of low long-term interest rates and the instruments designed to control, ration and steer capital into priority fields, such as social housing and regional investments. These objectives were achieved mainly through direct government allocation till 1950, but later indirectly by a variety of state banks and public funds, getting their capital direct from the government. To realize these ambitions the Labour government raised the household and company taxes to levels matched only by Sweden, and in some years by Denmark and the Netherlands,[3] in the belief that income equality was a good thing and on the presumption, less often expressed, that government planning would result in better investment decisions than those taking place in the private sector. As a result, taxes to local and central government inched upwards every year, from 28 per cent of GNP in 1949, up from 16 per cent in 1938,[4] to 47 per cent in 1975.[5]

So far no one has yet attempted a full assessment of the postwar growth record, though Odd Aukrust has compared the 1920s with the planned reconstruction staged by Labour after 1945.[6] He concludes by saying that the favourable economic outcome in the latter period was mostly due to more enlightened Keynesian planning by the Norwegian authorities, notably the maintenance of high investment and employment levels. In praising Labour's policies, Aukrust failed to consider possible negative aspects, among them the high taxes, disincentives to save, the effects of rapid income re-distribution and the erosion of the value of the currency. After Aukrust, the debate apparently turns on the degree to which the favourable outcome, a trebling of *per capita* incomes, should be ascribed to socialist planning or to market forces. In a recent volume on the postwar era professor Edvard Bull, a leftwing historian, has also tackled the matter.[7] He suggests that the Labour government by trading in socialism for economic growth, has betrayed its socialist heritage. Both Labour and the trade union chiefs succumbed to the lure of more jam on the cake, and despite their ideology and plans, they in effect precipitated the final victory of 'organized capitalism' at the expense of solidarity and other traditional values. In Bull's view then, planning was a permissive, not a decisive factor; the decisive elements were capital, modern technology and free trade. A further issue would be to assess how much the outcome depended on internal decisions and how much on international factors, including foreign markets and capital.

In attempting to account for the remarkable period of growth, we will here proceed, first by considering 'stylised' macro-economic evidence, including statistics on production, employment, investment, and demand, and in the following chapter go on to review selectively the performance in individual sectors.

Growth of the Work Force

Among the factors that contributed to the material improvements we first consider growth of labour inputs. When labour inputs and total output are viewed together, the obvious inference is the gap in growth rates between the two: Table 11.1.

Table 11.1: Average Yearly Growth Rates of GNP and Employment 1950-1979

	1950/5	1956/61	1961/5	1965/9	1969/74	1974/9
Yearly growth of GNP	4.2	3.8	4.8	4.2	4.2	4.7
Yearly growth of employment	0.1	0.2	0.6	0.8	0.8	1.2
Yearly GNP-growth per man year	4.1	3.6	4.2	3.4	3.4	3.5

Source: Å. Cappelen & A. Hellesøy, 'Strukturelle endringer i norsk økonomi etter krigen', *Vardøger* no. 11, 1981, p. 145.

Table 11.1 underlines the modest increase in the labour force that occurred in the two first postwar decades. It also reveals the new trend that became apparent in the 1970s when the labour force increased by a yearly 1.2 per cent during 1974/9. The new trend in the 1970s reflects in part the entry into the labour market of the big postwar generation, in part the invasion of women as participants in the labour force. In 1950 a mere 24 per cent of women between 15 and 65 years held jobs outside the home, by 1960 the percentage had dropped to 23 per cent, in 1970 it reached 28 per cent, but in 1980 had jumped to 41 per cent against 68 per cent for men. The number of women gainfully employed soared from 404,000 in 1970 to 783,000 by 1980, up 52 per cent, whereas the total labour force increased by a mere 30 per cent, up from 1.5 million to 1.9 million. Against the stagnating percentage share during the sixty years 1900-60, the growth of female participation in the economy was a dramatic feature of the labour market of the 1970s. Of the 379,000 women that entered the work force in this decade about 90 per cent have found employment in low paying jobs such as catering and shop work, and in the public sector, notably in education and health care. The long term changes for women in the labour force are set out in Table 11.2.

Table 11.2: Women in the Labour Force 1900-1980 (In thousands)

	1900	1910	1930	1950	1960	1970	1980
Total labour force	870	921	1163	1388	1406	1462	1906
Women	271	274	314	328	321	404	783
Women in %	31	30	27	24	23	28	41

Source: NOS. *Statistical Yearbook, Economic Survey*, NOS, 1981, pp. 5, 7; *Historical Statistics 1978*, p. 22. Note that labour force is defined as total number of persons 15 years and over, from 1970 persons over 16 years.

Norway used to be a country exporting surplus labour. In the period 1840-1914 only Ireland sent a larger share of its population to the USA as emigrants. In the postwar period the old situation was reversed. Norway became a net receiving country of immigrating labour, 16,000 in 1950 and 80,000 by 1980. Still, in comparison with Sweden, the Norwegian government has followed a rather cautious and restrictive immigration policy. The percentage of immigrants in the population was 1.2 per cent in 1950 and 4.2 per cent in 1980, against 5.1 per cent in the latter year in Sweden. Of recent origin is the influx of immigrants from Asia. Of a total of 80,000 immigrants in 1980, Asians numbered 11,000, of which 6,200 came from Pakistan. The majority, however, had their origin in Europe (52,000) and North America (14,000). A temporary ban on unregistered immigration has been in force since 1970.

Looking again at the postwar growth record, we may perhaps say that since the labour force has increased only modestly, the bigger contribution stems from higher skills on the part of the labour force, which in turn has had continual access to more productive capital and technology. *Per capita* growth (table 11.1) has varied between a yearly 3.4 per cent and 4.2 per cent in most of the years 1950-79. A growth rate of 4 per cent per year means a doubling every 18 years, a rate of 5 per cent a doubling every 14 years. So in terms of material welfare *per capita* output 1950-70 just about trebled. Who can afford to scoff at the achievement?

Occupational Structure

The sustained boom 1950-70 depended on far-reaching changes in occupational structure, and in the way the nation utilized its natural resources and stock of real capital. Equally, the boom saw significant changes in the kind of products and services that were offered in response to demand shifts at home and abroad at a time when private incomes just about trebled. Ultimately, of course, growth and structural changes should be conceived as mutually dependent processes, both reflecting the overall commitment to change, and the concern to adopt institutions favourable to change. The salient changes in the occupational structure are brought out in Table 11.3, which offers figures for the years 1930-80.

Table 11.3: Employment by Sector 1930-1980 (1,000 persons and in %)*

	1930	1950	1960	1970	1980
Agriculture, forestry, fishing	417	360	274	170	160
Mining, manufacturing & construction	308	507	513	545	566
Services	434	514	614	744	1179
Total	1163	1398	1406	1462	1905
			in per cent		
Agriculture, forestry, and fishing	35.8	25.9	19.5	11.6	8.4
Mining, manufacturing & construction	26.5	36.5	36.5	37.3	29.7
Services	37.4	37.1	43.8	50.9	61.8
Total	100.0	100.0	100.0	100.0	100.0

Source: *NOS. Historical Statistics 1978*, Table 6. *Economic Survey 1981*, p. 7.
*Due to a small group whose employment is unknown, the figures do not add up exactly in the extract given here.

Table 11.3 suggests occupational shifts characteristic of an economy undergoing rapid economic growth. They were no less dramatic. While the primary sector declined by two thirds, from 26 per cent to 8 per cent between 1950 and 1980, and secondary sector employment retained a stable share of around 37 per cent, at least till 1970, the service sector by contrast increased its employment by two thirds, up from 37 to 62 per cent of the total by 1980. This pattern of change is a pretty invariant feature of all the present high-income countries. Measured by the employment distribution Norway had become a service economy around 1965 when more than half the workforce was occupied in the provision of services.

Origins of the National Output

Naturally, as the occupational distribution changed, so did the sectoral origins of the national output. The secondary sector contributed a fairly stable share of just over a third of total output, its share being 39 per cent in 1950 and 34 per cent in 1979. The share stemming from the primary sector — agriculture, fishing and forestry, was 16 per cent of GNP in 1950 against 5 per cent in 1970. This means that services, the tertiary sector, was point of origin of 45 per cent of GNP in 1950 and 60.3 per cent in 1972.[8] As returns to labour were higher in industry, the workers in the primary sector tended, when job opportunities arose elsewhere, to emigrate from lower to higher productive types of employment. The sectoral income gap has been estimated by Einar Hope,[9] who measured the average hourly return to labour in agriculture in per cent of hourly pay in manufacturing:

1938	1950	1955	1960	1965	1969	1975
21%	53%	44%	54%	57%	63%	70%

Long term pay to labour in agriculture has improved relative to manufacturing, but only in the 1970s. Up to 1970 the improvement was achieved mainly by voluntary reduction of the labour force. By contrast the gains for agriculture in the 1970s, approaching by 1980 a state of parity with wages in manufacturing, were due to the decision in the Storting in 1976 to subsidise the farm population more heavily than before. The reduction of surplus labour in agriculture, halted in the interwar years, occurred more rapidly in the fifties and sixties at a time when investments in manufacturing provided ample job opportunities at higher pay. Surplus labour here may be defined as the share that was available, but not economically necessary for maintaining the same output. Thus, manufacturing helped to raise productivity levels in the aggregate economy in two ways, directly by creating expansion in high productive types of employment, indirectly by reducing employment in sectors of the economy with low productivity. These inter-sectoral shifts, often termed transfer gains, may have been quite substantial, although they do not in themselves constitute causes of growth, but merely mirror differences in productivity and factor returns, activated when workers move between sectors..

Transfer Gains

Calculations of the order of magnitude of the effect of inter-sectoral shifts on output growth, are bound to involve somewhat arbitrary assumptions. In the standard computation following Colin Clark, the economy is divided into primary, secondary and tertiary sectors, viz. agriculture, industry and services, and on the basis of gross production value and employment in each sector, one derives a measure of gross production value per worker in each sector in the first and last year of an observation period. To measure the productivity gains between the two points that stem from inter-sector shifts, one multiplies the sectoral estimates of GNP per worker at the beginning of the observation period by the figures for the work force at end of observation period. The resulting measure is the hypothetical GNP per worker that would have been achieved in each sector if labour had been as productive at the end of the period as at the beginning. Next the real sectoral GNP figures at end year are summed up to yield the average GNP per worker for the whole economy, and the difference between the GNP averages for the two years will then indicate the gain achieved through inter-sectoral shifts alone.

In a new study[10] of the magnitudes of the transfer gains in the Norwegian economy, the following results were achieved (in per cent and fixed prices):

	1910-20	1930-9	1950-60	1960-70
Productivity gains	74.2%	64.7%	87.8%	84.0%
Transfer gains	25.8%	35.3%	12.2%	16.0%
Total	100.0%	100.0%	100.0%	100.0%

The results are in fairly close agreement with other scattered estimates of the transfer gains, based on conventional procedure.[11] The long run tendency is for the inter-sectoral gains to diminish, which in turn is compatible with the expectation that the smaller the agricultural sector, the smaller the transfer potential. Swedish data bear out the expectation. In a study of the transfer gains in Sweden, Yngvar Åberg, using the calculation method described here, found that the transfer gains were 36 per cent of *per capita* GDP growth in the period 1871-90, against 19 per cent during 1901-15, 25 per cent in the period 1921-40 and 5 per cent in the period 1946-5.[12]

The validity of the measure involves acceptance of two fairly strict assumptions, one, that agricultural *output* would have remained unaffected by the exodus of labour; second, that *productivity* in the labour-receiving sectors would have remained unchanged at the end of the period whether or not labour had moved into them. However sceptical one is of the methods used to measure the transfer gains, there is no reason to discard the notion itself, namely that a good deal of the performance gains achieved are due to inter-sectoral shifts between agriculture and other sectors; indeed, these shifts are only one example of those that constantly take place within individual sectors, notably those between growth industries and stagnating industries.[13]

We have already noted that employment grew only modestly in the postwar period, hence, the high rate of growth of total output remains unexplained if analysis is confined to a study of labour inputs. What of capacity utilisation? Again we have observed that unemployment averaged 1 per cent of the total labour force between 1950 and 1970; so, the growth record cannot be accounted for by variations in capacity utilisation. We therefore turn to capital and capital formation in a search for an explanation of the postwar boom.

Capital Formation

Capital, by provding new equipment, not only allows increased employment for a growing labour force; new capital also embodies the new technological improvements in the form of products, tools and processes, which permit the work force to be more productively employed as well. Capital investment, its volume and composition, is central to the causation chains in economic growth.

While the labour force, as noted, increased by a yearly rate of growth of 0.3 per cent between 1946 and 1974, real capital grew by a yearly 4.0 per cent.[14] The figures suggest a strong capital-deepening process, with each worker getting equipped with more real capital than earlier averages. The postwar boom was very much an investment boom, which is perhaps best revealed in figures for investment levels in Norway in comparison with investment figures for other OECD member countries. If we exclude housebuilding, we note that non-residential investments soared 54 per cent higher in Norway than the OECD average in the fifties and 31 per cent higher in the sixties (Table 11.4).

Table 11.4: Non-Residential Fixed Investment as Per Cent of GNP at Current Prices 1920-1970

		Average of ratios for years cited	
	1920-38	1950-60	1960-70
Austria	6.1	16.4	20.2
Belgium	—	12.4	15.5
Denmark	8.9	14.0	16.9
Finland	—	19.6	20.0
France	11.8	13.7	17.4
Germany	9.7	16.1	19.3
Greece	7.5	11.7	18.2
Ireland	—	13.1	15.1
Italy	13.6	15.1	14.5
Netherlands	—	18.0	20.3
Norway[a]	12.4	23.7	23.8
Sweden	10.5	15.5	17.3
Switzerland	—	14.1	20.0
UK	5.7	11.6	14.2
Average Western Europe	9.6	15.4	18.1

Source: A. Maddison, 'Economic Policy and Performance in Europe', in *Fontana Economic History of Europe*, vol. 5.2, p. 487.
a) The elements of repair in the Norwegian national accounts are excluded, so as to make comparisons valid.

The figures for investments, quoted in Table 11.4, do not take account of housebuilding. Since this has been a heavy investment item in all postwar years, averaging 15 per cent of GDP 1950-80, the gross investment figures would demonstrate even more convincingly the abnormally high gross investment levels in Norway, which placed the country in the lead in all international comparisons till the middle sixties when Japan moved ahead.

Next we want to know where the capital was invested. Information is offered in Table 11.5 which traces the development through the seventies to 1980.

Table 11.5 provides a vantage point for surveying the investment profile in the postwar era. Beginning in 1950, we note how shipping towered

Table 11.5: Composition of Gross Fixed Capital Formation 1950-1980.
Percentage distribution

	1950	1955	1960	1965	1970	1975	1980*
Agriculture	6.8	7.1	6.7	4.3	4.6	4.2	6.1
Forestry	1.1	0.9	1.5	0.9	0.7	0.5	0.5
Fishing	2.4	2.8	2.5	2.1	1.5	1.2	0.9
Mining	1.1	0.9	1.3	0.9	1.0	0.6	0.8
Manufacturing	18.8	16.3	17.7	16.0	15.2	13.1	12.9
Oil and gas prod.	—	—	—	—	1.5	13.1	8.5
Electricity	7.6	6.9	7.8	7.2	8.1	6.4	9.8
Construction	0.8	1.4	2.2	2.3	2.0	0.2	2.2
Drilling of oil	—	—	—	—	—	1.8	2.2
Trade	2.4	3.6	4.5	4.7	6.9	7.1	7.9
Dwellings	18.0	18.1	15.5	13.1	18.5	15.9	19.4
Ships	25.6	27.5	24.0	21.3	13.4	12.7	3.9
General govt.	10.8	12.8	14.7	14.7	11.5	10.3	12.1
Other	4.6	1.7	1.7	12.5	15.1	12.9	12.8
Total	100.0	100.0	100.0	100.0	100.0	100.0	100.0

Sources: *NOS. National Accounts 1865-1960; NOS. Statistical Yearbook* and
NOS. Economic Survey 1981.
*Provisional figures.

as the single biggest investment area, a position maintained till 1965
when it began to slip behind. By 1970 dwellings was front runner, as it
was also ten years later in 1980. General government, central and local,
has maintained a stable percentage of 10-14 per cent of the total. The
primary sector, including agriculture, forestry and fisheries, maintained
a 10 per cent share till the mid-sixties when a drop followed , bringing
the share down to 7 per cent, which proved lasting. Manufacturing,
narrowly defined, provided investment outlets for a little less than a
fifth of the total in 1950, but the share shrank steadily thereafter,
down to 12.9 per cent by 1980. If manufacturing is taken to include
oil and gas production as well as oil drilling in the North Sea, we see
that manufacturing, after dropping to second place, by 1975 was again
the biggest investment field, absorbing 23.7 per cent of gross capital
formation in 1980. Water power development, taking between 7 and
9.8 per cent of the cake, clearly has been a stable, high-priority field
throughout the period, despite the much publicized protests, sit-ins
and demonstrations staged by self-appointed environmental protec-
tionists in the seventies.

To gauge the relative importance of the public sector investments,
one may compare them with private investments.

Table 11.6: Gross Fixed Capital Formation in Public and Private Sector Activities 1946-1975, in %

	1946	1950	1955	1960	1965	1970	1975
Private sector	76.8	76.4	75.8	72.8	71.3	67.3	69.7
General government	23.2	23.6	24.2	27.2	28.7	32.7	30.3
of which							
in enterprises	12.9	13.9	11.5	14.3	14.0	15.2	16.3
public consumption							
capital	10.3	9.7	12.7	12.9	14.7	17.5	14.0

Sources: *National Accounts 1865-1960,* Table 9, pp. 114-15; *NOS. Statistical Yearbook.*

Table 11.6 shows that over the years 1946-75 the vast majority of investment decisions, between 83 and 90 per cent, were made as ordinary business decisions in the expectation of normal profit margins. Only those under the heading public consumption capital, which refers to hospitals, schools, rest homes etc., were exempt from market forces in this context. The percentage distribution between the private and public sector investments in Table 11.6 is thus somewhat misleading, in as much as public enterprises were also expected to operate at a profit. From this one may go on to say that about nine tenths of capital formation reflected market forces, the rest may be ascribed to planning. As a result of growing international competition following trade liberalisation in the 1950s management, whether in private or public companies, was increasingly forced to take into account the shifts in demand that surfaced when private incomes began to rise. This brings us to a brief consideration of the relationship between income levels and demand patterns.

Income Elasticities of Demand

A long observed feature of economic growth is that demand increases more for some goods than others when disposable incomes rise. The demand shifts are not random, but tend to move from necessities to non-necessities, from the desire to stay alive to the desire for better health, education, travel or entertainment. The general contours of the shifts in demand were first quantified by the German statistician Ernst Engels in the 1880s, who found that the smaller a person's income, the greater the proportion spent on food. Although this is empirically confirmed in the aggregate, the products destined to experience a boom are not known, and cannot be known, in detail *ex ante*, hence the irreducible element of risk and uncertainty in a market economy. A market may exist, equally it may be created. A convenient formula for expressing the degree of the responsiveness of demand to a change of income is the income elasticity (ϵ), which expresses the relation between a percentage change in realised demand and a percentage change in income. The relation may be one of three types, either $\epsilon = 1$ when incomes and demand chage uniformly, or $\epsilon > 1$, when demand changes more than proportionately, or finally $\epsilon < 1$, when demand changes less than proportionately with any given percentage change in income. From numerous statistical investigations carried out in Great Britain, Norway, the United States, Denmark and Sweden, it appears that demand with respect to necessities, including food, is inelastic ($\epsilon = 0.4 - 0.7$), but with respect to personal hygiene, a private home or a private car, demand is greater than unity ($\epsilon = 1.0 - 4.0$). A recent Norwegian study by Arne Amundsen for household expenditures 1930-59, typically yields an $\epsilon = 0.9$ for all food items in the period 1952-9, against $\epsilon = 2.7$ for private cars, $\epsilon = 2.1$ for furniture, and $\epsilon = 2.1$ for radios.[15]

The implications are far-reaching. For one thing, demand structures in effect determine that in a high-income country, agriculture in the absence of exports is bound to shrink relatively with respect to value creation and employment. The universality of the generalisation approaches the force of physical laws. On the aggregate level we note that food took 31 per cent of total household expenditures as late as 1958,[16] but the share dropped to 25 per cent in 1970 and 21 per cent by 1980.[17] For the original English cost of living index, first issued in 1914, food similarly was given a weight of 60 per cent whereas the index of retail prices, with 1962 as its base, gave food a weight of only 35 per cent. On the individual level we note that the average Norwegian consumed 77 kg cereals in 1960 and 69 kg in 1970, he consumed 212 kg potatoes in 1900, 130 kg in 1950, and 87 kg in 1960. By contrast the sweet tooth consumed 3.3 kg sugar annually in 1866, 14.6 kg in 1900 and 45.7 kg in 1970.[18]

If demand exhibits a uniform dependence on levels of income, one concludes when analysing the causes for the postwar boom that the volume of investment is perhaps less important that its composition. What mattered as much was investment in human capital i.e. training the labour force to master the new technologies behind for instance travel and transportation, telecommunication or electrical household goods, that became major sources of demand once private incomes rose in the fifties. Travel and transportation took 5.8 per cent of total private consumption expenditures in 1950, but 11.0 per cent twenty years later, and 14.7 per cent in 1980.

Investment in Human Capital

We have already observed the gap between growth of total output and the labour force, output increasing 4.7 per cent, labour by 0.3 per cent per year between 1946 and 1970. The gap suggests that size and capacity utilisation of the labour force has been less important than its qualitative improvement in this period. To begin with the presence of Labour in government after 1945 allayed the traditional mistrust among the trade union chiefs regarding rationalisation and productivity research. Not only did the trade union leadership collaborate with the employers' organisation in time and motion studies and other productivity experiments, it also initiated its own education programmes at Sørmarka, outside Oslo, to train local spokesmen in measuring productivity, and devising ways to translate the gains into pay rises for their colleagues on the shop floor.[19] The work went hand in hand with experiments in industrial democracy, a field where Norway's trade unions have been pioneers. After several experiments in the 1960s, the Labour government under Trygve Bratteli in 1972 proposed legislation that gave the workers a legal right to representation on the boards of their firms. Since January 1973 employees of firms with 50 or more on the company payroll can, on request, elect a third of the directors, and in any event at least two directors must be worker representatives. In companies employing more than 200 the new concept of a 'bedriftsfor-samling' or corporate assembly — analogous to the Aufsichtsrat (supervisory board) of German companies — has been introduced, consisting of one-third employee and two-thirds shareholder representatives. This in turn elects the board.[20]

With rewards like this, the trade unions, at least till the 1970s, have taken a positive view of technological change, and labour relations have been, if not cordial, at least conducted in an atmosphere of mutual understanding. Strikes for instance have not posed serious problems, though some politically inspired wildcat strikes occurred in Oslo in the late 1970s. To illustrate, in the twenty years 1920-39, only one year saw the number of days lost in labour conflicts drop below 100,000. That was in 1922. But in the thirty years between 1950 and 1980, when the industrial workforce was higher by fifty per cent, only nine years saw the number of days lost in strikes exceed the interwar figure.[21] The contrast is quite striking. Healthy labour relations contributed in other words to a fairly rapid assimilation of new methods, processes and practices in industry in the postwar period.

At the same time, educational levels have been raised. Elementary education, paid through taxes, was increased from seven to nine years by legislation in 1955 and 1969, with the option for a tenth year. The number of graduates from the secondary level *gymnasium*, covering the age groups between 15 and 19 years, was 5,700 in 1946 and 17,000 in 1975.[22] Student enrolment at universities rose from 8,000 to 41,000, and at teachers' seminars from 1,000 to 7,000.[23] It was the age of the educational explosion. The students do not pay tuition fees, and liberal scholarships or loans are awarded for maintenance, hence nearly all costs are covered through general taxation.

Technological Research and Development

Science and technology have been promoted and sponsored in the postwar years over an everwidening front, in a wave of public enthusiasm and private necessity that only recently shows signs of abating. In 1945 the country boasted one university (Oslo) in addition to the Technical University at Trondheim, but in 1946 Bergen University was founded, followed by Trondheim and Tromsø Universitys, both in 1968. All these carried out research besides teaching, though little in the way of applied research or development.

The Storting in 1946 gave a strong boost to 'collective research' when it set up national research councils to act as umbrella organisations in three fields: Norges almenvitenskapelige forskningsråd (NAVF) for the humanities, Norges landbruksvitenskapelige forskningsråd (NLVF) for agriculture and Norges teknisk-naturvitenskapelige forskningsråd (NTNF) for research in the physical sciences and technology. The focus here is limited to the last.[24] Funded by government money, in part by the Norwegian Football Pool (a national weekly lottery), the NTNF has a 30 member council appointed by the government; of these eight are from the ministries involved, 11 from business and 11 from the academic institutions. NTNF seeks to fulfil its functions by continuous assessment of the need for research equipment and new technical and scientific staffs, by setting up new research institutes in response to changing market and societal demand, by evaluating and monitoring projects under way in its affiliated institutes, by promoting co-operation between the participating research institutes, and by help-ing to disseminate the fruits of research in industry in general. By 1970 NTNF, besides acting as a funding agency, had altogether 17 affiliated research institutes, engaged in research over a wide spectrum, ranging from atomic energy, industrial research, building and ship construction, to geotechnics, electrical supply, transport economics and computers.

Besides the universities and the research councils one comes across the increasing number of private and co-operative institutes for spon-sored research. Of these Veritas, a shipping classification agency which recently has taken up oil geology in the North Sea and China, origi-nated in 1864. The Christian Michelsen Institute (CMI) in Bergen dates from 1935, but for the most part the private institutes, basing their activities on contract work, have proliferated in the postwar period. Among the latter are SINTEF (the Engineering Research Foundation at the Technical University of Norway, Trondheim), set up in 1953, Statens Teknologiske Institutt (STI) established 1916, but revived in the postwar period, and Sentralinstituttet for Industriell Forskning (SI), established 1950 in Oslo. The latter institution acts in part as a service centre for other research institutes in order to facilitate efficient utili-sation of total capacity in its main fields, which are high polymers, food, chemistry, metalography, chemical engineering, structural chemi-stry, vacuum technology and control engineering.

In this forest of technological infrastructure one also notes Norsk Produktivitetsinstitutt (the Norwegian Productivity Institute), estab-lished in Oslo in 1953 by the government, partly founded with Marshall money in understanding with the Marshall Aid authorities, with the concrete task to promote productivity, in the interest of workers, con-sumers and business. It has a council of 25 members, appointed by the government, and a board of nine responsible for daily operations. The board is composed in such a way that labour, industry and the aca-demic side are adequately represented. Since its beginning the institute, backed by sympathetic media, besides preaching the gospel of more productivity, has conducted research and co-ordinated productivity re-search both in government and private business, including retraining courses for workers whose skills have become obsolete. Another early programme was to send managers and staff personnel to the USA for a period of up to 12 months to study American production methods and thus help the country catch up with best-practice products and pro-cesses. Bridging the technological gap after the war was a national pri-ority.

Research and development gained if possible added prestige with the surfacing of the human capital-school in the 1960s, the decade of the Soviet-American space race to the moon. All research and educational programmes were radically enlarged. The trade unions apparently had few reservations in endorsing continued research in cost cutting innovations, perhaps because unemployment posed no threat at that time, while the micro-processor, just invented in USA, could be ignored. Apart from the newspapers the postwar years witnessed the appearance of new professional journals and publications that aimed to inform and entertain special groups of professional readers. Dissemination of best-practice methods was also helped by meetings, congresses and seminars, organised by scientific and professional organisations.

Expanding Technological Education

The national drive to close the technological gap received expression also in efforts to widen programmes for technological education. The technical schools, the technical evening schools and the apprentice schools taught a total of 11,000 students in 1938,[25] 11,500 in 1947, against 21,000 in 1962[26] and 32,000 in 1967.[27] Subjects were updated, training periods lengthened, while increasingly general aspects were favoured at the expense of practical application in the belief that this was the best way to prevent obsolescence. At the same time the higher and medium levels of technical education have been expanded. The technical University of Norway (NTH), Trondheim, *Alma Mater* for engineers, had an enrolment of 761 students in 1938, 1,500 in 1960, against 2,835 in 1966 and 4,552 by 1978.

Nor did incentive structures or status considerations act as barriers against the entry of first rate candidates. The engineering profession had high social esteem, NTH at Trondheim enjoyed high status, and so did admission as a student there. As for pay, engineers ranged near the top for academic personnel. Besides, the availability of student loans from a state loan fund set up in 1947 enabled a wave of bright working class boys of which NTH had its quota, to move up the social ladder. In short, recruitment to technical and engineering jobs was no bottleneck.

What of Commercial Expertise?

The foregoing reveals the dominance of engineers and technologists and the weakness of the economic side. The onesideness is understandable if one takes an historic approach. Hauling up fish, felling timber, digging the ore and harnessing the waterfalls called for engineering rather than commercial skills. As long as the country was semi-industrialised with a raw material bias, the engineering approach was natural, and the lack of marketing skills no great drawback. But when the country moved to the specialised manufacturing products that characterise a fully industrialised economy, the lack of expertise in international marketing, which is neglected by NTNF when deciding which projects to fund, is at present an increasing handicap.

The number of annually graduated engineers and economists tells the story this way:

	1950	1955	1960	1965	1970	1980*
A Civil engineers (NTH)	226	251	281	383	746	4802
B Civil economists (NHH)	48	52	62	90	183	1248
B as per cent of A	21	21	22	23	25	26

*Students enrolled

The relative paucity of candidates with commercial and business training is documented by statistics for the postwar period; by 1980 business students, whose number did increase in the seventies, still numbered only a quarter of engineering students on university level. The imbalance has received little or no attention in Norway, despite the fact that successful innovation depends as much on non-technical factors, such as good management, forecasting and marketing, as it does on technical ones.

The Costs of R & D Efforts

Information on the level and structure of R & D expenditure sponsored by private industry was first collected in 1963. The survey showed that expenditure was 111 million kroner, of which 25 per cent was spent by the chemical industry, and 24 per cent by the electrotechnical industry. Of the total, 77 per cent was devoted to development, 2 per cent to basic and 21 per cent to applied research.[28] Adding 222 million provided by public authorities, we find that total R & D expenditure was 332 million kroner in 1963. The research personnel counted 2,050 persons, 30 per cent of whom had an academic degree. OECD collected information on private and public R & D efforts in

1967. In that year total expenditure was 1.2 per cent of GNP against 3.4 per cent in USA, which headed the list, and 2.4 per cent in the United Kingdom, trailing second behind USA. Of a total of 770 million kroner ($107 million) spent in 1969, the government provided 465 million while 265 stemmed from private business. This equalled 1.0 per cent of GNP that year.[30] Of the R & D money spent, about 25 per cent went into the electrotechnical industry, always the most research-intensive area, another 25 per cent was used in the chemical industry, while the primary iron and metal industries took about 10 per cent, as did the iron and metalworking industries. In a comparative setting, despite the expansive sixties, Norway in a 1975 survey was ranked by OECD among the countries . . . 'with small industrial R & D efforts'.[31] The countries referred to were Spain, Norway, Denmark, Austria, Finland, Ireland and Portugal. Together they spent $823 million in 1975, representing a mere 2 per cent of the OECD total.

Patents and Technology Imports

However, the amount of research money spent is hardly the interesting yardstick in assessing R & D efforts; if that was the case, economic growth would follow from dumping money in the sea. A more sensible yardstick, as the British-French Concorde project suggests, is the amount of useful and commercially viable products resulting from the research efforts. One aspect of technological innovation is successful borrowing, another the product development achieved within the country itself. One indicator of the importance of technological borrowing is the number of foreign patents and their share of total registered patents. The amount of technology imports after the war is indicated in Figure 11.1, which brings the numbers up to 1980.

Granted that patent data may be reasonable approximations to reality, several observations can be made from Figure 11.1. Total number of patent applications rose from 2,534 in 1945, an abnormal year, to 5,249 in 1968, the record year, after a smooth uninterrupted twenty year ascent. Since applications from Norwegian citizens declined almost as smoothly in the same period, it follows that the patent share of foreign origin rose steadily, up from 53 per cent of total number of applications in 1947 to 82 per cent in 1968, at which level it hovered through the following decade. By 1980 the foreign share was still 82 per cent.[32] As a very rough observation one may say that borrowing foreign technology has been a mainstay in the postwar effort to bridge

Figure 11.1: Patents in Norway

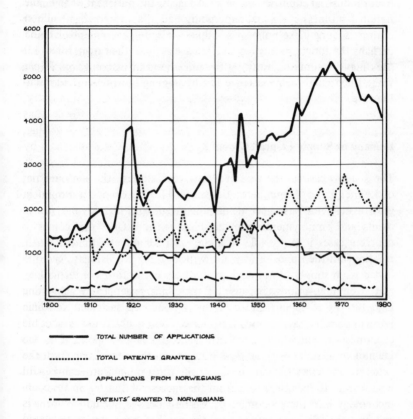

TOTAL NUMBER OF APPLICATIONS

TOTAL PATENTS GRANTED

APPLICATIONS FROM NORWEGIANS

PATENTS' GRANTED TO NORWEGIANS

Source: Bjørn Basberg, *Norwegian Patents 1840-1980*, Working Paper, Norwegian School of Economics, May 1981, p. 5.

the technological gap.

In the light of the 50-year Kondratieff-cycles, the fourth allegedly beginning in the early forties, it is interesting to note that the patent evidence shows a culmination in the late sixties, which coincides quite accurately with the culmination point of the fourth Kondratieff, roughly twenty five years after its inception. It is equally interesting to observe the steep decline in patent applications that set in afterwards. The turning point preceded the oil crisis of 1973 and has continued almost without interruption ever since. Again, this coincides with the downturn of the fourth Kondratieff. The coincidence is the more remarkable as the patent statistics in question are not local; they stem from the major industrial countries and as such suggest the pulsebeat of the international business cycle that supposedly had disappeared together with oldtime scourges like polio or smallpox. Despite government planning, perhaps the longterm business cycles have a life of their own; for a time they may be conjured away by the priesthood of planning, but after a while they make their existence felt by coming out of the shadows of the cave.

Demand or Supply-induced Growth?

The shadow cast on the wall in recent years suggests the contours, not of Keynes, but of Schumpeter. Contrary to Keynesian postwar opinion, growth may not have been demand-induced, with high savings, investments and employment following high demand. Once one comes to concrete cases it is possible to argue with Schumpeter that the chain reaction ran the opposite way. Growth, in other words, may have followed from supply of new and qualitatively better forms of technology and from innovations. Because of their high productivity gains, and high returns to labour and capital, they induced sustained and high levels of demand, savings and investments. Presumably, this was what the economists meant when in the fifties and sixties they spoke of the US technological superiority *vis-à-vis* Europe and the need for the latter to catch up and close the gap. In this chain of reasoning European growth would seem to have followed from the successful transfer of American technology into the economies of Western Europe, including Norway, and to have lost momentum once the gap had been closed. In such a perspective the remarkable growth period would appear to be the outcome of a combination of non-repeatable factors and therefore assumes the nature of an episode rather than the beginning of a new economic dispensation. Perhaps, given the difficulties of indexation and adding, the big causal chains cannot be unravelled on the macro-level. On that level one merely observes correlations, but correlation tells us nothing of causation, let alone its direction. If so, we are justified in demonstrating the possibility of supply-induced growth by examples. These remarks serve as justification for the episodic and selective sections in the next chapter.

Notes

1 Angus Maddison,'Economic Policy and Performance in Europe 1913-1970', *Fontana Economic History of Europe*, 1976, vol. 5.2, pp. 476-9.

2 *NOS. National Accounts* (fixed prices).

3 OECD. *Public Expenditure Trends*, Paris, 1978, p. 46.

4 Sverre Thon, *Økonomisk politikk i Norge 1945-1965*, Oslo, 1965, p. 44.

5 OECD. *Public Expenditure Trends*, Paris, 1978, p. 16.

6 Odd Aukrust, *Norges økonomi etter krigen*, Oslo, 1965, pp. 410-18.

7 Edvard Bull, *Norge i den rike verden. Tiden etter 1945*, Oslo, 1979, pp. 155-67, 182, 185, 186.

8 *NOS. Historical Statistics 1978*; OECD. *Economic Survey. Norway*, Paris. 1963, p. 29. Only USA and Australia exceeded the Norwegian figure in 1972.

9 Einar Hope, *Næringsøkonomiske oversikter*, I, p. 186.

10 Ole Jakob Aarland, *Transfer gains in the Norwegian Economy 1900-1970*, Norw. School of Economies, 1982, seminar paper.

11 See St. meld. nr. 71, 1972-3, p. 44 (Parliamentary report no. 71, 1972-3, p. 44); Preben Munthe, *Sirkulasjon, inntekt og økonomisk vekst*, Universitetsforlaget, 2nd ed., 1981, p. 293.

12 Yngvar Åberg, *Produktion och produktivitet i Sverige 1861-1965*, Uppsala, 1969, p. 24.

13 *OECD, The Growth of Output 1960-1980. Retrospect, Prospect and Problems of Policy*, Paris, 1970, p. 38-40.

14 Preben Munthe, *Sirkulasjon, inntekt og økonomisk vekst*, Universitetsforlaget 1981, 2nd ed., p. 262.

15 Arne Amundsen, *Konsumelastisiteter og konsumprognoser bygd på nasjonalregnskapet*, Art. no. 7 from CBS, Oslo, 1963 Table 1.

16 *Historical Statistics 1978*, Table 53.

17 *Statistical Yearbook 1981*, Table 115.

18 *NOS. Statistical Yearbook; NOS Historical Statistics 1968; UN Statistical Yearbook.*

19 *Labour Relations in Norway*, Oslo, 1975, p. 98.

20 Ibid., pp. 93-8.

21 *Statistical Yearbook 1982*, Table 94, p. 69, and *Historical Statistics 1978*, Table 50, p. 87.

22 Ibid., Table 352, p. 623.

23 Ibid., Tables 355, 357.

24 *Forskning, teknisk utvikling og industriell innovasjon. En vurdering av den offentlige støtte til teknisk-industriell forskning og utvikling Norge*, NOU 1981: 30 A+B, Univ. forlaget 1981, 2 vols. Especially *Government Support for Industrial Research in Norway. A SPRU Report*, Appendix 4, pp. 195-311.

25 *NOS. Statistical Yearbook 1940*, Table 254.

26 *do. 1962*, Table 350.

27 *do. 1963*, Table 350, *do. 1968*, Table 388.

28 *OECD. Scientific Research, Norway*, Paris, 1965, p. 19.

29 Einar Hope, *Næringsøkonomiske oversikter. Sekundaernaeringene*, vol. II, p. 167.

30 *Statistical Yearbook 1971*, Tables 74, 405.

31 *OECD. Trends in Industrial R & D in selected Member Countries 1967-1975*, Paris 1979, p. 75.

32 Patent data are published weekly by Styret for det industrielle rettsvern (The Office for Patent Rights Protection), Oslo. The data here obtained from B. Basberg and Aa. Svinndal, ed., *Styret for det industrielle rettsvern 5Går 1911-1961*, Oslo 1961, p. 325.

12 SECTORAL TRENDS 1950-1975

Winners and Losers in Manufacturing

An outside study of manufacturing trends in Norway for the period 1949-66 discerned two phases.[1] The first was characterised by low degrees of value adding in general. The second, beginning in the sixties, showed a markedly higher degree of transformation. Exports reflect the transition well: in 1949 intermediate products at lower stages of transformation with value adding less than 50 per cent of sales value, provided nearly four fifths of Norwegian merchandise exports, with processed fish, pulp and paper each providing one fourth of the total. Manufactured goods, in which value adding exceeded 50 per cent of sales value, accounted for 9.2 per cent, less than one tenth. Engineering industries as yet did mostly repair work in the home market. Consumer goods industries, hatched in the isolationist thirties, were equally oriented towards the home market, enjoying some protection throughout the fifties. The verdict was that Norway in the early postwar period showed features characteristic of a semi-industrialised country.

The EFTA agreement of 1960 challenged Norwegian industry to adapt to complete free trade in industrial goods by 1969. The climate of competition ushered in a new phase. Survival in the market place required willingness to change. No longer sheltered, industrial firms were forced to seek out niches, either in the home market or in foreign markets, where cost reductions were obtainable in large scale production. Those unable to cultivate such niches were unable to compete and were driven to the wall. Usually those who succumbed were tied to the home market.

The rationale in a growth perspective is that in industries enjoying economies of scale productivity tends to increase with increasing production and employment. Growth in industry of this type, paying above the average, will absorb labour from other sectors. As a result productivty will go up both in industry and in the outside sectors, losing surplus labour. Hence, the larger the growth of manufacturing, the larger the growth of the economy as a whole. This is usually termed Verdoorn's law. Equally, the larger the growth of employment in industry relative to growth of total employment, the larger the growth of productivity in the economy at large.[2]

Bela Balassa's assessment above catches the main trends up to 1970. If we apply his scheme to individual industries, we find among the winners, i.e. industries with expanding output and employment,

— printing and publishing
— basic metal industries
— chemical industry
— machinery excl. electrical
— electrotechnical machinery, apparatus etc.
— transport equipment

Stagnating trends in output and employment were seen in consumer goods, that catered mainly for the domestic market, notably the manufacture of:

— tobacco & cigarettes
— textiles
— garments and apparel
— furniture and fixtures
— leather and leather products.

In general, industry survived in the open economy by utilising natural resources, like cheap energy, fish and forests, or competitive skills in engineering and other modern high technologies. Manufactured goods, defined as goods in which value adding exceeds 50 per cent of market value, rose from 9.2 to 38 per cent of merchandise exports between 1949 and 1970.[3] Both thrusts were compatible with high wages. Complementing the trend towards export specialisation, there has been an inrush from abroad of consumer goods, for instance shoes, apparel, furniture, cosmetics, that gradually ousted the Norwegian producers by price, quality or design. Exceptions occur, of course, but general trends are not in doubt. The old distinction between the home market and export markets has been blurred. The major exception has been agricultural products and also fish — a situation that goes back to the 1930s.

Aluminium and Power Intensive Industries

If heavy industry in the traditional sense failed to gain a footing, the combination of water power development and aluminium smelting came close enough. After a lull in the early fifties, the aluminium mania picked up again in the late fifties. Elkem, a large Norwegian industrial corporation, resulting from the merger of Elektrokemisk A/S and Christiania Spigerverk A/S, went into partnership in 1956 with the American aluminium giant ALCOA on a 55-45 per cent baisis. With government concessions and promise of cheap water power energy, they built a huge aluminium smelter at Mo, Nordland county, Mosjøen Aluminiumsverk (Mosal), which started operations in 1958. Ten years later the two partners, again on a 55-45 per cent basis and again on the initiative of the government, built Lista Aluminiumsverk, near Farsund on the south coast, operative in 1971. Both these plants employed a workforce of about 900 men.[4] Anxious to secure foreign venture capital, the Labour government under Einar Gerhardsen in 1959 sent abroad Trygve Lie, former UN Secretary General and former Foreign Minister of Norway, to coax international companies to invest in Norway. The bait was cheap electricity at fixed prices for contracts up to 40 years. The result of his goodwill tour was the incorporation of Sør-Norge Aluminium, an aluminium smelter at Husnes on the west coast, established 1962, in which DnC, playing the role of a *banque d'affaire*, participated with 19.5 per cent, IAAG or Alusuisse with 74.8 per cent and Serpindus with 13 per cent. The latter was a holding company in Luxembourg. Husnes went into operation in 1965. DnC divested itself of its Husnes shares in 1973 by selling them to a competitor, Norsk Hydro. Husnes, as a result of double expertise, developed into one of the most profitable aluminium companies of Europe.[5] Another deal resulted in the incorporation of Norsk Hydro A/S Karmøy Fabrikker, an aluminium smelting company at Karmøy on the west coast, not far from Husnes, established 1963 and operative 1967. Behind this venture was Norsk Hydro (51 per cent) and Harvey Aluminium Co of the USA (49 per cent).

Trygve Lie also negotiated with the international oil companies, which led to the construction of two oil refineries, one by ESSO (or Exxon) at Tønsberg, the other by SHELL outside Stavanger. By 1970 the ESSO refinery ranked fifth, the SHELL refinery number nine among the 500 largest industrial companies of Norway. Foreign capital, among socialists always a touchy subject, counted for 15 per cent of total owner capital in Norwegian industrial companies in 1952. The share increased to 22 per cent in 1968.[6]

The intimate relationship with international finance in the sixties was underlined in 1966 when the non-socialist ministry of Per Borten sanctioned a deal between the state aluminium company ÅSV and

Alcan Alum. Ltd, whereby Alcan took over 50 per cent of ÅSV's shares in return for the sale of a substantial amount of Alcan stock to ÅSV. In 1975 the Norwegian government repurchased from Alcan one half of Alcan's ÅSV holdings, and in 1979 the remaining half. ÅSV now ranks as a 100 per cent government-owned company.

In a world setting Norway, whose aluminium production increased from 47,000 tons in 1950 to 522,000 by 1970, was the world's second largest exporter and the fifth largest producer, trailing behind the USA, the Soviet Union, Japan and Canada. The aluminium smelters were in the first division, very capital intensive, with a workforce each of about one thousand. Another feature in common was that all the raw materials, except the energy, were imported; thirdly, they served as cornerstone establishments in the periphery, the sole income source for a local community, and fourth, exports made up 90-95 per cent of output. As long as operating profits were satisfactory in crude metal production, anxiety remained dormant, that is, till the late 1970s.

The other part of the power intensive industry, privately owned by home and foreign capital, comprised magnesium, carbide, ferro alloys, zinc, chemical fertilizers and copper. Like aluminium these products resulted from large scale operations, and depended on export markets for 90-100 per cent of output. Magnesium production got under way in 1954 at Norsk Hydro's plant at Herøya, exports soaring from 40,000 to 489,000 tons between 1954 and 1973. The figure placed Norway as second among the world magnesium producers, while in ferro alloy products the country ranked first.[7] Chemical fertilizer exports, increasing from 42,000 tons in 1950 to 838,000 twenty years later,[8] remained a mainstay of Hydro's operations, helping to cover the costs of its expanding activities into plastics, urea, ammonia, and later into North Sea oil. Diversification helped spread risks, while increasing the potential for profits.

Setback for State Industry 1963

In addition to iron, steel and aluminium the state industry in the sixties came to include coke refining. In 1960 the Gerhardsen government proposed to build A/S Norsk Koksverk, a state coke works at Gullsmedvik in northern Rana, in the vicinity of the state steel mill at Mo. Labour, riding the familiar saddle, wanted to transport coal, dug by the Kings Bay Kulcompagnie at Svalbard, refine it at the coke works at Gullsmedvik, and use the cinders as input for steel refining at

Jernverket in Mo. The gas resulting from the distillation, was to provide raw material for an ammonia plant to be built in the Mo region. The arguments to go ahead were compelling: the project would serve national self sufficiency, save foreign currency and provide jobs in a region threatened by depopulation. Against 29 votes from the Conservative Party the Storting (14 march 1961) voted 80 million kr. for the coke works, and another 60 million for the ammonia plant on 12 June the same year. The latter vote was unanimous.

Building costs ran to 195 million rather than the 140 million kr. appropriated by the Storting. The government in 1962 asked for another 55 million, which galled the non-socialist parties. Worse, on 5 November 1962 the coal mine accident at Kings Bay in Ny Ålesund, Svalbard, cost the lives of 21 miners. The accident occasioned a heated national debate on security meaures, control and responsibility for their implementation, which brought up the larger constitutional issue of the conflict between the need for democratic control and operating efficiency in state industries run by government bureaucrats. The issue led to a vote of no-confidence against the Gerhardsen ministry in the Storting in August 1963, the resignation of the Labour government and a four-week coalition ministry, 28 August-25 September 1963, led by John Lyng (1905-78) of the Conservative Party.

In retrospect the confidence in state industry suffered a lasting setback. The dilemma of reconciling efficiency with control and responsibility has haunted the state-owned companies to this day. The coke works however, after a bad start and several writedowns of capital, developed into a going concern, with a yearly production of 340,000 tons of coke, 55,000 tons ammonia, 15,000 of raw tar and 5,000 of benzine. In 1978 its sales amounted to 126 million kroner and its workforce was 332. Based on sales it was number 96 on the list of the 500 biggest industrial companies in 1975.[9]

Hydro Power Development

Continued hydro power development went hand in hand with investment in aluminium throughout the fifties and sixties. Both areas reveal the effects of political planning and decision making. The water power plants were owned, and the capital provided, either by counties or the central government. The government share of owned capital in industry climbed from 0.4 to 15 per cent between 1939 and 1963.[10] To some degree, obviously, the postwar growth is explained by planning; however, besides providing energy for electrolytic smelting processes, the electricity development campaign also aimed at providing electricity for households. Harnessing water-falls, erecting pylons and stretching the electricity wires were a top priority welfare objective. The coast is lined by 50,000 islands, 2,000 of them inhabited. The gradual completion of the electrification pro-gramme, which also encompassed those inhabited islands, is seen in the gradual decline in the number of persons without network connection at year's end[11]

        1940: 700,000
        1945: 640,000
        1950: 420,000
        1953: 200,000
        1960: 20,000
        1970:   1,000

A long dark coast was lit up. As if by magic, radio, telephone and, after 1960, television brought the coastal people into immediate contact with the rest of the world. Their lives were never the same thereafter.

Aggregate production of hydro electricity rose by leaps and bounds. This is indicated in Figure 12.1 which brings the record up to 1981. It should be emphasized that imported coal and coke were still important sources of energy in industry and households at the end of the war. Electrification, based on water power, drove coal practically out of sight. The coal mines at Svalbard yielded around 850,000 tons of coal a year, but the coal was not used as an energy input, but as a raw material for steel and ammonia production at Mo in Rana. Thermo-electricity, dominant in other industrial countries, is non-existent in Norway, except for the nuclear test reactor at Halden. Total electricity output increased by a rate of growth of 6.2 per cent per year between 1950 and 1970, up from 17 Twh in 1950 to 57 Twh in 1970 and 84 Twh in 1980. *Per capita* energy consumption in Norway by 1980 is exceeded only by the United States and Canada. As seen in Figure 12.1, the power intensive industries in 1970 bought 44 per cent, other manu-facturing industries 18 per cent, households 37 per cent and transport 1 per cent.[12] Households tended to increase their share in the seventies. By 1980 it was 51.4 per cent.[13] In terms of cost electricity based on water power was the best alternative. Cheap heavy oils, imported by the international oil companies, gained some headway in the sixties, in the heating of houses, but after the oil crisis of 1973 the oil price dis-

Figure 12.1: Annual Production of Hydro Electricity

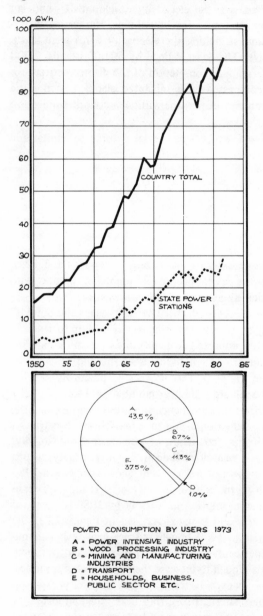

POWER CONSUMPTION BY USERS 1973

A = POWER INTENSIVE INDUSTRY
B = WOOD PROCESSING INDUSTRY
C = MINING AND MANUFACTURING
    INDUSTRIES
D = TRANSPORT
E = HOUSEHOLDS, BUSINESS,
    PUBLIC SECTOR ETC.

Source: NVE: *Vår Virksomhet* (Annual Report) 1981, p. 19.

couraged their expansion outside transportation.

Export figures tell the story this way: aluminium counted for 3.1 per cent of total commodity exports in 1950 at a time when fish and fish products represented 32 per cent, but twenty years later fish products had declined to a modest 10 per cent while aluminium alone had increased its share to 11 per cent; if one adds the other non-ferrous metals, the percentage had climbed to 19.[14]

Looking back after thirty years, Labour deserves credit for starting and upholding the electrification programme. Up to 1970 the power intensive industries offered well above average returns to capital and labour. Proof here is that apart from ÅSV, most of the share capital was privately owned. In the longer run the verdict is less favourable. The sales contracts for state energy have been seen to subsidise the smelting companies to a degree that appears unjustified and was exacerbated by the ongoing inflation. State participation, moreover, hampered product innovation and international marketing to an extent that would have been unthinkable for managment in privately owned companies. In the longer perspective aluminium smelting tied the labour force to low-degree skills, and brought the Norwegian workers to compete with crude aluminium from low-income third world countries. By 1980 these aspects had come into full view.

Engineering Industries

Engineering industries, including the manufacture of metal products, machinery, electrotechnical machinery and transport equipment, are the hallmarks of a mature industrialised country. Even in the 1950s these were mostly geared to repair jobs in the home market. No sector demonstrates better the galvanising effect of complete free trade that came with the opening of the sixties.[15] On the one hand, the engineering industries got access to the large market of Western Europe; on the other, they faced competition from the EFTA partners on the home market. Lukewarm so far to the idea of a Scandinavian customs union, Norwegian industrialists now felt confident that they could stand up to Swedish competition. In that belief they supported the idea of EFTA. Ample profits in the fifties had helped modernise techniques and equipment. The first reduction of customs duties within EFTA — 20 per cent on industrial goods — became effective 1 July 1960, and to keep pace with the EEC, the original EFTA plan for tariff reductions was shortened. Hence free trade was a fact for most manufactured goods by

1966, three years earlier than originally scheduled.[16] Table 12.1 indicates that in 1950 about a quarter of all industrial establishments was in engineering (23 per cent), employing a little less than a third of the workforce in manufacturing. It contributed 18 per cent of the gross production value, and 22 per cent of the value-added activity. The Table offers figures that place in relief the rise of the engineering industries up to 1975.

Table 12.1· Engineering Industries and their Place in Manufacturing 1950-1975. Mill. current kroner

Year	Number of firms Total manuf.	Employment Total manuf.	Gross prod. value Total manuf. Mill. kr	Value added Total manuf. Mill. kr
1950	1,391	72,859	1,586	876
	5,984	249,859	8,726	3,990
1955	5,065	89,797	3,228	1,681
	21,667	307,213	15,646	6,764
1960	4,445	93,863	4,555	2,291
	19,485	317,156	21,721	8,685
1965	4,577	115,623	7,875	4,046
	17,762	371,612	33,765	13,670
1970	3,337	115,834	12,286	5,665
	14,516	370,510	49,924	20,879
1975	2,275	131,911	31,161	11,132
	8,494	367,229	97,916	30,762
Engineering in per cent of total manufacturing				
1950	23	29	18	22
1955	23	29	21	25
1960	23	30	21	26
1965	26	31	23	30
1970	23	31	25	27
1975	27	36	32	36

Sources: *Historical Statistics 1978*, Tables 133, 134 (mining not included) *Industristatistikk 1976*, NOS A 949, Oslo, 1978; *Statistical Yearbook 1977*, Table 171.

In 1950 engineering had 29 per cent of the industrial workforce, a figure that changed very little till 1970, but in this period its share of total production by value jumped from 18 to 25 per cent and the share of value added from 22 to 27 per cent; indeed, by 1975 the latter had soared to 36 per cent of total value added in manufacturing. The same occurred in employment. These figures testify to a strong industrial transformation.

In a growth perspective it is interesting to observe that in terms of gross production value, or value added, engineering increased faster than overall manufacturing, and both faster than GNP. A similar trend is observed in other OECD countries. Table 12.2 provides figures for 12 OECD countries during the 1951-73 period.

Table 12.2: Annual Average Rates of Growth of Aggregate Output (Q) and Manufacturing Output (Qm) 1951-1973

	Q %	Qm %		Q %	Qm %
Austria	5.0	5.5	Italy	5.1	7.1
Belgium	3.9	4.9	Japan	9.5	13.6
Canada	4.6	4.9	Netherlands	5.0	6.1
Denmark	4.2	4.8	Norway	4.2	4.3
France	5.0	5.5	UK	2.7	3.4
Germany	5.7	7.4	USA	3.7	3.9

Source: John Cornwall, *Modern Capitalism: its Growth and Transformation* London, 1977, p. 64. Figures derived from T.F. Cripps & R.J. Tarling, *Growth in advanced capitalist Economies 1950-1970*, London, 1973, pp. 45-56.

We note that manufacturing (Qm) without exception exhibited growth rates higher than GNP (Q). Table 12.1 moreover permits calculations to show that in engineering, employment and output growth were even higher. The evidence confirms 'Verdoorn's law' mentioned earlier. Growth was highest in those sectors offering the·best opportunities for economies of scale and hence productivity gains. In other words, manufacturing acted as a strong engine of growth till the 1970s.

To some extent the engineering industries simply expanded with the spread in the fifties and sixties of the automobile, electric household goods, air transport, broadcasting, television and telecommunications in Western Europe. Mass consumption of household machines reflected the disappearance of hired help in the households. Before the war the housemaid or the nanny, or both, were present in every sixth household. Now rising wages created new openings for the women while destroying the venerable profession of the housemaid. The electric household machines represented one set of revolutions, in which the washing machine, the refrigerator, the dishwasher, the deep freezer or the electric stove reduced the work of the housebound mother. Another revolution was that in telecommunications, with radio, the radio-link, and from 1960 television.

All the machines mentioned came to be manufactured in Norway, though poor marketing, forecasting, advertising and design prevented successful lasting export. The weakness in marketing handicapped Norway throughout the postwar period, whether in household electronics, furniture, bicycles or ready-made garments. Salesmanship, like catering, or the waiter's job, has traditionally lacked appeal, nor have the media or the school curriculae granted marketing the recognition it deserves. Customers abroad bought Bang & Olufsen rather than Tandberg radios or television sets, although Tandberg's products were in the opinion of experts technically superior.

From 1960 car imports were finally decontrolled, releasing a transportation revolution and a bonanza for car repair shops, driving schools, road-building and gasoline stations. In 1950 there was a car for every fortieth inhabitant, in 1970 one for every fifth, in 1980 for every fourth. All cars were imported; still, they boosted engineering skills, notably the mechanical firms building the bodies of lorries and buses. So did the air transport revolution. In 1949 the three state-owned airline companies of Denmark, Norway and Sweden joined together in establishing the Scandinavian Air Lines System (SAS). The company pioneered regular passenger flights across the North Pole, and earned a satisfactory return on capital. With 15,000 employees and sales of 5 billion 1973 kroner, SAS in the seventies ranked sixth by turnover among the European airlines, and ninth among international airlines.[17] Internal air traffic exploded: in 1950 there were 56,000 passengers who experienced the thrill, speed and convenience of air transport, against 1.4 million in 1970, which yields a rate of growth of 17.5 per cent per year.[18] Again, commercial aircraft production did not develop, but the rise of the international aircraft industry still had considerable effect on engineering skills, notably through government purchase contracts of military aircraft, which usually provided for the participation of Norwegian firms, among them Kongsberg Våpenfabrikk (KV). Small runways for regional and local air traffic proliferated.

From the point of view of originality very little of the engineering skills indicated so far was indigenous. Apart from Tandberg and a few other exceptions, they drifted in, so to speak, with the products themselves, borne on a buoyant and strong wave of mass consumer demand. Absorbing American mass production techniqes in these fields, Western European manufacturing was able to reap rapid productivity gains up till the seventies when the technological gap had closed, or was on the point of closing. Norwegian engineering partook in this expansion.

Along the way Norwegian engineering industries also developed some specialities. One was the innovation to cut out labour intensive clinking in shipbuilding. The new welding method, optical control flame cutting, was developed in the fifties by Bergens Mekaniske Verksteder (BMV), Bergen, in collaboration with Kongsberg Våpenfabrikk, the state munitions and research establishment. This innovation was followed by the numerically guided drawing and cutting technique, developed at Kongsberg, which dramatically increased building efficiency. Henceforth ships were built in modules and assembled afterwards.[20] Both were commercialised and sold on licence worldwide. Between 1950 and 1971 the export share of engineering jumped from a few percentage points to 21 per cent of total output. The expansion is best dealt with in the next section devoted to shipping.

Shipping & Shipbuilding

Few if any countries are more oriented toward the seas than Norway, in fishing, hunting, sea transport and seaborne trade.[21] Given the country's character, its geographical location and history, this is all natural. Once international peace was restored, the merchant fleet was rebuilt, and in the two decades to 1970 it swelled rapidly.

	Total tonnage		Oil tankers		Dry cargo	
1950	5.7 mill.	gr. tons	2.5	44%	2.5	44%
1955	7.8	"	4.2	54%	2.6	35%
1960	11.4	"	6.1	54%	4.3	38%
1965	16.0	"	8.4	53%	6.5	41%
1970	20.1	"	9.7	48%	7.7	38%
1975	25.8	"	13.9	54%	10.9	39%

Between 1950 and 1970 the fleet's tonnage quadrupled from 5.7 to 20.1 million gross tons.[1] In a world setting this was about 10 per cent of world shipping tonnage in 1968, the peak year. The share has since averaged 8 per cent. Apart from the flag convenience countries, Norway maintained its position as fourth among the world's shipping nations. By contrast, the country has 0.1 per cent of the world's population (Figure 12.2).

Not only did the fleet expand; in terms of age, average size and type it was also transformed. As for age, the Norwegian shipowners intensified the contracting policies begun in the thirties. In 1950 about a third

Figure No. 12.2: Developments in Number of Ships, Gross Tonnage and Employment

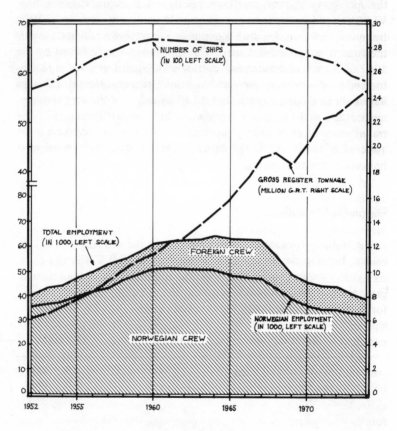

Source: *OECD Economic Surveys Norway, 1976*, p. 40.

of the fleet was less than five years old, 51 per cent less than ten years. In general the entire fleet is renewed every nine years. Rapid turnover was a necessary part of survival in a high-cost country. Naess Shipping apart, almost all the ships of the fleet continued to be operated from Norway with the relatively high wage and tax burden which home registration meant.

As for size, the ships got bigger and bigger, dwarfing all traditional notions. One third of the fleet was under 400 gr. tons in 1946, about 90 per cent under 10,000 gr. tons. In the fifties came the ships of 50-60,000 tons. In the early sixties they were overshadowed by giants over

100,000 tons. Before the decade was over, monsters of almost 300,000 tons had been built in a number of countries, among them Norway, at the Aker Group's Stord Shipyard on the west coast. These were the VLCC's — very large crude carriers, the supertankers in international oil transport, that appeared after the closing of the Suez Canal in 1967 and the Arab oil embargo against the UK, USA and West Germany, also in 1967 in the wake of the Arab-Israeli war. Manning requirements failed to keep pace with the change: the supertankers generally have a crew of 35, or about the same as a 4,000 ton dry cargo-vessel in 1950. Employment in the fleet engaged in ocean transport, exclusive of the coasting trade, was 34,000 in 1950. It culminated around 57,000 employees in 1964 after which the figure tumbled to 34,000 in 1973. The figure bottomed out at about 30,000 of whom 300-400 are women.

As for type of ships, the orders reflect new market trends. Dry cargo and liner trades stagnated, while oil transport increased. The shift is mirrored in the share of tankers, over 50 per cent of the fleet's tonnage. New cargoes were chemicals and liquid gas. In these markets Norwegian shipping companies captured a world market share of 50 per cent before 1970. Other types developed in response to new lifting and transport technologies on shore, among them the fork lift which triggered the roll on-roll off ships. Wage cost considerations paved the way for the dry bulk ship: grain-ore or even ore-grain-ore. Grain, coal, ore and oil account for 75% of world ocean freight transport, which explains the new combinations.

As for builders, the fact is that during the 1946-73 period some 75 per cent of ships in ocean freight markets, newly delivered to Norwegian owners were built by foreign shipyards.[22] Still, the home yards expanded rapidly in the sixties, with orders from domestic as well as foreign customers. In the peak year 1972, the Norwegian shipyards built 428,000 gross tons, up from 58,000 gross tons in 1950, and new ships represented 17.6 per cent of total commodity exports, up from zero twenty years earlier. Adding the rest of the output from the engineering industries sold abroad, the percentage climbed to 25 of total commodity exports.[23] The expansion was strongest along the west coast, at Stavanger (Rosenberg), at Stord (Aker), in Bergen (BMV), at Florø (Ankerløkken) and at a number of smaller yards on the Møre coast. The seventies demonstrated that the expansion was without solid foundation. Of the eighty — yes eighty — shipyards that operated by 1981, most were in trouble.

Turning to markets for engineering products, EFTA countries bought 51 per cent in 1959 and 61 in 1972, of which Sweden alone took 31 per cent, while the EEC's share had declined from 19 to 17 per cent and that of the rest of the world from 31 to 23. In other words, Europe was the most important market, taking 77 per cent (1972). Growth, in short, for a time was highest precisely in those industries in which level and rate of growth of productivity was highest. It was a textbook case. Still Norway was a laggard here in Western Europe: engineering in West Germany in 1971 contributed 16 per cent of GNP, in Great Britain 14 per cent, in Sweden 12 per cent, in the Netherlands 10 per cent, but in Norway a mere 8 per cent. This was less than the contribution of shipping.

To illustrate the place of shipping in the Norwegian economy, we may use the same measure, the share of gross freight earnings relative to total output.

Figure 12.3: Developments in the Shipping Sector's Share of GDP, Investment and Exports

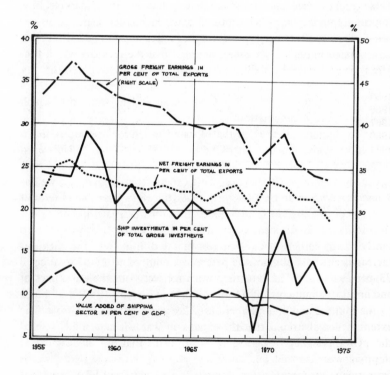

Source: *OECD, Economic Surveys, Norway 1976,* p. 41.

Figure 12.3 traces the development of shipping to 1975. It appears that value added of shipping culminated in 1957 at 16 per cent of GNP. Till 1967 its share fluctuated around 10 per cent, and declined thereafter. To gain perspective on this, we note that value added from shipping to GNP in 1973 was 1.02 per cent in Finland, in France 0.28 per cent, in West Germany 0.19, in Japan 0.42, in Sweden 1.02 and in the Netherlands 1.12 per cent.[25] In the longer perspective, however, the position of shipping in the economy has deteriorated, whether one considers the relative share of its freight earnings, investments or value added. In 1957 for instance, its gross freight earnings were 37 per cent of total exports, goods and services, but in 1968 that share had fallen to 30 per cent and by 1975 to 25 per cent. Shipping, that is, remained a highly risky trade, with little stability in either employment or earnings. Still, when the going was good, returns to labour and capital towered above those in other sectors, as indicated in Table 12.3.

Table 12.3: Wages per Man Year in Shipping, Export-competing and Import-competing Manufacturing Industries. Current Kroner

Year	International ocean transport (1)	Export-competing industries (2)	Import-competing industries (3)	1:2 (4)	1:3 (5)
1963	27,800	20,800	18,000	1.34	1.53
1965	33,200	23,800	21,600	1.39	1.54
1967	42,800	28,300	26,100	1.51	1.64
1969	52,100	33,000	30,400	1.58	1.71
1971	72,500	41,800	37,700	1.73	1.92

Source: Ib Eriksen & Victor Normann, 'Skipsfarten i norsk samfunnsøkonomi', *Statsøkonomisk Tidsskrift 1974*, no. 2, p. 131.

According to Table 12.3, columns 4 and 5, wages have been consistently higher in shipping than in other sectors, and the gap has increased all the time. In 1971 wages for shipping employees averaged 73 per cent and 92 per cent higher respectively than wages in export- and import-competing industries.

An indication of superior earning capacity is that to a considerable extent new building has been financed by foreign banks. Looking at the period 1946-73, we find that 60 per cent of the investment in shipping was financed out of current and past profits, while proceeds from selling used ships covered some 25 per cent. Only 11 per cent was financed through net borrowing — almost entirely from foreign banks, prominent among which was Hambro's Bank, London — but due to large advance payments on new ships, gross borrowing was considerably higher. Hence, by the end of 1972 net indebtedness corresponded to about one-third of the value of the fleet, while gross debt, 16.3 billion kroner, was equivalent to about 50 per cent.

The government, pressed by the most influential trade union, the Iron and Metal Workers, in the 1960s eased the mortgage situation for the Norwegian shipyards by co-operating with the three biggest commercial banks, DnC, BB and Christiania Bank og Kredittkasse (CBK) in setting up a loan institute to provide mortgage loans for ships, in which most of the share capital was held by the banks, while the government guaranteed the bonds issued by the loan institute. To prevent unfounded concern abroad, about state subsidies to Norwegian shipyards, the banks the government and the shipyards negotiated a new arrangement in 1965 whereby the Bank of Norway placed some of its American assets at the disposal of Hambro's and other British banks which, thus secured, proceeded to offer second priority loans to Norwegian shipowners who contracted at Norwegian shipyards, among them the towering Hilmar Reksten, Bergen (1897-1980). More importantly, the Norwegian commercial banks from the sixties onwards incorporated subsidiaries abroad, notably in Zürich, Amsterdam, Luxembourg and London. In this way they were able to arrange credits for shipowners directly, gaining international experience into the bargain, not least in the buying and selling of currencies on the spot market, in which DnC soon ranked as a world leading institution. The road to internationalisation thus followed once again in the wake of ocean-going ships.[27]

Mergers and Managerial Capitalism

To cope with the competition from EFTA partners, the engineering firms in the sixties found it advantageous to enter into various working agreements, which in many cases paved the way for outright mergers. Offensive or defensive, these agreements in response to competition aimed at securing economies of scale in contract bidding, production or marketing in export markets. To outsiders it looked like a replay of the 1890s when large scale capitalist enterprise, unable to survive cut throat competition, sought shelter in cartels or monopolies. The merger movement this time encompassed not only engineering industries; retail and wholesale trade were also overhauled, as was the banking structure, and the forest product industry. To insiders the merger movement was not a repetition of the past: it was a belated and necessary kind of rationalisation to stand up to new tastes, demand and competition in an open economy. It was business doing voluntarily what Labour had sought to drive through by mandatory legislation in 1952-3, but had given up when private business balked.

According to a report by Norges Industriforbund (National Association of Industry) the decade of the sixties saw a total of 227 registered mergers and 193 formal agreements in manufacturing alone, which in view of the total number of firms (about 4,000) amounted to a pretty strong overhaul of the corporate landscape, affecting every tenth firm or so.[28] Based on voluntary information, the report may underrate the real figures. Engineering boasted 4,445 establishments in 1960 (Table 12.1). Fifteen years later its number had declined to 2,275 firms, down one half. Some had folded, some had changed names, most had been swallowed up. Equally, the private commercial banks numbered 68 in 1960 against 28 in 1975, down by more than one half in fifteen years.

Out of the rationalisation race there emerged a handful of bigger banks and bigger concerns, among the former, Den norske Creditbank, Christiania Bank og Kreditkasse and Bergen Bank, among the latter the Aker Group or the Kvaerner Group, which may stand comparison with the multi-divisional concerns typical of international manufacturing today. These pursue a philosophy of growth rather than profit maximisation; they have a vertically integrated, decentralised structure and run subsidiary companies in several countries, carry out R & D activities and are of necessity oriented towards the export markets. Kvaerner, Norsk Hydro, Aker ar ÅSV are in this division, though they are far from being vertically integrated; in fact, none of the Norwegian concerns is fully integrated. Yet internationalisation is a reality. Kvaerner by 1975 had engineering and sales offices in Bremen, London, Newcastle, New York and Spain.[29] ÅSV, one of Europe's biggest aluminium producers in 1975, operates three smelters in Norway and processes aluminium at eight other Norwegian concerns, five in Sweden and four in Denmark. In 1981 it employed a workforce of 7,809, of whom 1,326 were women, 878 employees in Sweden and 656 in Denmark. Total external sales soared from 1.1 to 3.6 billion kroner between 1972 and 1980.[30] The Aker Group expanded its total external sales from 1.1 to 3.5 billion kroner between 1970 and 1979, the peak year, while its workforce increased from 8,500 to 11,200 (1980). Besides building ships and marine engines the Aker Group in the 1970s expanded into oil rigs in the British and Norwegian part of the North Sea, which was a help when shipbuilding went into depression after 1974.[31]

Management, typically, is in the hands of professional careerists with diplomas from a technical university like NTH, Trondheim, less often from a school of economics, like NHH, Bergen. Managerial capitalism has to some extent taken the place of the Buddenbrooks, the family firm of yesterday, though to a lesser degree in Norway than elsewhere. Professionalism has largely ousted amateurism. Though in sheer numbers the individually owned firms dominate with 70 per cent of the total, according to the industry census of 1964, the stock companies overshadowed them completely in regard to capital and employment. In the year mentioned the latter employed 66 per cent of the workforce and controlled 78 per cent of fixed real capital in manufacturing against a mere 15 per cent held by the individually owned firms. Still, internationally the Norwegian concerns are not much in evidence. Only Norsk Data and Norsk Hydro are listed on the London Stock Exchange. The former is a rapidly expanding computer company. Using employment as a yardstick, international comparisons reveal the predominance of the small-scale industrial structure in Norway. In 1961 West Germany had 41 per cent of its industrial workforce in establishments employing 500 and over, Great Britain 48 per cent, Sweden 30 per cent against a mere 19 percent in Norway.[32] Despite the strong industrial expansion later, the structure in Norway changed little, for it turns out that establishments employing 200 or more represented 36 per cent of the manufacturing workforce in 1964, against 39 per cent in 1970 and 40 per cent in 1975.[33]

The transition to managerial capitalism in manufacturing may have boosted the tendency to finance growth through external borrowing rather than through internally generated profits; but so may inflation, stiff company taxes, anti-pollution legislation, dividend regulation or high wages. Whatever the reasons, the fact is that equity capital in Norwegian manufacturing firms was on average 33 per cent of the total in 1950 against 19 per cent in 1966,[34] and 16 per cent by 1978,[35] which is in strong contrast to the situation in other industrial countries. Equity capital in 1964 was 46 per cent in Germany, 48 per cent in France, 60 per cent in Great Britain and 61 per cent in the United States.[36] Clearly, the supply of risk capital in Norway has come forward more tardily than elsewhere, and among industrialists the opinion is that the main culprits are inflation, government regulations and taxes, while cash wages, which do not of course include all wage costs, remained a stable 50 per cent of total value added through the sixties with no upward tendency till well into the seventies.[37] Still, workers in engineering enjoy the highest wages among industrial workers. They have been pace setters. Despite these special features, the overall trend, as elsewhere, is from resource-bound to knowledge-based industry. The biggest gains in profits and sales recently have accrued to engineering and consulting companies, selling high-performance technology or advanced technological knowledge.

The Forest Products Industry

The forest products industry, once the country's industrial pride, proved unable in the sixties to effect the necessary modernisation. Flushed with its success in the recent Husnes aluminium project, DnC, under its chief executive Johan Melander (b. 1910) in 1965 bought a substantial amount of stock in Union Co, one of the leading concerns. In the six following years DnC tried to restructure the pulp and paper companies in the Drammen and Skien regions, in order to step up their competitiveness *vis-à-vis* Finland, Sweden and Canada.[38] Existing units — Drammen alone had 25 — were too small to be able to afford the adoption of the most efficient technology. All interests would be served by co-operating in a planned rationalisation. DnC, trying to convince the parties involved, found itself blackballed and its motives misrepresented by local politicians, the press, trade unions, the government, and above all by the infighting going on among former members of the board of Union, wishing to pull out 20 million kr from the company as accumulated reserves. The rationalisation scheme, including the planned merger of Follum and Union, involved something like 10,000 jobs in the Telemark and Buskerud counties, and one quarter of all jobs in industry in the latter county.

In the end DnC gave up its attempts at rationalising the industry. The belated reorganisation, when it came in the late seventies, was instead shouldered by the forest owners through their joint company, Norske Skogindustrier, dating back to 1962. The forest owners were in a strategic position at a time when the capacity of the pulp and paper industry far exceeded the supply of timber. In 1977 the forest owners set on foot a forest company, Nye Tofte Cellulosefabrikk, a flagship of corporative capitalism, in which the forest owners through Norske Skogindustrier had 50 per cent, the other leading concerns around the Oslofjord 8 per cent each, among them Follum, Sagbrugsforeningen and Union, and the last 26 per cent was taken up by the Odvar Nordli government at the insistence of the local trade union. Constructed at the colossal cost of 1.2 billion kr. Nye Tofte proved a white elephant by 1982 and went into bankruptcy in October of that year, at which point the government capital of 918 million kroner was lost. The mixed economy, clearly, worked both ways.

Export-oriented Growth

We are now in a position to summarise our overall review of growth and its causes in the postwar period. We noted that the growth of the workforce lagged far behind growth of total output; hence, we turned to figures for the growth of capital and capital formation. As the effect of labour and capital is measured jointly, efforts to estimate their separate contribution involve a violation of reality. The conventional method is to estimate the increase in the two factors separately, and consider additional output growth a result of technological progress, involving qualitative, not merely quantitative changes in input factors. In Table 11.5 above we have provided separate figures for the growth of capital, labour and total output in the postwar period 1946-74. GNP increased by a yearly 4.4 per cent, labour by 0.3 and capital by 4.0 per cent. If on empirical grounds to our best knowledge, two thirds of output growth is ascribed to labour, one third to capital, we obtain a measure of the contribution of labour and capital to yearly output growth:

$$0.67 \times 0.3 + 0.33 \times 4.0 = 1.5$$

As total output growth from 1946-74 was 4.4 per cent per year, we are faced with a residual difference (4.4-1.5 = 2.9), which is responsible for 66 per cent of yearly output growth in the period.[39] This 'rest' is conveniently ascribed to technological progress. Similar results are obtained from corresponding figures for other mature economies.

Next, we have observed that capital formation in Norway was far higher than in other OECD countries, which is seen in the extraordinarily high capital coefficient. Yet, growth of total output in Norway was just under the average for OECD countries. This suggests a low return on investment in the short run. Responsibility lay with the build-up of power intensive industries, the sevenfold increase in hydro-electric production and large investments in shipping, all yielding benefits in the longer run. The housing drive throughout the fifties and sixties also contributed. Now, as growth is essentially a matter of increasing the productivity of factor inputs, and industry is best able to reap economies of scale, it is clear that productivity gains would accumulate in the economy with increased production in industry. Since the rate of growth of both employment and production was higher in industry than in the overall economy (Table 12.2), we see that industry in general, the engineering and the power intensive industries in particular, acted as a major engine of growth till 1970. To these may be added shipping, which, operating on competitive terms in the international markets, was able to offer returns to capital and labour consistently higher than both import- and export-competing industry (Table 12.3).

The causal reasoning need not stop here, for the rationale, as seen, for the build-up of electricity and power intensive industries was always the possibility of selling in foreign markets. Access to the export markets was indeed its official justification. The earliest long-term programme by Labour in 1947 was, in fact, a recipe for export-led growth. So the outcome, a quadrupling of GNP and a trebling of *per capita* income 1947-70, may in a sense be ascribed to the trade liberalisation policies inaugurated in the fifties under the aegis of the United States. Enlarging on the point, we may say that the *desire* for reconstruction and economic growth was there, as Labour's programmes make clear, but admittance to the international markets was by an outside effect, the one a permissive, the other the decisive factor. So, if in line with common linguistic habits we consider that factor decisive, which men regardless of their motives, do not control, we could say that exports have not only been the necessary condition but also the sufficient cause of the post-war growth. We turn to some additional evidence to test the strength of the conclusion. Table 12.4 relates exports to GDP in twelve OECD countries.

Table 12.4: Annual Average Rate of Growth of Total Exports ($\dot{E}$) and GDP ($\dot{Q}$) 1951-1973 (in constant prices)

	$\dot{E}$	$\dot{Q}$		$\dot{E}$	$\dot{Q}$
	%	%		%	%
Austria	10.7	5.1	Italy	11.7	5.1
Belgium	9.4	4.4	Japan	15.4	9.5
Canada	6.9	4.6	Netherlands	10.1	5.0
Denmark	6.1	4.2	Norway	7.2	4.2
France	8.1	5.0	United Kingdom	4.1	2.7
Germany	10.8	5.7	United States	5.1	3.7

Source: John Cornwall, *Modern Capitalism*, p. 162.

As shown in Table 12.5, our conclusion is compatible with the predictable fact that in Norway and 11 other OECD countries exports increased at a rate faster than that of total output every year in the period 1946-70. In turn, the export share of GNP has inched upwards, though at an uneven rate, from about a third to a little less than one half in the late seventies. Imports have about the same dimension; hence, the foreign trade totals together now match GNP. Among the OECD member countries, only the Netherlands is in this league, if we except a transit economy like Luxembourg. In this sphere continuity has prevailed. Around 1970 the country as an open economy was more open than at any other peace time in the past. The seventies, however, have witnessed renewed protectionist tendencies, *vis-à-vis* textile imports for instance.

Foreign Trade

Among the trading partners West European countries dominate, as they always have. Of total commodity exports in 1972, the Nordic countries took 26 per cent, EFTA 47 and EEC 24 per cent, USA 7 and Canada 1 per cent, the Soviet Union 0.08 per cent and developing countries 10 per cent. Conversely, of total merchandise imports the Nordic countries contributed 29 per cent, EFTA 44 per cent, EEC 26 per cent, USA 6 per cent and developing countries 9 per cent. If one looks specifically at the 24 OECD countries in the 1970s, which include Australia, Japan, Switzerland, Turkey, Greece and Spain as well, we find that these purchased 86 per cent of Norway's total commodity exports, and contributed 87 per cent of Norway's imports.[40] Replacing Sweden, the United Kingdom in the seventies became Norway's biggest customer, taking 30 per cent of total commodity exports alone in 1976 and 35 per cent in 1978. Oil and gas exports to EEC countries in the seventies have increased their role as foreign trading partners. This trend is likely to increase; in 1981, indeed, EEC took 53 per cent of Norway's commodity exports, a doubling in nine years.[41] The entire Comecon group in 1978 represents a mere 3 per cent both on the import and export side.

Very little need be said of the terms of trade, as they have fluctuated around 100 in most postwar years, and the deviations have at any rate been too small to have had any effect one way or the other. Nor did currency changes affect trade till the decade of the seventies, when the IMF structure began to crumble.

Notes

1 Bela Balassa, *Industrial Development in an Open Economy: The Case of Norway*, CBS, Articles no. 30, Oslo, 1969, pp. 5-23.

2 John Cornwall, *Modern Capitalism. Its Growth and Transformation*, London, 1977, pp. 122-36.

3 Bela Balassa, *Industrial Development*, pp. 11-12.

4 *Norges 1,000 største bedrifter*, Oslo, 1975, pp. 38-9.

5 Francis Sejersted, *et al., En storbank i blandingsøkonomien. Den norske Creditbank 1957-1982*, Oslo, 1982, pp. 94-103.

6 Einar Hope, *Naeringsøkonomiske oversikter*, II, p. 230.

7 *Aftenposten*, 22/10-1974, p. 21.

8 *Historical Statistics 1978*, Table 144.

9 *Norges 1,000 største bedrifter 1975*, Oslo, 1975, p. 40.

10 Sverre Thon, *Statsdrift i Norge og andre land*, Oslo, 1960, p. 10.

11 Johan Vogt, *Elektrisitetslandet Norge*, Oslo, 1971, p. 216.

12 *NVE. Vår virksomhet 1973*, Annual Report pp. 40, 42.

13 *NVE. Elektrisitetsforsyningen i Norge*, Oslo, 1982 (booklet).

14 *Statistical Yearbook 1952*, Table 186, *do.* 1972, Table 186.

15 Onar Onarheim, *Tanker omkring norsk verkstedsindustri. Perspektiver og forutsetninger for utvikling*, Lehmkuhl Lecture, NSE 1973.

16 Odd Aukrust, *Norges økonomi etter krigen*, CBS, Oslo, 1965, pp. 179-80.

17 Knut Hagrup, *SAS og den internasjonale luftfart*, Lehmkuhl Lecture, Norwegian School of Economics, 1974.

18 *Historical Statistics*, 1978, Table 224.

19 Onar Onarheim, *Tanker omkring*, p. 37.

20 Håkon With Andersen, 'Fra klink til sveis, Noen synspunkter på en teknologisk endring i skipsbyggingsindustrien', Paper at Technology Seminar Trondheim, 1981, Univ. of Trondheim 1981.

21 A. Strømme Svendsen, *Norges skipsfart*, in E. Hope, ed., *Naeringsøkonomiske oversikter*, vol. III, pp. 89-196.

22 *OECD. Economic Survey. Norway*, Paris, 1976, p. 42.

23 Onar Onarheim, *Tanker om norsk verkstedsindustri*, p. 5.

24 Ibid., p. 5.

25 *OECD. Maritime Transports 1973*, Paris, 1974.

26 *OECD. Economic Surveys. Norway*, Paris, 1976, p. 42.

27 Helge Pharo, 'Internasjonalisering og skipsfinansiering', in F. Sejersted *et al., En storbank i blandingsøkonomien*, pp. 224-30.

28 Einar Hope, 'Norges Industri', in *Naeringsøkonomiske oversikter*, vol. II, p. 208.

29 Kjell Langballe, *Kvaernerkonsernet. Oppbygging og egenart*, Lehmkuhl Lecture, NSE 1975, Bergen, 1975, pp. 6,35.

30 *ÅSV. Annual Report*, 1975, 1981.

31 *Akergruppen. Annual Report*, 1973, 1980.

32 Einar Hope, 'Norges Industri', p. 216.

33 *Industrial Statistics 1964*, Nos A 157, Oslo, 1966, Tab. 2 *Industrial Statistics 1970*, Nos A 485, Oslo, 1972, Tab. 9. *Industrial Statistics 1976, Nos A 949, Oslo, 1978, Tab. 15.*

34 Einar Hope, 'Norges industri', p. 148.

35 Egil Abrahamsen, *Kreativitet, innovasjon og konkurranseevne*, Lehmkuhl Lecture 1980, NSE, Bergen, 1980, p. 17.

36 Einar Hope, 'Norges industri', p. 213.

37 *Historical Statistics 1978*, Table 131.

38 F. Sejersted, 'En banque d'affair', in *En Storbank i blandingsøkonomien.*

DnC 1957-1982, Oslo, 1982, pp. 112-30.
39 Preben Munthe, *Sirkulasjon, inntekt og økonomisk vekst*, p. 284.
40 *Nos. Utenrikshandel 1972*, (External trade), Oslo, 1973, Table VII.
41 *Norges Eksportråd*, (Norway's Export Board), *Aftenposten* 23/9-82.

13 GOVERNMENT AND THE ECONOMY

Planning Priorities

It is a truism to say that government has increased its role in the post-war mixed economies. Government, central and local, took charge of 26 per cent of GDP in 1950 against 48 per cent in 1976 and 50.6 per cent in 1980. The increased public sector activity stems in part from socialist ideology, in part from a universal demand for more equality, possibly more from the steering needs of an increasingly complex industrial civilisation in which higher frequency of market failure, regardless of political creed, requires collective action. On the formal level the various governments tended to justify their interventions in the economy by pointing to their programmes which outlined their mandate from the voters. One lasting political cleavage was that between Labour and the non-socialist parties. Till 1970 observers nevertheless noted a great amount of consensus among the parties in key areas, such as the desirability to maintain full employment, equitable income distribution, economic growth, balance in the foreign sector, reasonable cost/price stability, and above all regional balance. In the seventies protection of the environment gained urgency. Objectives here blended with a shift of emphasis towards quality of life standards, away from mere material affluence.

The upward march through the wants hierarchy is reflected in the government's long term programmes that appeared every fourth year, permanently from 1954.[1] Priorities at first mirrored the reconstruction tasks, housing and elementary consumption, and moved to sports, arts and culture in the late sixties, followed by anti-pollution measures and preferential legislation for the handicapped in the seventies. A perennial objective was the conservation of the regions. Perhaps the Norwegian political establishment, one generation from the farm, has sentimentalised more than other elites about the rural past, which would explain the nostalgic cross-party protection granted the primary occupations of the regions — farming, forestry, and fishing. The dualism between the modern and the traditional culture runs deeper and stronger in Norway than in neighbouring states in Europe. This was amply demonstrated during the anti-EEC campaign in 1972. Below we review main areas of (mostly) Labour government efforts to eliminate market mechanisms or compensate for market failures, as part of the goal of implementing Labour's conception of the welfare state, the secular equivalent of the heavenly city of antiquity.

Credit Policy

Efforts to uphold a regional and sectoral balance required channelling resources, by non-market measures, into agriculture, fishing, housing and welfare. Efforts in these fields justified the Labour government's credit policy. Two phases may be discerned.[2] In the period 1951-65 the government's credit policy relied on joint responsibility between the authorities and the private credit institutions. From 1951 the annual credit targets were fixed by talks in a high-level forum, Samarbeids-nemda (the Co-operation Board), that included representatives from the Ministry of Finance, the Bank of Norway and the Bank Inspection on the one hand, and representatives from the banks and, from 1955, the insurance companies on the other. The credit ceiling had to be set so as to allow for continued government subsidised housing and similar political priorities, but this required voluntary restraint in private lending to avoid overheating, inflation or currency devaluation. The banks co-operated in this form of corporate capitalism to prevent the worse alternative of mandatory credit legislation or even nationalisation. The system, re-negotiated every second year, worked tolerably well. In 1955 the government, bowing to credit demand pressures, raised the discount rate from 2.5 per cent to 3.5 per cent. As part of the package the private banks agreed not to raise their lending above the 1955 volume in the following two years, and also agreed to hold a fixed amount of low-yielding government bonds in their portfolios. In 1957 total lending by the state banks, thus favoured, exceeded that of the private banks. The resulting shift to low-productive credit targets may have accounted for the moderate GDP growth experienced in the late fifties.

In 1965 the new money and credit act shifted sole responsibility for the credit policy over to the authorities. Henceforth the government had discretionary power to dictate quotas for total lending by the credit institutions; additionally to set liquidity reserve requirements and command banks to place up to 60 per cent of asset growth in government bonds. By these instruments it was hoped one could curb private bank lending, control inflation and at the same time provide continued financing of the state banks. The discount rate was raised to 4.5 per cent in 1969.

A third step in state control of banking was Labour's campaign to nationalise the private banks, in practice by pushing through legislation in 1977, effective from 1 January 1978, that gave the Storting the right to appoint a majority of the members of the banks' *representantskap* (Committee of Shareholders). As these appointed the bank boards, the banks in reality had been socialised, though Labour preferred the term 'democraticised'. Robbed of responsibility and influence, the stockholders were granted the option of selling their bank shares to the government at their going market value. Some did, but there was no stampede. In practice the credit policy was not much affected, but remained subject to familiar attempts at control, including changes in the discount rate. The rate was raised to 5.5 per cent in 1974 and 6 per cent in 1976.[3] The state banks in 1978 had 42 per cent of all bank loans to industry and private persons, the commercial banks 34 per cent.[4] Moving to the aggregate level, we find that in 1978 total credit supply originated as follows: 22.3 per cent from abroad, 28 per cent from state banks, 34.4 per cent from insurance, credit associations and the bond and stock market, 7.4 per cent from the savings banks and a mere 7.9 per cent from the commercial banks.[5] The Conservative government under Kåre Willoch reversed the 1977 bank legislation in March 1982, by giving the stockholders the majority again in the banks' decisions.[6]

The credit policy was the meeting ground for several mutually irreconcilable objectives. The efforts to channel capital towards social priority goals clashed with the objective to maintain stability in prices and safeguard the external balance. However, the foreign national debt posed no problem. The funded government debt in foreign currency was 1.0 billion kr in 1950, 2.5 billion in 1965, but was brought down to 1.9 billion by 1970. Lending abroad for oil investments did not pick up till 1975; but did not at any point reach dimensions that caused embarrassment for the government in the money markets abroad. The government's foreign funded debt increased to 9.6 billion kr in 1976 and 31.5 billion at end of 1979. By then oil had immensely raised the credit rating of the government.

Summing up the experience in this sector, the fact that the state banks in recent years have far exceeded the private banks as credit suppliers testifies to the determination of Labour to gain control over credit supply. The justification for the policy takes us into the sheltered economy.

Agriculture — a Sheltered Sector

Total farm area in 1949 was 10 million decares or one million hectares, about 3 per cent of the land area. The total number of farms was 345,000, of which 132,000 were over 5 decares. Through the next twenty-five years a total of 106,000 small farms, representing 2.9 million decares, was discontinued. The population exodus implied has if any-thing accelerated over the years:

1949-59	20,228	holdings were discontinued	. . . .	538,000 decares
1959-64	18,238	" " "	. . . .	438,000 "
1964-9	33,345	" " "	. . . .	930,000 "
1969-74	34,139	" " "	. . . .	1,014,000 "
1949-74	105,950	holdings		2,920,000 decares

The reality for farming was less bleak than these figures suggest. Most of the land has been continued as farm land, assimilated into other larger holdings; besides, new land has been cleared. Indeed, so far from declining, the total agricultural area has tended to increase. In 1980 it was 9.4 million decares, up 0.6 per cent since 1974. Farms over 5 decares, still tiny family plots by any standard, went down, however, to 112,000 by 1979. The reduction occurred most extensively in out-lying areas where the average farms were smallest beforehand. In the south-eastern part of the country the average farm size in 1973 was 140-150 decares, which compares with European standards.

Owner occupation, cemented by the allodial rights, dominated as before, with 79 per cent of the farms run by the owner and his family, pertaining to 85 per cent of the agricultural area in 1969. The work force in agriculture has continued downwards. In 1973 the actual labour input was estimated at about 128,000 man-years, down 23 per cent in five years. Much of farming is part-time, with fishing as an additional occupation in the north, forestry in the east. Road construction and hydro power dams have also offered stable additional work and incomes for farmers who, like any middle class commuter, show up at construction sites on Monday mornings and return in their own cars Friday afternoons. In 1972 an average of nearly 40 per cent of the income of farm-holders stemmed from wages and salaries earned out-side agriculture.

Production and farm incomes continued to be concentrated around animal products. Of total agricultural first hand sales of 5.6 billion kroner in 1972, two thirds pertained to meat and milk products, with milk giving the largest single income (36 per cent). All the sugar, nearly all the fruits and breadgrain and half of the feedgrains were imported, much as before the war, while very little was exported apart from fur and cheese, one third of which went for export in 1973. In terms of calorific balance self-sufficiency in 1972 was about 40 per cent for agricultural products, and 52 per cent if fish is included. However, if production based on imported feedgrains is left out, the degree of self-sufficiency, excluding fish, would drop to about 30 per cent.[7]

The market for agricultural products is shot through by politics over the whole gamut of farm products. The basic document since 1952 has been the Main Agreement for Agriculture, by which the agricultural income targets, production and productivity targets and the regional policy targets are co-ordinated. The overall aims include economic, demographic and nutritional objectives. The economic objective has been to have farms large enough to provide full employment throughout the year for a skilled man and his family with an annual income on a par with average industrial wages. The production target has been to cover the domestic market of livestock products, preferably on the basis of home-grown feed. To ensure adequate supplies of milk and meat in remote areas, special incentives are provided in the form of a two-price system for concentrated feed and prices on products. The productivity targets include the raising of incomes in agriculture by means of viable farm holdings consistent with an optimal use of resources, including tourism, hunting, mountain grazing and farm land use. The regional and demographic target is to stimulate a decentralised settlement structure by means of economic incentives and transfers to rural areas, so as to hold back depopulation of the countryside and prevent over-congestion of towns.

To achieve these objectives, a general import ban is in force for products of interest to domestic agriculture. For meat and dairy products the ban, going back to 1930 in fact, is in force the year round, while it is in force in off-season periods for fruits and vegetables. Grain and flour, as will be recalled, have been subject to state monopoly trading by Statens Kornforretning (the State Grain Corporation) since 1928 and are not covered by the import ban. Equally important, subsidies for agriculture were called for, including a support for basic prices for farm products and a system of differentiated support, paid individually to producers, so as to achieve income parity for farmers irrespective of regions, types of production or size of holding.

Ever since 1952 the farm support programme has been negotiated by the two farm organisations and the central government, represented by the Department for Agriculture, and concluded for two years, subject to approval by the Storting, which has the final say on appropriations. The Main Agreement is harmonised as far as possible with the wages and tariff awards for trade union workers, and provides a clause for renegotiations on the basis of the cost of living index. About 130 support schemes are open to the farmers (1982). The programmes swelled to about 8 billion kr annually by 1980. The Storting in 1976 agreed on an income escalation deal intended to bring farmers' incomes in line with industrial wages over a four-year period. The programme, involving more farm subsidies than ever, was a remarkable victory for the farm interest organisations. By 1979 the average man-year in agriculture received about 67,000 kroner in subsidies per year, a little less than the average annual wage in industry.

With a secure income basis and cut-off from market competition, the farmers have been able to invest in new machinery and buildings at a rate that has amply compensated for the emigration of farm hands. The mechanisation and market specialisation, which also included forestry, amounted to a revolution, which also benefited the consumers. Milk yields illustrate the productivity gains: between 1950 and 1970 the annual yield per cow jumped from 1,800 to 4,300 litres.[8] According to the latest figure, the yield by 1981 had climbed to an average 5,000 litres. This is just about the highest average annual yield anywhere in the world. Meanwhile the number of milk cows dropped from 700,000 to 380,000 between 1950 and 1980. (See Figure 13.1.) Surpluses of milk products became a constant problem by 1980.

Curiously, the single most important marketing innovation originated outside the agro-monopolies. Heavy glass milk bottles were used for milk distribution between 1946-60. From 1960 the privately financed Elopak A/S, a Norwegian firm, possessing a production licence for a US-patented milk carton, revolutionised milk distribution. Risk money was provided by the Andresen family behind Tiedemann, the tobacco concern. From milk the Elopak unbreakable cartons went on to invade other market segments, yoghurt, fresh water, preserves, and even wine. After twenty years the Elopak Company sells its packing systems in 33 countries in Europe, the Middle East, the Soviet Union and North Africa. In 1981 its turnover was 1.1 billion kroner, 4 billion cartons, and included 10 subsidiary companies abroad, employing 1,100 workers.[9]

Figure 13.1: Milk Production 1949-1971

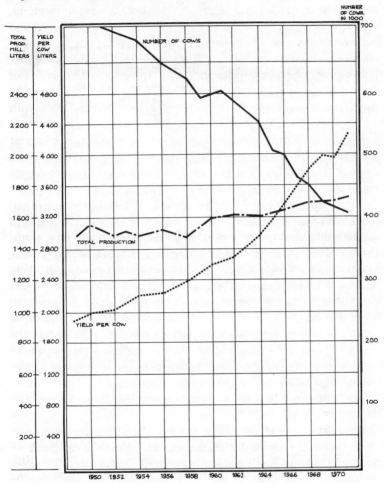

Source: *Budget Board for Agriculture*. Cited from *Norske Meieriers Landsforbund* (NML) Annual Report 1971, p. 14.

Fisheries and Depletion of Resources

The transformation in agriculture is echoed in the recent development in the fisheries: while labour inputs have declined by two thirds, the total catch has more than doubled, as a result of vastly more efficient boats, gear and equipment. The decline in labour inputs affected the part-timers more than full-timers:

	Full timers	%	Part timers	%	Total
1940	34,000	28	88,000	72	122,000
1950	26,000	26	72,000	74	98,000
1960	21,000	34	40,000	66	61,000
1970	21,000	49	22,000	51	43,000
1980	17,000	49	18,000	51	35,000

Full-timers by 1970 counted 49 per cent of the fishermen, up from 26 per cent twenty years earlier. Fishing had become a full-time occupation for professionals, one sign of which is the range of new gear and equipment that came into use. In the fifties the deck vessels installed radio and asdic, a sonar device, and these were followed by radar, telephone and other all-weather navigation wonders. The nets were made of synthetic fibres, nylon or perlon, while hemp became history. In the late fifties and sixties the trawlers, steel-decked vessels of 100 feet and over, added the 'power block', a lifting winch that revolutionised the haul-up of nets and catch. There were 161 of these 'trawlers' in 1952 and 414 in 1975. The vacuum pump came in the sixties, allowing the live fish or herring to be sucked, not hauled, through the vacuum nose directly into the cargo room in a matter of minutes. The purse seine nets got longer and deeper, which boosted the catch capacity of the bigger vessels enormously. Soon the fishermen on ocean-going 'factory fishing' trips fished in a sitting position on the bridge, turning knobs, pulling levers, worrying about overweight problems and payments on the next mortgage!

Landings soared in the fifties. Notably the winter herring fisheries showed all-time records that peaked in 1957. The total catch culminated in 1967 when the fishermen hauled up 3 million tons, after which the landings levelled out around 2.3 million. This gives Norway a fifth place among the world's top fishing nations, after Japan, the Soviet Union, China and Peru. Overfishing reduced the fish resources before 1960. The problem, a permanent one since 1960, was acute for the high quality species like salmon, trout, winter herring, cod and from 1975, mackerel. The blue-fin tuna from the Mediterranean, coming in big shoals in July and August to feed on herring along the Western coast, disappeared around 1960 with the decimation of the herring stock. Barred by resource constraints in these directions, the trawlers instead cast their nylon purse seine nets after lower-quality fish, capelin and Norway pout, which later accounted for the bulk of the landings. Their monopoly trading company 'Norsildmel' was set up in 1964 as a co-operative for herring oil and herring meal producers (50 per cent) and the fishermen's organisations (50 per cent), with export sales of 1.0 billion kroner in 1978. 'Norsildmel' ranked third among trading companies that year.[10] Exports represent 95 per cent of total landings. A mere 2.4 per cent is for fresh consumption; three quarters goes into meal and oil, less than one per cent into canning, 10.5 per cent into freezing, and 6.6 per cent into salting. Aquaculture in the seventies has opened new vistas for fishing in the future.

In the national economy the fisheries represented 1.3 per cent of GNP in 1968, 1.4 per cent in 1974 and a mere 0.9 per cent in 1978. The 17,000 full-timers represented 0.9 per cent of the 1975 labour force of 1.8 million. Their political influence remains, however, out of proportion to their economic significance. The anomaly is rooted in history, in the all-party concern to maintain the fishing communities in the north, and stems also from the widespread localisation of the fishing fleet and of the processing and reception concerns scattered along the coast from Egersund in the south to Vadsø in the north. Fishing is part of politics in all the coastal counties. Besides, legislation in the 1930s gave the fishermen's organisation, Norges Fiskarlag, a monopoly over all first hand sales of fish and shellfish through its 13 legally protected co-operative sales organisations. A special Fishery Ministry was established 1 July 1946, the first of its kind anywhere, headed by Reidar Carlsen (b. 1908), a colourful, unconventional politician from the north. Through these corporative channels the fishermen, like the farmers through theirs, exert a direct influence on governmental fishing policies, including the negotiations for state subsidies. The support continued along lines staked out in the 1930s, and gradually expanded. An agreement concluded in 1964 between the government and the fishermen's association Norges Fiskarlag, patterned on the farmers' agreement, put the support programme on a permanent footing and linked it with the aims of the regional policies.

Support for fisheries is rendered in three fields, for investment, processing and operations. Though no regular support scheme for financing the construction of fishing vessels exists, the State Fishery Bank of 1920, with funds from the government, offers first mortgage loans up to 60 per cent of the total investment, for a maximum period of 15 years at an interest rate (7.5 per cent) below the market rate (in 1979).[11] A special government fund for regional development, Distriktenes Utbyggingsfond, was established in 1961, to replace the earlier development programme of the 1952 North Norway Plan. Its director

(1961-78) was Reidar Carlsen. The Regional Development Fund also offered credits for fishing vessels till 1975 when this was discontinued. Instead the fund provided assistance on easy terms for fish-freezing projects and other processing plants, mostly for rationalisation and modernisation of existing plants and for pioneering new products. The fund also offers guarantees for loans granted by private credit institutions.

More important to the fishermen, and the taxpayers, are the subsidies to support landing prices of certain species of fish. The price subsidy is given to the sales organisation which administers the grants. Price subsidies amounted to 15 per cent of first hand landing value in 1960, increasing to 21 per cent in 1968.[12] Fishing gear purchase was subsidised, so was bait. Support for experimental work in quality and efficiency improvements is also channelled through the Fishery Directorate, Bergen (est. 1900) and its off-shoot the State Ocean Research Institute, Bergen, established 1949.

Most important of all, the government through the fishery agreement guarantees a minimum weekly income for fishermen. The aim is to secure a minimum income in case the fishing fails. If the income falls below this amount during the season, the difference is covered by the guarantee. To ease marketing difficulties in Nigeria for the stock fish industry in 1977, the government through the Bank of Norway granted loans of 150 million kroner to stockpile the products and pay for alternative utilisation of catches. The fishermen in many ways are state pensioners. At any rate by the late seventies government subsidies amounted to just under an average annual wage in industry. The subsidies received by the farmers were of similar magnitude.

Again, with security of incomes regardless of what happens to the fish, and cut off from the market, the fishermen need not stay in tune with trends in consumption abroad; nor have marketing and the export side been sufficiently heeded. The mentality of the hunter collided with the modern world in 1962 when Freia Ltd, a Norwegian chocolate concern, sold its filleting plant 'Findus' at Hammerfest to the Swiss multinational Nestlé. Unwilling to shoulder the costs of building up an international marketing organisation, Freia withdrew to its chocolate, while Nestlé already owned an international sales network. Still, the local fishermen, suspicious of far-away foreigners and foreign capital, staged a protest strike against the sale. Their action received national backing. On 1 January 1963, for the first time in history, 30,000 vessels from Lindesnes to North Cape refused to go out. After seven days and promises of increased subsidies, state guarantees and other support measures, the fishermen's national organisation called off the strike, whereupon the Gerhardsen government, in compliance with the concession laws, sanctioned the Freia-Nestlé transaction. This was a forewarning of the battle staged in 1972 between the modernists and the traditionalists, and involving Norway's membership in EEC.

A Dualistic Society

Regional Development

Structural change implied urbanisation. Just after the war 50 per cent of the population lived in towns or densely populated areas. The urban share climbed to 66 per cent in 1970 and 70 per cent in November 1980. The migrations have threatened to depopulate the regions, particularly the sparsely populated North. Disparities in income levels (see Figure 13.2) and income opportunities were believed to be the main factors behind migration. Accordingly, regional policies have aimed at compensating for income gaps, in the main by subsidising capital and labour on the periphery, and more recently, by placing restrictions on the free establishment of business in urban areas. National and regional policies are here combined, though in the national budget the regional bias crops up in diverse places, in special appropriations for regional infrastructure investments, communications, electricity, housing, education, welfare, industry, fishing and agriculture. The seventies was the decade of environmental protection, of anti-pollution and the countercultures. One sign was the establishment of a separate ministry, the Ministry of Environment, in May 1972, which co-ordinated aims, means and policies. The instruments used to achieve the decentralisation goals are as follows:

Regional Development Fund 1961.[13] Incorporating earlier schemes the RDF, under its first director Reidar Carlsen, swelled to become 'the main special body in charge of implementing the Government's regional policy'. It obtained nearly all its funds from the government in the first years, but from 1969 the tax law allowed private taxpayers to deduct from their income returns funds invested in certified RDF projects. The aim was to channel capital into the districts, if necessary at the expense of market outlets. This loophole for tax avoidance remained generally unknown till the late 1970s. Meanwhile, money was provided from the national budget. Acting as top financing credit institution, RDF offered easy loans, guarantees, investment grants up to 35 per cent and other aid for industrial or commercial ventures in regions defined as having a weak or narrow economic base. During the 1961-77 period RDF paid out

Figure No. 13.2: Regional Pattern of Income and Employment
Employment Change by Sector and County 1961-1970, Annual Rate
and Relative Income Level by County

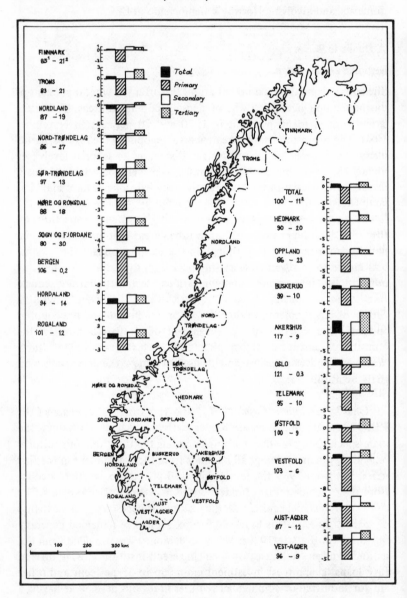

1 Index for assessed taxable income *per capita* (1968) compared with the
national average equal to 100.
2 Primary industries' share of total employment (1970)
Source: *OECD Economic Surveys Norway 1972*, p. 13.

a total of 7.7 billion kroner, of which 4.7 million were loans, 1.1 billion guarantees and 1.9 billion grants, to a total of 7,178 projects. According to region, 34 per cent went to North Norway, 27 per cent to the West coast, 21 per cent to the East, 13 per cent to Trøndelag and 5 per cent to the South coast.

SIVA – The State Industrial Estates Corporation. This state-funded corporation was established in January 1968 with head offices in Trondheim, to develop and lease industrial floor space in chosen areas as part of a policy of decentralised growth and development. After assessing locations in regard to labour, communications, building sites, education, the health service, etc., SIVA by 1978 had erected and leased 14 industrial estates, in places like Kongsvinger, Tynset, Førde in Sunnfjord, Kleivi in Hallingdal, Verdal, Namsos, Fauske, Ballangen and Alta in Troms. The terms are favourable in order to attract private businesses.

Legislation. Other measures of regional policy include a special Building and Planning Act of 18 June 1965. This provided the legal basis for regional planning formulated by counties and municipalities within their areas. The goal is a general plan for each of the country's 449 municipalities. By 1978 seventeen counties had forwarded plans to the Environment Ministry for approval. In June 1971 the Storting approved of a scheme for regional transport subsidies to particular districts, mostly the northern and west-coast counties, where long transportation distances place producers at a competitive disadvantage. The subsidies are graded according to need, highest priority being given to the northernmost parts. By 1980 the subsidies had swelled to 2.2 billion kr. Milk price subsidies are differentiated on similar considerations. Legislation passed in 1973, and superseded by a permanent Establishment Control Act 1977, introduced a restrictive licensing system for industrial establishments. Under this scheme the authorities' approval is required for the construction, extension or reconstruction of a building or plant requiring a work input of above 100 man-years, a minimum labour force of 100 workers, or where construction costs exceed 25 million kr. The act is intended to be applicable to all types of economic activities.

The above sketch, far from exhaustive, suggests the range of instruments available both for national and specifically regional policies.[14]

A 'Red – Green' Alliance defeats EEC-Membership 1972

The question of joining the EEC came on the agenda in 1961 when Britain, the biggest EFTA partner, applied; it resurfaced briefly in 1967, again in the wake of Britain's second application for EEC membership, and came to a traumatic head 1970-2. The Nordic alternative was again aired 1969-70, but again dismissed. Along with Great Britain, Ireland and Denmark, Norway in July 1970 sent a formal application for EEC membership. The EEC negotiations were complete by January 1972. Before making its decision the Storting and the government had promised a national advisory referendum. When the results of the referendum, held 24th – 25th September 1972, were in, a majority of 53.5 per cent was found to have voted no to membership. The turnout was 78 per cent. Although consultative, the referendum was felt binding on the course of action to be taken by the government. The membership issue was shelved, and Labour premier Trygve Bratteli resigned. He had formed a Labour government when the coalition government of Per Borten of the Center Party broke up the year before.

Britain, Ireland and Denmark joined the EEC in 1972, while Norway negotiated an EEC trade agreement in 1973, which was quite generous in the circumstances. The negotiations were shouldered by a caretaker government of Lars Korvald, from the Christian Democrats. By 1982 it would appear in retrospect that Norway, small enough to get away with it, obtained the advantages of EEC membership without joining, while retaining the advantages of sovereignty.[15] The latter pertained especially to the extension of the offshore fishing limit, the introduction of the trawling-free zone in the northern waters in January 1975, and the establishment of an economic zone of 200 miles in 1976, effective from 1 January 1977

The contrary outcome in Norway came as a surprise both to the country and to Europe. How could the pro-marketeers fail to carry the country into the EEC? Pro-marketeers represented 86 per cent of the workforce, 95 per cent of GNP, and the country's political, bureaucratic and economic elite. They had the support of Labour (74) and the Conservative Party (29), a solid majority in a Storting of 150 representatives, even if some Labour representatives were to bolt to the no side. They argued, as they had since 1961, that EEC and NATO would serve peace and stability by cementing military and economic ties between the United States and Europe. In view of its large foreign trade, Norway could hardly afford to stay out if the other EFTA partners joined.

The anti-marketeers counted essentially the farmers and fishermen, 5 per cent of GNP and 14 per cent of the work force. They controlled the Center Party (20), one half of the divided and crumbling Liberal Party (13), some of the Christian Democrats and some of Labour. The Communists and the Socialist People's Party were not represented in the Storting 1969-73. Anti-marketeers were in command, however, of the national interest and sales organisations of farmers and fishermen, notably the Norske Melkeprodusenters Landsforbund (the Norwegian Milk Manufacturers' Federation) (NML). Chairman of the organisation, Hans Borgen, was also founder of the 'People's Movement against Norwegian Membership in the EEC'. This was a campaign organisation created in May 1971, with 5 million kroner in campaign money handed over by the NML, the milk farmers' federation. The anti-marketeers launched a single-issue, extra-parliamentary, cross-party campaign. With skilful slogans they argued for national sovereignty and the preservation of the rural way of life and condemned capitalism in its EEC version.

The vote results expectedly showed that in towns an average 56.2 per cent voted yes. In the country 62 per cent voted no, but the percentage was over 71 in the three northern counties where King Fish ruled. The traditional conflict cleavages between the political parties vapourised for a moment, with non-socialist farmers, Christians and rural traditionalists cuddling up to outspoken anti-capitalist, anti-Christian, urban socialists on the one hand, and Labour chiefs appearing arm in arm with Conservative politicians on the other.

As for explanations, Edvard Bull finds that anti-capitalism was the common rallying point.[16] The political scientists, following in the footsteps of Steinar Rokkan, see the outcome in the light of six conflict dimensions. They distinguish between territorial, cultural, moral, religious, economic and class lines. The EEC issue lit up tempers along all dimensions. Taking account of them all is an explanation in terms of a 'red-green' alliance between socialist radicals in towns and the primary interests on the rural periphery, represented by farmers and fishermen.[17] This is also the explanation offered by foreign observers.[18]

The Welfare State

The welfare state in the post-war era manifested itself in three areas in particular, housing, education and programmes for social security. Behind programmes in these fields there was a majority till the seventies, hence their rapid expansion. If one relates public expenditure growth to growth of GDP one may gauge the elasticity of demand for public expenditure. An OECD study from 1978 for twenty of its members shows that the elasticity, measured in current prices, was greater than one for all the countries studied. In the years 1960-76 the unweighted average was 1.21, for Norway 1.25, for Sweden topping the list, 1.38.[19] Belgium, Denmark, Ireland, Australia and the Netherlands also exceeded the Norwegian figure. This suggests the universality of the social demands released during rapid change in the present high-income countries. The demand explanation for the public-sector growth would be that as long as enough voters felt they received a net gain over the taxes they paid themselves, public sector expenditure continued to grow. The demand theory rivals with a supply theory. According to one school of thought the growth of public sector expenditures is due to the influence of high-status pressure groups who, being in a position to define need, succeed surreptitiously through the corporative channel in foisting new public services upon the voters, while creating new high-salaried jobs for themselves.

Education

In 1948 the Storting established a state loan fund, Statens Lånekasse, that offered loans to students without conventional collateral in the form of personal security or mortgage. Based at first on a means test, the loan scheme was gradually extended to new age and income groups. It paved the way for a massive expansion of education for new social groups whose upward horizon so far had been blocked by poverty and lack of motivation. Legislation in 1954 and 1969 extended compulsory basic training to 9 years. About 700,000 persons, 18 per cent of the population, were in school in the seventies. Estimates on the returns of education to the individual over a lifetime have also been made on the basis of Norwegian material.[20] Interpretation of findings is difficult as only economic returns are included, which precludes any definitive statement either on the welfare aspect or the efficiency gains to be harvested from education now and in the future by the individual and society. In the 1962-74 period OECD countries spent on average 3.2 per cent of the their GDP on education, Norway spent 4.1 per cent, or 28 per cent more. Only Finland spent more than Norway (4.8 per cent).[21]

Housing

From any viewpoint housing investments, taking between 13 and 18 per cent of total investment 1950-80,[22] deserve our attention. Here we underline their stabilising effect and the degree to which they have been controlled by the authorities. Of a total 567,000 flats built 1946-64, 57 per cent were financed by the government housing bank, Statens Husbank, established in 1946.[23] The authorities announced that dwelling costs should not exceed 20 per cent of annual wages of industrial workers. The rule was repeated in the bank's annual report as late as 1977.[24] Dimensions of credits, loans, floor-space, and rate of interest were scaled accordingly. Average floor space for Husbank-flats was 68m^2 in 1957, 71m^2 in 1967 and 81.1m^2 in 1977.[25]

Demand exceeded supply, hence queues were normal, which fostered a mentality of paternalism and standard type architecture. Both blighted town landscapes for more than a generation. Families with children were preferred; singles, less socially useful, were cold-shouldered till the late sixties. Shortages dictated the building of blocks, supposed to be cheaper, rather than single bungalows or even semi-detached homes in urban areas. Olav Selvaag, a building enthusiast, in vain demonstrated that the latter were cheaper. Pennypinching bureaucrats in charge of planning, building sites, building rights and credits, could not quite see poor folk in bungalows. Bowing to their socialist heritage, Labour premiers like Einar Gerhardsen, Trygve Bratteli, and Odvar Nordli, have always lived in blocks of flats in the capital. By contrast single houses were the rule in the rural areas. In 1976, 41 per cent of Husbank-financed dwellings were single homes.[26]

First mortgages at the state housing bank were initially 2.5 per cent for up to 50 years. By 1977 the average had risen to 5.57 per cent at a time when car loan interest rates averaged 12 per cent.[27] The subsidy element persisted, in other words, and so did the queues. In 1978 when the state housing bank financed 80 per cent of all new flats and homes, the original justification, social housing, had long since disappeared. Only the secondary one, that of maintaining an obsolete bureaucracy, remained, or seemed to remain. Adding to queuing were the countrywide price and rent controls for flats and dwellings, upheld by Labour in the name of solidarity right up till the 1981 election, thirty-six years after the war. Since market values exceeded the licensed assessed price, a black market for co-operative flats persisted till the new Conservative government under Kåre Willoch, from 1981, took steps to decontrol the housing market the following year.

Social Security

The postwar income maintenance and health programmes more than anything embody the idea of welfare and the solidarity ideals of old: to each according to need, from each according to ability. Among the new main developments of the social security net after the war, we note in 1946 the introduction of child allowances, universal disability pensions 1960, rehabilitation and invalidity pensions 1961, survivors' and maternal benefits 1965, and the people's pension or National Insurance 1967. The latter, incorporating all the existing programmes under one umbrella, was a major event in ensuring everyone in need against unforeseen loss of income. Financing has followed along prewar lines, with the majority of the programmes paid, part way, not fully like ordinary insurance premiums, by the employees, the employers and the government into a common fund. One portion continues as straightforward social assistance. The present National Insurance includes five, mostly premium-paid schemes:

- Health
- Occupational injuries and workers' protection
- Unemployment
- Old age, disability
- Family welfare

Expenditures in these fields were 7.2 per cent of net domestic product in 1948, 17 per cent in 1970 and 30.5 per cent in 1977.[28] In 1981 old age pensioners over 67 years numbered 531,000, the total number of pension recipients under the National Insurance 822,000, respectively 13 per cent and 20 per cent of a total population of 4 million.[29] With a workforce of 1.9 million there is now a pensioner for every 2.3 workers. In an OECD context there is little remarkable about the Norwegian figures, for in 1974 public health expenditure in 24 OECD countries averaged 4.5 per cent of GDP, against 5.3 per cent in Norway. Five countries exceeded the Norwegian figure.[30]

Cost Explosion in Health Care

There was at first ample justification for public spending on social security. For one thing, Labour inherited the commitment to remove the stigma of poverty from its voters and from society in general. That goal was reached by most standards in the post-1945 period. Next, health expenditures tended to go up with changes in the age structure, with urbanisation and changes in attitudes. Those over 65 years, for instance, represented 8.7 per cent of total population in 1930, but 14.2 per cent in 1980. The increasing percentage of elderly tends to expand public expenditures in health. Moreover, relatives, living in cramped town flats, were unable to provide care for older relatives to the same extent as in rural environments. Unmarried, living-in daughters disappeared into the work force. An increasing unwillingness among younger folk to provide home care for the older generation was another factor that pushed costs upwards. Then there is the issue of the validity of yardsticks for assessing need. The ideal one is the subjective satisfaction of the individual seeking help.

Factors like those mentioned would seem to push up costs, regardless of opinion on the marginal value of continued investments in publicly paid health programmes. The choice of yardsticks is not without consequence. If life expectancy is used, the value of investing more money in health would appear doubtful. Life expectancy for men at birth was 71 years in 1951/5, 71 years in 1961/5 and 72.3 years in 1979/80. For females the figure was five to six years higher. That is, the average life expectancy for men has stayed pretty constant in the last quarter century, despite the steady increase in public expenditures, facilities and personnel in the health sector. Society paid more for getting the same. The seventies saw a particularly heavy expansion, but 56 per cent of the increase went to compensate for inflation, about 20 per cent simply improved the pay and working situation for health personnel and a mere 24 per cent represented increased volume and standard of services that benefited patients.[31]

Indeed, a growing concern is that health programmes are not so much demand-induced as supply-induced. Health and welfare maintenance, measured in man-years, was the source of livelihood for 82,000 employees in 1969; by 1980 for 161,000; and new building apart, a gross 2.7 billion kroner was spent in the former, 16.5 billion in the latter year.[32] No other sector bears comparison. Relevant evidence is provided by statistics on employment trends and government expenditures. Let us consider them in turn. Table 13.1 offers figures for man-years by sector in the seventies. Health care personnel had an estimated 6 per cent total man-years in 1969, but 12 per cent in 1980, fifty per cent more than total labour inputs in agriculture.

In the seventies employment in local government services went up by 74 per cent, in education and research by 47 per cent, but it almost doubled in health care (96 per cent). In the eyes of inside observers health care has been transformed into a pressure group interest, in which expenditure no longer bears a clear relation to its primary justification.

Table 13.1: Employment by Sector 1969-1980 in 1,000 Man-years

	1969	1975	1980	% change 1969-1980
Agriculture	166	117	108	− 35
Forestry	13	10	9	− 31
Fishing	30	21	21	− 29
Mining*	9	11	12	+ 33
Industry	371	389	373	+ 0.5
Trade, wholesale & retail	201	210	230	+ 14
Education & research	77	92	106	+ 47
Health & welfare	82	119	161	+ 96
Central govt. services	106	117	133	+ 25
Local govt. services	137	190	238	+ 74
Total man-years	1285	1289	1348	+ 5

*Incl. gas and petroleum extraction.
Source: *National Accounts 1969-1980*, NOS B 222, Oslo, 1981

Income Redistribution

Paying for the welfare state involved steeply progressive personal taxes, creeping inflation that threatened to pass out of control after 1973, a swelling bureaucracy and the erosion of incentives to work. Absenteeism received an initial strong boost when trade union members from 1978 could absent themselves from their job with full pay for three days six times a year. By the mid-seventies non-active members of the workforce received benefits that almost equalled the take home pay of those working. On less than precise evidence, income equality, roughly speaking, appears to have become a practical reality.[33] The subject is surrounded by strong value judgements, and they persist because the right evidence, relevant to an assessment of all the determinants of income distribution, is never assembled. Lack of specification adds to the confusion: the distribution of incomes at any given moment is not necessarily the same as the distribution of life incomes over time. Again, the income distribution for individuals may not coincide with that of households.

Ambiguities adhere also to the term 'income'. Incomes in the market from work and capital holdings used to be sufficient evidence for a judgement on the income distribution. Recent work, however, has also drawn attention to the effects of non-market forms of income, and the effects arising from redistribution achieved through taxes, subsidies and transfers, including payments for education and infrastructure, which also have strong bearing on the income distribution. Besides, income, whether measured in the above narrow or wider sense, is not necessarily identical with welfare. Besides, who defines welfare? In this conceptual morass, a recent Norwegian study on income distribution despairs of hard answers, mainly for lack of reliable evidence of non-market incomes.[34] When this much is said, one is left with impressionistic evidence, which suggests that after taxes and including subsidies and transfers, a rough equality of material incomes has been achieved. In a situation when 512,000, a quarter of the total number of personal taxpayers in 1979, had a marginal tax of 54.9 per cent and over, it is hard to see how much further it is possible to use the income tax as an instrument for further income equality.[35] The tax leviathan continued to make inroads on the private sector in the seventies. Figures in Table 13.2 offer evidence on how much.

Table 13.2: Total Taxes and Transfers by Category 1969-1981. Million kroner in current prices and in %

	1969	1970	1975	1980	1981	% change 1969-81
Total taxes	28,532	32,889	82,342	143,472	159,221	458
Direct taxes	10,654	10,591.	29,464	61,191	65,277	513
Social security taxes	6,704	7,730	21,866	34,176	38,946	481
Indirect taxes	11,174	14,568	31,012	48,105	54,998	392
Transfer, total	11,335	13,902	35,303	61,056	68,940	508
of which social						
security	6,685	8,956	20,904	35,836	41,617	523
other consumer						
benefits	1,098	828	2,775	5,717	6,211	466
subsidies	3,552	4,118	11,624	19,503	21,112	494
In % of gross domestic product						
Total taxes	41.1	41.1	48.2	50.6	48.5	
Direct taxes	15.3	13.3	17.3	21.6	19.9	
Social security taxes	9.7	9.7	12.8	12.1	11.9	
Indirect taxes	16.1	18.2	18.2	17.0	16.8	
Transfers, total	16.3	17.4	20.7	21.5	21.0	
social security	9.6	11.2	12.2	12.6	12.7	
other consumer						
benefits	1.6	1.0	1.6	2.0	1.9	
subsidies	5.1	5.2	6.8	6.9	6.4	

Source: *Skatter og overføringer til private*. Rapporter fra Statistisk Sentralbyrå 82/19, Oslo, 1982, Tables 1 and 2. (Taxes and Transfers to Private Individuals.)

During 1969-81 total taxes (in current kroner) increased four and a half times, against 513 per cent for direct taxes and 392 per cent for indirect taxes. Relative to gross domestic product total taxes increased from 41 per cent in 1969 to 50.6 per cent by 1980. The following year saw a drop to 48.5 per cent. Incidentally, Table 13.2 shows that payments under social security exceeded taxes paid into the social security funds. As a result the funds by 1980 had been emptied. The pretence that nationl insurance payments referred to real insurance, however, was upheld; the fraud might otherwise create a howl among the voters, some of whom have paid their dues during thirty years.

Inflation

The vast machinery of redistributing other people's incomes meant *inter alia* that the number of public servants went up from 243,000 man-years to 371,000 during 1969-80 (Table 13.1). This 52 per cent increase over a decade implied a concomitant increase in low-productive jobs. Maintaining existing jobs, regardless of their economic justification, became a fixation, which helped fan inflation. Inflation averaged, as noted, 4.3 per cent per year 1950-70, but jumped to 9.8 per cent as yearly average 1975-80. The depreciation of the currency, the krone, is best expressed by using the cost of living index as deflator. With 1950 equal to 100, the value of the krone was as follows:

    1950 = 100 øre
    1955 = 74 "
    1960 = 64 "
    1970 = 41 "
    1980 = 19 "

Till 1970, after twenty years, the value had gone down three fifths, by 1980 just over four fifths. Inflation was cemented into an independent force in the form of a general expectation of continued inflation. With the rates in the income tax schedule remaining fixed, taxes tended to increase automatically.

Hitting back, the taxpayers invented the 'black economy' as a subterfuge. According to recent estimates based on the currency method, the 'black economy' by 1980 may have reached an order of magnitude of 10 per cent of gross domestic product in Norway and 13 per cent in Sweden.[36] Excessive redistribution has its price; the

retreat of taxpayers into the hidden economy is at the same time a protest against a law that is no longer felt to be binding, because it is no
longer just.

Wages and Income Policies

And yet, Atlas has not shrugged, perhaps because the working people
have also benefited. Paid holidays were increased to three weeks in 1947,
four weeks in 1964 and five weeks for workers over 60 years in 1980.
The average working week of 48 hours, dating back to 1919, was cut by
degrees after 1945 to 42½ hours by March 1959 for shift workers,
in 1969 for all. From 1971 the farmers benefited from the introduction
of a farmers' vacation scheme, giving eligible farmers a 12 day paid vacation from the farm. Miners already had a 40 hour week by 1950, continuous shift workers from 1972, and during 1975-7 the working week was
cut to 40 hours for all manufacturing industries. By the mid-sixties
industrial workers had Saturdays off. They were soon followed by
other groups in the early seventies.

Using the national accounts figures to gauge their gains, we find that
between 1969 and 1975 the average *per capita* GNP growth was 3.3 per
cent yearly (in 1970 prices), and 3.7 per cent yearly in the following
period 1975-81 (in 1975 prices).[37] As for the Norwegian incomes
policy, the trade unions arranged for central tariff agreements in every
year 1963-74 and again 1976-80. The alternative was free collective
bargaining. Central-bargain deals tended to reduce strikes. Once the
strongest trade unions of LO, the iron and metal workers, had arrived
at a satisfactory deal for the following two years, the others fell in
behind, farmers, fishermen and public-sector servants, bowing to what
LO leaders called the solidarity principle. At a time of high wage drift at
the local level, the pacesetting unions could declare solidarity at very
little expense to their members, but they did help raise the low-wage
industry workers. To speed up matters, a special expert committee was
set up with members from both sides to prepare statistics acceptable to
both parties. Another innovation was the 'Kleppe-packages' in the seventies, which involved income tax reductions or government subsidies to
help sell the pay package negotiated centrally. Strikes were kept low, but
inflation was not braked.

How much Affluence?

The mid-seventies saw widespread signs of affluence in the form of suburban living, private cars, two for many families, holiday trips to the Canary Islands and the Mediterranean beaches, seminars at mountain hotels, holiday houses on the mountainside and on the coast. According to one investigation 61 per cent of people between 15 and 64 years went on holiday in 1970, against 74 per cent in 1974 and 77 per cent in 1978.[38] An increasing number went abroad. A more debatable, but equally ubiquitous sign of affluence was the rising divorce rate: by 1978 every third marriage in Oslo was headed for a divorce. Foreign tourists, notably the English, came in reduced numbers; the Norwegian prices were too high. But the international recession and the crushing weight of income redistribution soon caught up with the wage earners. As is clear from Table 13.3, there have been no real income gains for wage earners in the last seven years if the national average figures are used, but of course, average figures hide the most interesting things, the gains for holiday-making farmers and the health sector workers, the decline for other public sector servants, absolutely, and relative to employees in the private sector.

Table 13.3: Average Wages in Cash and Real Wages per Man-year 1976-1981*

	1976	1977	1978	1979	1980	1981
			kroner			
Wages in cash	59 977	66 000	71 477	74 092	81 471	91 198
			1979 = 100			
Consumer price index	80.9	88.2	95.4	100.0	110.9	126.0
Deflated index of wages	100	101	101	100	99	98

*Average wages per manyear are computed as the ratio between the wage figures in the national accounts and the estimated number of man-years. Real wages is the wages in cash deflated with the consumer price index.
Source: *Wage Statistics 1981*, NOS 8306, CBS, Oslo, 1982. Table 2.

We noted above that real GNP *per capita* grew by a yearly 3.7 per cent between 1975-81. Yet Table 13.3 suggests that real wages paid out to members of the workforce remained more or less static in those years. There is no paradox. The GNP figure above referred to the whole population, the wages figure in Table 13.3 to the workforce alone. Moreover, the former figure covers investments, social security taxes, capital depreciation, government borrowing to balance the budget etc, while the wages figure below refers to the average cash wages paid out to employees. This offers an illustration of the dimensions of the income redistribution going on in the name of the welfare state (Table 13.3).

How much do the Norwegian per *capita* figures amount to in a comparative setting? According to *The Economist* Norway by 1970 had reached ninth place in the world league table of wealthy nations.[39] In 1982 it ranked Norway third on the same table.[40] This brings us to oil, the main factor for the continued buoyancy of the Norwegian economy in recent years.

Oil – the New Growth Sector in the 1970s

Neither Britain nor Norway in the 1950s suspected the existence of oil or gas on their continental shelf. At the 1958 Geneva Conference on the rights of the sea, for instance, the Norwegian delegates argued against assigning sovereignty over the sea to the coastal states. Their view was defeated. Norway was saddled with sovereignty over waters she had not asked for. Yet the Oklahoma-based Phillips Petroleum Company in 1962 approached the Norwegian government for permission to start exploration on the Norwegian shelf.

At a time when Trygve Lie campaigned abroad for foreign capital investments in Norway, Phillips asked for exclusive rights of exploration, drilling and production. No answer could be given. There was no offshore boundary. Following Britain, Norway in May 1963 proclaimed sovereignty over the continental shelf in respect of exploration for and exploitation of natural resources. In accordance with the Geneva Convention of 1958 her soverignty extended to the median line relative to other countries. Details were settled in 1965 with Britain and Denmark and with Sweden in 1968, but so far there has been deadlock in the negotiations with the Soviet Union.

BP and Mobil in 1964 obtained exploration concessions from the British government to start looking for gas, and the following year the Norwegian government licensed off the first round of blocks on the Norwegian shelf. Nobody thought much of it, and the government was in no hurry. But 32 holes and 750 million kroner later Phillips in December 1968 discovered gas condensate and later oil in the Cod field, which became part of the later Ekofisk. This was the beginning of the oil bonanza. By the end of 1974 altogether 22 discoveries had been made in the Norwegian sector, among them Ekofisk in 1969,Valhall 1969, Tor and Vest-Ekofisk 1970, Frigg 1970, Heimdal 1972, and Statfjord 1974, blocks 33/9 and 33/12. Then followed the Norwegian part of Murchison 1975, the huge Troll gas field 1979, stretching over four blocks 31/2, 31/3, 31/5 and 31/6, Flathead 31/2 in the same year, and Gullfaks 1981 in the Gold block 34/10, so-called because all prior seismic indicators suggested the existence of oil and gas in the block (Figure 13.3.)

By this time oil had in many ways been turned into a state industry.[41] The first concessions, carrying state participation, were negotiated in 1969. A state-owned oil company, Statoil, was organised 14 June 1972 to manage the state interests in respect of oil exploration, transport, distilling, marketing and the petrochemical industry at home and abroad. It was a fledgling giant. An Oil Directorate was organised at the same time to look after security and technical standards. In 1978 the Oil and Energy Department was established, in recognition of the growing importance of energy and energy problems in the nation's affairs. This was at the time when OPEC shocked the world by setting up a world cartel of oil-producing countries and raising the price of oil from $3.01 in October 1973 to $11.65 in December that year.

The political instability of the Middle East, while threatening oil supplies to the West, increased the attractiveness of the North Sea oil fields, located near markets and characterised by a stable political climate. The higher oil prices made fields feasible which at a lower oil price had been ruled out. Norway now embarked on a course that aimed at maximising the government's gain in taxes and duties. At the same time, Labour turned Statoil, the state company, into a virtual monopoly company among the Norwegian private oil companies that had mushroomed around 1970-2. In the Norwegian offshore sector Statoil was ensured a major interest in all new rounds of licences, varying between 50 and 75 per cent. Apart from Norsk Hydro and Saga, the others were barred from participation. State capitalism was the name of the game. So it was elsewhere: in 1976, 40 out of 100 leading industrial concerns in 16 OECD countries had strong state participation.[42]

As OPEC continued to drive up the oil price to $39-40 per barrel by 1978, the Norwegian government, beginning in 1975, revised existing contracts with the oil companies in order to trim the collossal and, in the government's view, unjustified excess incomes that now accrued to the oil companies. In June 1975 the maximum tax ceiling was first

Figure 13.3: Oil and Gas Fields in the North Sea 1980

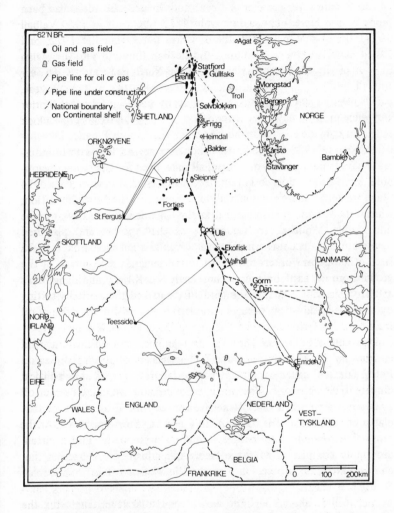

set at 90 per cent of net income, but this was hastily scaled down to 83 per cent. The taxes at present vary from company to company, depending on their opportunities for expenditure deductions, but the ceiling is 83 per cent in any case. Taxes paid by the oil companies include a 23 per cent municipal tax (collected by the state), a 27.8 per cent state tax, a 35 per cent petroleum revenue tax, a 0.7 per cent investment duty, and in addition a share of the oil, called a royalty, that the companies hand over to the state. For blocks leased before

1972 the royalty was 10 per cent of gross production; for subsequent blocks it varies between 8 per cent and 16 per cent, depending on production volume. For gas the royalty is 12.5 per cent.

This looks draconic. Still, the idea was not to tax the companies out of existence but to harmonise the greed of the state with the desire to protect the commercial viability of the North Sea activity. To this end all production expenditures are deductible, that is, the oil companies pay the state and municipal company taxes out of net incomes, and each project may be written off over six years from production start. Though the companies howled when the Labour Finance Minister Per Kleppe in 1975 cut down their bonanza profits, they continued to make good money. But of course, all incentives for the companies to hold down production costs vanished. A cost escalation set in after 1975 that threatened the economic viability of many of the North Sea fields, which but for the continued rise in the oil price, would have proved unworkable. Another consequence was that the oil and platform workers rose to become a much envied high-salaried elite, which stimulated other union workers to raise their pay demands.

Offshore oil exploitation in the North Sea is risky and dangerous, and any accident contains the seed of catastrophe. In April 1977 an uncontrolled blow-out occurred on the Bravo-platform on Ekofisk, caused by human rather than technical failure. Oil spills spread over a considerable area; worse, the existing equipment for dealing with the disaster failed. The famous American specialist in capping oil wells, Red Adair, was called in, and after three failures, succeeded in bringing the fire under control.[43] The worst accident happened in the evening of 27 March 1980 when one of the five legs of the 'Alexander Kielland' platform on Ekofisk was torn off. In a howling hurricane the platform capsised, drowning 123 people. Only 89 were saved in the worst disaster in the history of the offshore oil industry.[44] Altogether 209 people have died in accidents in the Norwegian offshore oil sector during 1967-81.

But if the risks are high, so are the potential gains. The estimates of proven recoverable oil and gas reserves have been revised time and again, and in any case, since future oil prices are unknown, such estimates cannot be more than indications. In 1982 the Oil Directorate expects the total extractable reserves south of the 62nd parallel to be of the order of 5 billion toe, which with a yearly production of say 50 million toe, will last one hundred years. But the continental shelf north of the 62nd parallel is eight times larger, and is almost certain to contain oil and gas reserves.[45] Against a background of such perspectives, it seemed clear that oil would be part of Norway's economy for at least two or three future generations. Few would criticise the government's attempts to use oil as a lever for increasing future-oriented skills and technological knowledge. One debated move was to bring the old concession law to bear on the oil companies operating in the Norwegian sector, by making future licences dependent on the degree to which the companies used Norwegian workers and services, provided they were competitive in price and time.

Another debatable move was to make entry of foreign companies into the Norwegian sector dependent on offers of joint projects, involving industrial research and development, which held out the promise of raising levels of Norwegian competence in new industries. A much publicised example of a hastily concluded agreement of this sort was the Volvo-agreement between the Labour government of Odvar Nordli and Pehr Gyllenhammar of Volvo, announced 22 May 1978. In the end the Swedish shareholders of Volvo torpedoed the deal in January 1979, thereby preventing a confrontation between the non-socialist parties and Labour. The critics of the Volvo agreement argued that the capital gains for Norwegian industry were trifling in any case, and above all at the price and terms involved in this case. A more promising avenue would appear to be to hand over operator responsibility to Statoil or Norsk Hydro, in step with their maturing skills. In fact, there is a growing confidence among the offshore companies that Norwegian offshore technology has come of age.

The gradualist approach was adopted by the Norwegian authorities more by accident than by design. At first the policy seemed to pay off. By licensing rather than auctioneering a few blocks at a time, the government stayed in control, able to negotiate new terms in line with changing situations rather than risk having to sit on the fence like the British or Danish government, helpless once the blocks had been auctioneered or licensed off. The Danish government in 1963 gave exclusive rights on its shelf to A.P. Møller. The British government had already licensed off 65 per cent of the blocks in the British sector by 1975.[46] However, the Norwegian policy backfired in the late seventies. The Storting in 1974 decided on a moderate exploitation tempo, estimated at 90 million toe (ton oil equivalents) per year. The target was not reached: in 1978 the production had climbed to 48 million, and levelled out around 50 million in the three following years. The reason for the levelling out was the lack of a sufficient number new drilling permissions handed down in the intervening years. It is expected that the production volume will not pick up substantially above the present 50 million toe level till 1985, when the new gas and oil fields of Heimdal, Statfjord C, and Valhall will make their contributions felt. Statfjord B started operations in November 1982. Heimdal (Block 25/4) near Statfjord was discovered in 1972, but the gas field must await the completion of a pipe line from Statfjord to Ekofisk via Kårstø, south of Haugesund, before it can be exploited.

The Impact of Oil

To evaluate the impact of oil in the Norwegian economy so far, one might begin by placing oil and gas alongside existing sectors (Table 13.4).

Table 13.4: Gross Domestic Product by Industry 1973-1981. Million current Kroner

	1973	1975	1977	1979	1980	1981
Agriculture	3,641	5,176	7,053	7,534	8,157	9,452
Forestry	1,000	1,715	1,649	1,856	2,090	2,532
Fishing	1,699	1,345	2,323	2,322	2,468	2,621
Mining	797	972	966	1,070	1,119	1,261
Manufacturing	24,279	32,301	36,214	43,542	43,678	50,587
Oil and gas production	245	3,592	7,364	20,800	40,844	50,333
Electricity & water	3,451	5,037	5,984	8,805	9,666	11,885
Construction, incl. oil drilling	8,418	11,527	15,040	17,325	19,189	21,993
Wholesale and retail tra de	21,561	28,429	25,828	29,214	36,040	40,580
Water transport	9,591	8,481	9,075	10,929	12,587	13,711
Other transport & communication	7,278	9,437	11,629	14,549	16,348	19,170
Financing & insurance	3,076	4,452	5,938	7,656	9,226	11,889
Public services	20,324	27,874	38,214	45,487	51,225	58,982
Private services	6,494	8,363	9,423	15,246	17,695	24,204
Gross domestic product	111,854	148,701	191,534	238,668	283,512	327,970

*Incl. pipe line transport for oil and gas.
Source: *NOS National Accounts*. The krone in 1980-1 was 11.20 to the pound and around 5.50 — 6.00 to the dollar. In 1982 the dollar's exchange rate soared to kr 7.30 by November, while the pound exchanged for kr 11.50 — 12.20. By December 1982 the US dollar again was kr 6.99 and the pound kr 11.44.

Gross production value of petroleum and gas in the course of less than ten years shot up from 0.2 to 50.3 billion kroner, albeit inflated kroner. Relative to total output of the Norwegian economy its share increased 1972-81 from 0.02 per cent to 15.4 per cent, equal to the entire manufacturing sector, and surpassed only by public sector services. Oil production by value alone was three and a half times larger than the entire primary sector by 1981. The influence of oil now reaches far beyond the figures in Table 13.4. We note for instance how such activities as Construction and Other trasport & communication have gone up recently as a result of oil and gas drilling and pipe line transport of oil and gas.

Relative to central government revenue oil has made a splash indeed, up from zero in 1972 to one quarter of the total in 1981, or 27 billion kroner out of a total of 97 billion.

As regards employment, its impact was more modest. An estimated 2,000 workers were engaged in oil-related industries in 1972 and about 44,000 in 1982. This is just 2.3 per cent of a total workforce of 1.9 million.

Relative to total exports oil products shot up from 0.1 per cent in 1972 to 33 per cent in 1980, the single biggest item in the country's export books. Norway should soon become a net exporter of capital.

With such vistas the Odvar Nordli government in 1975 embarked on a strong anti-cyclical policy to cut through what it expected to be a temporary international recession. The objective was to maintain full employment by handing out selective easy loans, guarantees and grants to industry, which in turn piled up stocks. To this end the Finance Minister Per Kleppe, the central architect behind the policy between 1975 and 1979, went on a borrowing spree abroad that trebled Norway's foreign net funded debt, up from 35 billion to 104 billion kroner. The dramatic debt expansion after 1975 is illustrated in Table 13.5. About one third is by the government, two thirds by other domestic sectors. The policy amounted to spending money before it was earned.

By way of conclusion, it would seem that despite the strong stimulus provided by North Sea oil, the Norwegian economy by 1980 showed clear signs of stagnation; in shipbuilding, shipping, forest product industries and in the primary metal industries, including steel, ferro-alloys and aluminium. The seriousness of the situation is reflected in figures for unemployment; by third quarter 1981 the number of unemployed totalled 47,000, up from 32,000 as the average for 1976-9. Relative to a labour force of 1.9 million, this yields a rate of unemployment of 2.5 per cent, which is the highest since the thirties. The production

Table 13.5: Foreign Assets and Liabilities 1950-1981. Mill. current
Kroner. End of year

Year	Assets	Debt		Net debt	Debt in % of GNP
1950	2,793	4,551	–	1,758	11
1955	4,312	6,953	–	2,641	10
1960	7,155	10,578	–	3,423	9
1965	11,221	19,598	–	8,377	15
1970	20,397	29,497	–	9,100	11
1975	39,493	74,670	–	35,177	24
1976	37,804	92,292	–	54,428	32
1977	40,320	124,747	–	84,427	44
1978	47,485	146,498	–	99,013	46
1979	60,024	163,620	–	103,596	43
1980	81,922	175,190	–	93,268	33

Source: *NOS Statistical Yearbook*, and *NOS, Economic Survey 1981*, p. 103.

index for industry, oil excepted, was no higher in 1981 than in 1973, eight years earlier. (See Table 13.6). Manufacturing, the major engine of growth till 1970, in the following decade has failed to maintain the former brisk pace. (Figure 13.4). In a wider context this is what happened to the whole of West European industry: once the technological gap *vis-à-vis* the USA had been closed, the costs of developing new technologies with high productivity potentials seemed infinitely more difficult. The specific Norwegian causes for the slow-down, as indicated in the figures in Table 13.6, were a combination of high inflation, high taxation and new costly legislation to improve the working environment in industry, effective from 1 July 1977.[47] From Table 13.6 we observe that while gross production value per employee increased by a yearly 3.8 per cent during 1969-74, the rate dropped to just about nil in the subsequent five year-period.

Table 13.6: Production, Employment and Productivity 1961-1979 in Manufacturing. Average yearly rates of growth

	Gross value of product	Employment	Number of hours worked	Gross production value per employee	Gross production value per hour
1961-6	5.2	1.2	0.8	4.0	4.4
1966-9	4.7	– 0.1	– 1.8	4.8	6.5
1969-74	5.1	1.3	0.1	3.8	5.0
1974-9	– 0.6	– 0.9	– 2.6	0.3	2.0

Source: Harald Bergland & Ådne Cappelen, *Produktivitet og sysselsetting i industrien*, CBS Reports 81/23, Oslo, 1981, p. 10.

Figure 13.4: Labour Productivity per Man-year by Industry in 1980. Kroner

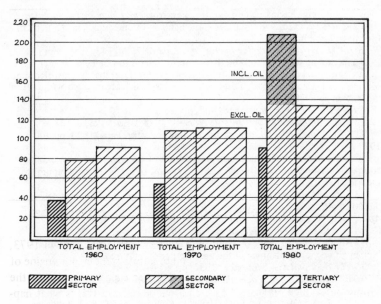

Source: *Makrogruppen. Produktivitetskampanjen 1982*, booklet, p. 13.

The effect of the oil bonanza, in short, by raising the cost/price level about 30 per cent above that of the country's competitors, was not entirely positive. Nobody much wished to see Norway transformed into a Kuwait economy and its industry reduced to a vast outdoor museum. By 1982 this prospect, however, is a serious possibility.

Notes

1 Longterm programmes since 1952 include eight planning periods up to 1982-5

Period 1954-7	Period 1970-3
" 1958-61	" 1974-7
" 1962-5	" 1978-81
" 1966-9	" 1982-5

2 Kaare Petersen, *Kredittpolitikken i støpeskjeen. Forretningsbankenes historie i etterkrigstiden*, Oslo, 1982, a recent review by an insider. (The credit policy in the melting pot. A history of the commercial banks in the postwar period.)

3 *Historical Statistics 1978*, Table 256.

4 Ibid., Figure 5.6, p. 477.

5 Johan Melander, *Oversikt ovr Den norske Creditbanks organisasjon og virk-somhet*. Lehmkuhl Lecture, NSE 1978, p. 27. (Survey of the DnC's Organisation and Activities.)

6 Trond Bergh, 'Bank og demokrati', in *En storbank i blandingsøkonomien. DnC 1957-1982*, Oslo, 1982, pp. 246-84. ('Bank and Democracy', in Big Bank in the Mixed Economy.)

7 *OECD. Agricultural Policy in Norway*, Paris, 1975, p. 14.

8 The rate of growth of productivity improvement must be held distinct from the absolute level of productivity. It is the relative low level that has justified the subsidies to agriculture, not its productivity gains, which are on a par with that of industry in general.

9 *Farmand* nr. 44, 6 November 1982, pp. 35-8.

10 *The 1,000 largest Companies in Norway 1975*, Oslo, 1975, p. 158.

11 *OECD. Financial Support to the Fishing Industry*, Paris, 1980, pp. 98, 102.

12 Gerhard Meidell Gerhardsen, 'Statsstøtten til fiskeriene', in *Økonomi og politikk. Festskrift til Ole Myrvoll*, Oslo, 1971, pp. 147, 154. ('State Support of the Fisheries'.)

13 *Labour Market Problems in Norway*. The Directorate of Labour, 1974, p. 160 ff; *OECD. Regional Policies in Norway*, Paris 1979, pp. 44-5; *OECD. Re-Appraisal of Regional Policies in OECD Countries*, Paris 1974, pp. 165-6; *OECD. Restrictive Regional Policy Measures*, Paris, 1977, pp. 21-5.

14 St. meld. nr. 75, 1976-7 'Long Term Programme 1978-81'. Appendix 1 'Survey of economic planning in the psotwar period', pp. 151-7.

15 *The Economist*, 4 September 1982, pp. 61-2.

16 Edvard Bull, *Norge i den rike verden 1945-1975*, Oslo, 1979, p. 465. (Norway in the Rich World.)

17 Nils Petter Gleditsch & Ottar Hellevik, *Kampen om EF*, PAX Publishers, Oslo, 1977. (The EEC Controversy.); Henry Valen, *Valg og politikk – et samfunn i endring*. Gjøvik 1982, pp. 55, 65, 288-295. (Elections and Politics. A Society in Transition.)

18 Hilary Allen, *Norway and Euope in the1970s*, Universitetsforlaget 1979, pp. 159-68; *The Economist*, November 15, 1975, special survey p. 11.

19 *OECD. Public Expenditure Trends*, Paris, 1978, p. 12.

20 Jostein Aarrestad, *Om utbyttet av å investere i utdanning i Norge*, Nor-wegian School of Economics, Bergen, 1969. (On Returns from Investments in Education in Norway.)

21 *OECD. Public Expenditure Trends*, Paris, 1978, p. 25.

22 Table 11.5 above.

23 St. Forh., St. meld. nr 79, 1967-8, p. 3. (Annual Report of the State Housing Bank.)

24 St. Forh., St. meld. nr 83, 1977-8, p. 4. (Annual Report of the State Housing Bank.)

25 Ibid., p. 10.

26 Ibid., p. 11.

27 *NOS. Kredittmarkedsstatistikk 1975-76*, Oslo, 1978, p. 54.

28 *Historical Statistics 1978*, Table 319, pp. 588-9.

29 *Statistical Yearbook 1982*, Tables 400, 401.

30 *OECD. Public Expenditure on Health*, Paris, 1977, p. 10.

31 Jan Grund et al., *Helseplan for 1980-årene*, Oslo, 1982, p. 62.

32 *National Accounts 1969-1980*, NOS B 222, Oslo, 1981.

33 *Levekårsundersøkelsen. Sluttrapport*, NOU 1976:28, (Investigation of Living Standards. Final Report.)

34 Tor Rødseth, *Inntektsfordeling i Norge*, NOU 1977: 44, 187 p., confer

Torstein Bye & Tor Eivind Høyland, *Inntektsbegreper og inntektsfordeling*, CBS Reports 81/31, Oslo, 1981. (Income Concepts and Income Distribution.)
35 Sverre Walter Rostoft, 'Lik-likere-likest', in *Myter i norsk politikk*, ed. Egil Bakke, Oslo, 1981, p. 29. ('equal − more − most equal', in Myths in Norwegian Politics.)
36 Jan Tore Klovland, 'In Search of the Hidden Economy. Tax Evasion and the Demand for Currency in Norway and Sweden', Discussion Paper No. 18/80. Norwegian School of Economics, December 1980; Arne Jon Isachsen & Steinar Strøm, 'The hidden economy: The labour market and tax evasion', *Scandinavian Journal of Economics*, vol. 82, 1980, pp. 304-11.
37 *National Accounts 1970-1981*, Nos B 313, Tab. 55, pp. 190-1.
38 Trygve Solheim, *70-årenes feriereiser*, CBS Reports 82/20, Oslo, 1982. (Holiday Travels in the 1970s.)
39 *The Economist*, November 15, 1975, Special Survey p. 3.
40 *The Economist*, September 4, 1982, p. 61.
41 St. meld. nr. 53 (1979-80). Om virksomheten på den norske kontinentalsokkel. (Parliamentary report on the activity on the Norwegian continental shelf.) Full bibliography of all earlier government reports and papers; Hans Christian Erlandsen, *Olje*, Oslo, 1982, an ABC about the Norwegian oil industry. Good bibliography; *Aftenposten*, 22 January 1982, *Olje*, (monthly supplement).
42 *Norges Industri* no. 15, 1976, p. 16, citing *Vision's* report on state capitalism in OECD countries.
43 *Bravorapporten*, NOU 1977:47.
44 *'Alexander L. Kielland' -ulykken*, NOU 1981:11.
45 *Muligheter og konsekvenser ved petroleumsfunn nord for 62° N*, NOU 1980:25. (Possibilities and Consequences of Petroleum Discoveries north of 62nd Parallel.)
46 *The Economist*, July 26, 1975, Survey p. 19 b.
47 Act concerning Workers' Protection and Working Environment of 4 February 1977, no. 4.

14 CONCLUDING REMARKS

When a country's *per capita* output grows at a yearly rate of three per cent, inhabitants in that country will experience a doubling of income every 23 years. If such a rate is maintained for sixty years, the inhabitants of the country will be three times better off at the end of the period — on the average. This is what occurred in Norway in the period we have reviewed in these pages. Between 1920 and 1980 *per capita* income has gone up from 12,000 to 69,000 kroner (in 1980 kroner). As the population also increased from 2.6 million to 4.0 million inhabitants, the growth rate for the aggregate output has been higher, around 3.5 per cent a year, in fact. Equally interesting is the tendency to acceleration observed in the statistics on long term economic growth (Table 10.7). Between 1865 and 1890 the national output showed a yearly rate of growth of 1.8 per cent, against 2.6 per cent during the following quarter century, 3.2 per cent in the interwar period and 4.4 per cent in the period 1946-74. The simplest way to interpret the signs of acceleration is to recall that while saving one krone out of ten may be difficult, saving ten out of a hunded is hardly noticed. The law of compound interest is at work here: like saving, investments over time tend to take a larger share of national income as that level is raised, and as a result of superior production capital, national income growth tends to accelerate.

When the Norwegian performance of the last thirty years is set in an international context, we have seen that the growth rates place Norway in the middle range. In respect of key economic indices, including output, investment, unemployment and inflation, Norway in the post-1945 period was remarkable only for its high gross investment ratios, 70-80 per cent higher than the OECD average till the mid-seventies. The excessive capital-output ratio observed in Norway (9.5 against an average 5.3 for eleven OECD countries 1949-62) points back to the high political priority accorded to social housing, hydropower development and shipping in the heyday of the fifties.

The last generation, which has witnessed the transition to affluence, has also experienced remarkable changes in its daily life. Occupational patterns, urban patterns, migrations, consumption, all testify to a strong structural transformation. Similar symptoms, however, are observed in all the highly industrialised countries. Consider some aspects of 'the future shock'. As for the occupational pattern, farmers and fishermen still counted 59 per cent of the nation's workforce in 1910, against seven per cent in 1980. Industry, construction and other secondary activities increased their share of the workforce from 26 per cent in 1910 to 37 per cent in the 1950s, the peak decade. The service sector, however, logged the biggest gains in employment, up from 32 per cent of the workforce in 1910 to 50 per cent in the sixties and 62 per cent by 1980. The time has come now to split up the tertiary sector into services and information. The fourth sector, involving information gathering, information processing and information propagation, is on its way to becoming the leading sector of tomorrow's super-industrialised society.

Parallel shifts are seen in the sectoral origins of value creation. As manufacturing had better opportunities for economies of scale, it was the biggest contributor to value adding by 1910, when 27 per cent of the national income originated in manufacturing. Conversely, the contribution by the primary sector dropped from 45 per cent in 1865 to about a fifth in 1910 and six per cent by 1974. Again, services soon overshadowed the other sectors, with a contribution of 45 per cent to the national income in 1950 and 65 per cent by 1980.

A third feature of the economic transformation was the spread of urban living. In 1910 four out of ten Norwegians lived in an urban setting against seven out of ten by 1980. Perhaps one could merely say that the agglomeration of people in towns and densely populated areas is the price people pay in return for the benefits of the division and specialisation of labour.

The motor of the postwar growth was above all manufacturing, notably mechanical engineering and power-intensive industries. Shipping was also source of substantial productivity gains, which were translated into returns to capital and labour higher than the average (Table 12.3). They have all been motors in the sense that they offered the best opportunities for reaping productivity gains through economies of scale. Emphasis on the supply side may induce the belief that economic growth stemmed from the harvesting of productivity gains only in industry. One should also recall the changes in wholesale and retail trade, in distribution and in communications. On closer inspection, moreover, the outcome depended not only on the supply side of the market, but on the demand side as well. We should round off the picture with a note on the role of demand. From this side one could say that the growth process is fuelled by our demands: without needs, there would be no problems, hence no growth. In support of the paradox, it is worth mentioning a special feature. Our needs are arranged by priority: as a result, when the level of incomes increases, demand released by the extra income shifts from food to other goods. Demand for food is inelastic, in the sense that we merely fill our bellies; hence provided incomes continue to increase, the share devoted to food will represent a steadily diminishing share of total consumption and incomes. Norwegians spent 42 per cent of their income on food in 1910. In line with the continued growth of private incomes, the share allocated to food dropped to 30 per cent in 1960 and 20 per cent by 1982. The presence of food subsidies requires that we regard the figures as approximate. They are, however, echoed in all high income countries. Clearly, the demand side has a decisive influence on the economic transformation. The climb up through the need priorities and the income ladder is very much determined by the nature and ordering of our preferences.

In these chapters we have analysed one implication in particular. From the point of view of demand a sustained rise in incomes can only be achieved if the producers continue to turn out the goods on which the consumers wish to spend their extra income. For a small country in particular that balance is heavily dependent on international trade. In any case continued economic growth requires a correspondence between types of production and types of demand at each level of income. In the case of Norway the pressure on the supply side was usually offset when free trade obtained in the world economy, e.g. in the period 1850-1914 and 1950-75. In these periods imports supplemented the rather restricted number of products marketed by Norwegian industries. When the protectionism forced the country back onto its own resources, income growth generally stagnated, e.g. during World War II 1940-5. There is every sign that the observation will also hold for the future. In the postwar era, an era of trade liberalisation, exports and imports have represented 40-45 per cent each of total national output, so that together the foreign trade totals now almost equal GNP. As a result, Norway has been able to increase *per capita* incomes by specialising in exports of shipping services, and selling a limited range of largely semi-processed products, among them fish, paper, chemical fertilizers, ferro alloys and aluminium but also mechanical engineering products, and, from the mid-seventies, crude oil, in exchange for a wide array of finished products and food stuffs.

One lesson of the above deserves underlining: economic growth, clearly, is not a gift, nor is it won once and for all. At each level a lasting setback or even reversal is a possibility. As seen, at each plateau continued growth depends on a robust interplay between shifts in consumer demand and continual changes in the range of goods and services offered, to match the proportions in which consumers wish to spend their additional income. Both sets of changes are necessary, none sufficient, for the maintenance of the growth process. Equally, in the absence of adjustments on either side of the market, the process will grind to a halt, or more seriously, slide into reverse, as happened in the interwar years, and as may happen again in the 1980s.

In view of the healthy GNP figures cited for the Norwegian economy in the seventies, such a negative forecast may seem out of place. Thus, in a period of deepening international recession after the OPEC oil shock in November 1973, Norwegian *per capita* GNP grew by 3.3 per cent each year 1969-74 and 3.7 per cent each year 1975-81. On the face of it the record is impressive. It has attracted international comment. A closer look, however, brings out that the result essentially reflects the discovery of a new natural resource, oil and gas, on the Norwegian continental shelf and the premature spending of anticipated oil revenues. While providing politicians with a welcome opportunity to play Santa Claus, the negative effects of oil may outweigh the positive ones, in so far as, till 1980 at any rate, the oil revenues merely halted the shake-out of dying industries, prevented labour mobility, failed to provide incentives to risk taking, and in general saddled the country with cost price levels, subsidies and welfare programmes that have rendered Norwegian products uncompetitive on foreign and domestic markets.

When the international recession seemed to threaten the traditional full-employment situation, the Labour government under Mr Trygve Bratteli began a counter-cyclical offensive in June 1974. In order to boost domestic demand, personal taxes were cut by 2 per cent from 1 June 1974, national pensions were raised and credit policies were made more expansive. The package assumed that the recession would soon pass, and that the country, by public sector spending, could pass through the trough at full utilisation levels. Inflationary pressure was foreseen by the Finance Minister, Per Kleppe, but it was thought the economy could take on the extra burden. If necessary, the government had no scruples at the idea of borrowing abroad to finance the counter-cyclical campaign. Thus began the process of spending the oil wealth before the oil had left the North Sea. The policy made no economic sense, but was justified on grounds of social welfare, above all by the need to avoid unemployment.

Indeed, unemployment stayed between 1.5 and 2.3 per cent 1975-

80. Domestic demand was maintained. For export-oriented firms, unable to benefit from the internal boost in demand, the government provided special relief measures by subsidising the interest expenditures involved in the accumulation of extraordinarily high stocks. Not only was unemployment held at bay; there were signs that the economy suffered from manpower shortages in a number of fields.

The unintended effects that soon surfaced were less welcome. The extra demand 1976-8, going way beyond the country's production, sent the inflation rate to 9-10 per cent on an annual basis. The Norwegian price level climbed about 30 per cent higher than that of Norway's trading partners. Worse, the level did not come down again. Norwegian products, in turn, lost market shares, both on the export markets and on the home market. Though direct wage costs on the average account for only 30 per cent of total production costs in industry, they nevertheless influence the other cost elements. All in all, wages are assumed to account for 70-80 per cent of total costs, including social security and other employers' taxes. The Central Bureau of Statistics in its 1982 survey estimated that wages in Norwegian industry, excluding oil, made up 80 per cent of production costs in 1977.

For a while during 1976 and 1977 oil created the illusion of an economic boom, while problems of inflation and competitiveness were simply subsidised away. After Labour was returned to office in the 1977 election, having won 76 out of 155 representatives, however, it became evident that the two assumptions behind the economic counter-offensive were wrong. The international recession was not shortlived, and the oil revenues turned out smaller and came later than expected. Some negative effects were now admitted. The campaign had involved foreign borrowing on an unprecedented scale: while the net foreign debt was 11 per cent of gross national output in 1970, it had climbed to 46 per cent by the end of 1978. Admittedly, most of the foreign debt represented private investments in oil related industries, but a third represented government borrowing for consumption and welfare purposes.

Mr Odvar Nordli had succeeded Premier Trygve Bratteli as head of the Labour government 15 January 1976. In February 1978 the Nordli government announced an 8 per cent devaluation of the krone, and at the same time tightened the credit polices to curb consumption. On 12 September 1978 the government declared a price and income freeze. The freeze was maintained through 1979. Taxes were raised, support to individual industries and companies were scaled down, the credit policy was tightened, all with a view to containing aggregate domestic demand.

On 30 November 1979 the Bank of Norway raised its discount rate from seven to nine per cent, the highest in its 163-year history. The squeeze at first seemed to work. During 1979 exports of oil and traditional exports soared, stocks were reduced, the high deficits on current account came down. Indeed, the foreign balance on current account showed a surplus for 1980 of 5.5 billion kroner, against record deficits of 20.4 billion in 1976, 26.8 billion in 1977 and 11.0 and 5.3 billion the two following years. Still inflation, reflecting the high wages in the oil industry, ran at a yearly 9.5-11.0 per cent. Norwegian products were rendered uncompetitive.The cost and price level, despite the wage freeze, settled on a plateau about 30 per cent above that of the country's trading partners in OECD. Money supply rose by 12 per cent a year between 1978 and 1980.

Mr Odvar Nordli resigned as Prime Minister on 30 January 1981. He was succeeded by Mrs Gro Harlem Brundtland, who soon faced a rising tide of Conservative sentiment. Though partially successful in rallying the voters to Labour in the national election in September 1981, the new government, headed by the country's first woman prime minister, failed to tackle the economic problems, notably the task of curbing the ballooning wage and cost levels. The new industries that had built Norway's prosperity in the 1950s and 1960s were swamped by the oil wealth: pulp and paper, chemicals, minerals and mechanical engineering. Another price freeze was announced by the Brundtland government in August 1981 for the rest of the year, to avert a new wage explosion. In the 1981 election the Conservative Party took 54 seats, 31.6 per cent of the vote, while Labour slipped from 42.3 per cent in 1977 to 37.3 per cent, down from 76 to 65 seats. With the backing of the Centre Party and the Christian People's Party, the Conservatives under Mr Kåre Willoch on 12 October 1981 formed a Conservative minority government. The voters, after eight years of Labour, were tired of the state bureaucracy, the high taxes and the Keynesian deficit planning, which seemed to intensify problems rather than solve them. We have seen, for instance, that despite the growth in *per capita* GNP, average real wages paid out remained at a standstill 1976-81 (Table 13.3). There is no paradox involved. The apparent contradiction reflects the oil revenues to the government, the inrush of women into low-paid health and welfare jobs and the excessive income redistribution maintained through the tax system, which included the regional subsidies to farming and fisheries in the districts.

One lesson from the failure of the latest social democratic planning experiment in Norway was that the trade unions, whose contributions to Labour's party chest remain a powerful lever, were led to believe that the government owed them a job, preferably one near home, preferably calling for old, familiar skills. Handing out vast amounts in subsidies to dying products and industries, the Labour governments thus helped postpone the necessity, unavoidable in any case, of switching to skills and products that promised to have a future in a high-cost country. In addition the handouts, by raising the domestic cost-price levels so as to render the country's exports uncompetitive, created difficulties for those industries that normally would have kept their foreign customers. Many of the difficulties are therefore the result, not of market failure, but of too much political steering, ill-advised, inconsistent and lacking continuity.

Another lesson of the recent failures was to raise doubts about the future of the welfare programmes. In fact the social security funds are emptied, and the payments, totalling more than a third of the net national product, are now provided in an *ad hoc* fashion by taxes and government borrowing, subject to party bargaining in the Storting. Nobody much wants to attack his parents' pensions, but the pro-grammes, notably the district subsidies, have swelled into a colossus that threaten the future of the whole edifice. What if the middle generation, as reflected in a fleeting coalition in the Storting, revolts? What security do public social security schemes in fact give? The programmes are compulsory. Nobody, except the very well off, can opt out and arrange their own old age insurance plan. The older generation thus seem to have been reduced to victims of whatever party majority happens to be in control of the Storting. A great many pension contributors deem such a prospect less than satisfactory as a guarantee for their future security.

Perhaps the ills of social democracy stem from the traditional marriage of strong trade unions and weak Labour party governments. The result, as was demonstrated in the 1970s, was that wages and con-sumption took precedence over savings, capital formation and risk taking in new products and new services. The myopia of the trade unions, though understandable, is morally indefensible. It won't do to criticise capital for maximising return on capital when in fact the trade unions pursue the very same goal of maximising gains for the workers. If the former is immoral, so is the latter. Greed is the defining criterion of both. But capital owners took risks, which justified their gains. The trade union worker by contrast claims a reward without any risk. The only force the unions bring to bear is the negative one of with-holding their labour. As long as the parties on the labour market were operating in a market setting, a certain power balance still remained. But when the trade unions in addition can call on the coercive power of the state, as has been the case in 29 out of the last 36 years, the balance is destroyed. Thus, while the Norwegian Price Act of 26 June 1953 calls for price control of all rents, interest rates, dividends, salaries and profits, the act excludes wages earned in the service of an employer. Equally, to bolster the monopoly position of the trade unions, the Norwegian Labour Disputes Act of 5 May 1927, art. 3, has made the personal wage contract subservient to the collective tariff contract, so in case of conflict between the two, the latter invalidates the former. In other words until the imbalance on the labour market is corrected, the combination of trade union power and weak party government promises more of the same. Wages will tend to go beyond their market value, inflation will continue, risk taking and flexibility will suffer. Oil in such a setting will hardly stop the process. Increasingly the central authority, the government and the Storting, has proved too weak to withstand the pressure of organised interest groups, unions, and the district interests. At best oil will grease the downward slide. In short, oil, once heralded as the new cornucopia, has so far, largely through political bungling, opened up Pandora's box. In consequence, the decade of the 1980s promises to be a stormy one.

CHAPTER BIBLIOGRAPHY

1

Hodne, F., 'Growth in a dual Economy. The Norwegian Experience 1814-1914', *Economy and History*, vol. 16 (1973)
——*Norges økonomiske historie 1815-1970* (Cappelen, Oslo, 1981)
Jörberg, L., 'The Nordic Countries 1850-1914', in Cipolla, C.M., (ed.), *The Fontana Economic History of Europe*, vol. 4.2 (Collins, Glasgow, 1973)
Schumpeter, J., *The Theory of Economic Development* (Harvard UP, Cambridge, Mass., 1934) (orig. 1911)
——*Business Cycles*, 2 vols. (McGraw-Hill, New York & London 1939)
Sejersted, F. *et al., Vekst gjennom krise. Studier i norsk teknologihistorie* (Universitetsforlaget, Oslo, 1982)
Stonehill, A., *Foreign Ownership in Norwegian Enterprises* (CBS, Oslo, 1965)

2

Amundsen, H., *Norsk Jernbaneforbund gjennom 60 år 1892-1952* (Oslo, 1952)
Bjerke, J., *Langtidslinjer i norsk økonomi 1865-1960*, (CBS, Oslo, 1966)
Bull, E. jr., *Norsk fagbevegelse* (Tiden, Oslo, 1968)
Christensen, C.A.R., *Fra verdenskrig til verdenskrig* (Aschehoug, Oslo, 1961)
Dahl, S., 'Norsk Arbeidsgiverforening 1927/28. Tilbaketog og revurdering', *Historisk Tidsskrift* (1981)
Danielsen, R., 'Høyreaktivismen i 1920-årene', in *Høyres historie*, vol. 2, forthcoming 1984
Furre, B., *Norsk historie 1905-1940* (Det norske Samlaget, Oslo, 1971)
Galenson, W., *Labour in Norway* (Harvard UP, Cambridge, Mass., 1949)
Hanisch, T.J., 'Om virkninger av paripolitikken', *Historisk Tidsskrift*, (1979)
Historical Statistics 1968, NOS XII, 245 (CBS, Oslo, 1969)
Johansen, P.O., *Menstadkonflikten 1931* (Tiden, Oslo, 1977)
Labour Relations in Norway, ILO Committee & Royal Ministry of Foreign Affairs (Oslo 1975)
Lafferty, W.M., *Industrialisation, Community Structure, and Socialism* (Universitetsforlaget, Oslo, 1974)
Langfeldt, K., *Moskvatesene i norsk politikk* (Universitetsforlaget, Oslo, 1961)
Maurseth, P., *Fra Moskvateser til Kristianiaforslag* (PAX, Oslo, 1972)
National Accounts 1865-1960, NOS XII. 163 (CBS, Oslo, 1965)
Ousland, G., *Fagorganisasjonen i Norge*, 4 vols. (Tiden, Oslo, 1949; paper 1975)
Stoltz, G., *Økonomisk utsyn 1900-1950* (CBS, Oslo, 1955)
Aarseth, S.B., 'Storstreiken 1921', *Tidsskrift for arbeiderbevegelsens historie*, vol. 1 (1977)

3

Bull, E. jr., *Klassekamp og fellesskap 1920-1945* (Cappelen, Oslo, 1979)
Egge, Å., 'Naeringslivet og paripolitikken', *Historisk Tidsskrift* (1974)
Engebretsen, E., *Norsk bankvesen (Oslo, 1939)*
Gerhardsen, E., *Unge år. Erindringer fra århundreskiftet fram til 1940*, (Tiden, Oslo, 1974)
Hanisch, T.J., 'Om virkninger av paripolitikken', *Historisk Tidsskrift* (1979)
Hveding, Ø., 'Opposisjon mot paripolitikken', *Historisk Tidsskrift* (1973)
—— 'Gjeldsforliket mellom Bondepartiet og Arbeiderpartiet 1934', *Historisk Tidsskrift* (1979)
Keilhau, W., *Vår egen tid* (Aschehoug, Oslo, 1938)
—— *Norsk pengehistorie* (Aschehoug, Oslo, 1952)
Kriser och krispolitik i Norden under mellankrigstiden, Nordiska historikermøtet i Uppsala 1974 (Almquist & Wiksell, Uppsala, 1974)
Petersen, E., *Den Norske Creditbank 1857-1957* (Fabritius, Oslo, 1957)
Petersen, K., *Forretningsbankenes historie i mellomkrigsårene* (A/S Hjemmet-Fagpresseforlaget, Oslo, 1982)
Roset, I.A., *Det Norske Arbeiderparti og Hornsruds regjeringsdannelse* (Universitetsforlaget, Oslo, 1962)
Rygg, N., *Norges Bank i mellomkrigstiden* (Gyldendal, Oslo, 1950)
—— *Norges Banks historie*, vol. 2 (Oslo, 1954)
Sejersted, F., *Ideal, teori og virkelighet. Nicolai Rygg og pengepolitikken i 1920-årene* (Cappelen, Oslo, 1973)
—— *Historisk introduksjon til økonomien* (Cappelen, Oslo, 1973)
—— 'Demokrati og rettsstat – er perspektiv på 1800-tallets politiske brytninger', *Historisk Tidsskrift* (1979)
Skånland, H., *Det norske kredittmarked siden 1900* (CBS, Oslo, 1967. English sub-texts)

4

Anker Olsen, K., *Norsk Hydro gjennom 50 år* (Oslo, 1955)
Bjerke, J., *Langtidslinjer i norsk økonomi 1865-1960* (CBS, Oslo, 1966)
Fasting, K., *Vintersildsoga. Norges Sildesalslag 1930-1960* (Bergen, 1960)
Hodne, F., *Norges økonomiske historie 1815-1970* (Cappelen, Oslo, 1981)
Hope, E., 'Jordbruket i Norge', in Hope, E., (ed.), *Naeringsøkonomiske Oversikter*, vol. 1 (Tanum, Oslo, 1972)
Karmly, D., *Norges kommunalbank 1927-1977* (Gyldendal, Oslo, 1977)
Nordstrand, L., *Fiskeridirektoratets historie 1880-1980* (forthcoming)
Rygg, N., *Norges Bank i mellomkrigstiden* (Gyldendal, Oslo, 1950)
Vogt, J. *Elektrisitetslandet Norge* (Universitetsforlaget, Oslo, 1971)

5

Basberg, B., *Innovasjonsteori, patenter og teknologisk utvikling i norsk hvalfangst 1880-1968*, thesis, NSE, Bergen 1980
—— 'Patents, Innovations, and Technological Development in Norwegian Whaling 1880-1968', *World Patent Information*, vol. 3 (1981)
Egeland, J.O., *Kongeveien. Norsk skipsfart fra århundreskiftet til Den annan verdenskrig*, 2 vols. (Aschehoug, Oslo, 1973)
Johnsen, A.O., & Tønnessen, J., *Den moderne hvalfangsts historie. Opprinnelse og utvikling*, 4 vols. (Sandefjord 1959-70)
—— *Norwegian Patents relating to Whaling and the Whaling Industry* (Oslo, 1947)
Keilhau, W., *Skipsfartens betydning for Norge* (Oslo, 1948)
Petersen, K., *The Saga of Norwegian Shipping* (Dreyer, Oslo, 1955)
Schreiner, J. *Norsk Skipsfart under krig og høykonjunktur 1914-1920* (Cappelen Oslo, 1963)
Skånland, H., *Det norske kredittmarked siden 1900* (CBS, Oslo, 1967)
Thowsen, A., 'Krise og krisetiltak i norsk tankskipsfart 1929-1936', *Sjøfartshistorisk Årbok* (1978)

6

Aldcroft, D.H., *From Versailles to Wall Street* (Allen Lane, London, 1977)
Egeland, K., & Ørjasaeter, T., *Mellomkrigstid* (Cappelen, Oslo, 1975)
Frøland, D., *Krise og Kamp. Bygdefolkets krisehjelp* (Universitetsforlaget, Oslo og Bergen 1962)
Furre, B., *Mjølk, bønder og tingmenn* (Det norske Samlaget, Oslo, 1971)
Ousland, G., *Fagorganisasjonen i Norge*, 4 vols. (Tiden, Oslo, 1949, Paper 1975)
Petersen, E., *Den norske Creditbank 1857-1957* (Fabritius, Oslo, 1957)
Rygg, N., *Norges Bank i mellomkrigstiden* (Gyldendal, Oslo, 1950)
Skånland, H., *Det norske kredittmarked siden 1900* (CBS, Oslo, 1967)
Stoltz, G., *Økonomisk utsyn 1900-1950* (CBS, Oslo, 1955)
Svendsen, A.S., 'Mellomkrigstiden', in Wasberg, G.C. & Svendsen, A.S., *Industriens historie i Norge* (Oslo, 1969)

7

Bjerke, J., *Langtidslinjer i norsk økonomi 1865-1960* (CBS, Oslo, 1966)
Dahl, S., & Hveding, Ø. *Økonomi og politikk. Emner fra norsk mellomkrigstid* (Tapir, Trondheim, 1979)
Egeland, J.O., *Kongeveien. Norsk skipsfart fra århundreskiftet til Den Annen verdenskrig*, 2 vols. (Aschehoug, Oslo, 1973)
Hanisch, T. *Hele folket i arbeid* (PAX, Oslo, 1977)
Hanisch, T.J., 'The economic Crisis in Norway in the 1930s: A tentative Analysis of its Causes', *Scandinavian Economic History Review* (1978)

Hovland, E., ' 'Smør' og margarin blir ett fett', *Historisk Tidsskrift* (1979)
Jahn, G., *Norges Bank gjennom 150 år* (Oslo, 1966)
Kindleberger, C.P., *The World in Depression 1929-1939* (Allen Lane, London, 1972)
Nordvik, H., 'Krisepolitikken og den teoretiske nyorientering av den økonomiske politikken i Norge i 1930-årene', *Historisk Tidsskrift* (1977)
Rygg, N., *Norges Bank i mellomkrigstiden* (Gyldendal, Oslo, 1950)
Schou, A., *Håndverk og industri i Oslo 1838-1938. Oslo Håndverks- og Industriforening 100 år*, (Oslo, 1938)
Seim, J., *Hvordan Hovedavtalen ble til. Staten, organisasjonene og arbeidsfreden 1930-1935* (Tiden, Oslo, 1972)
Sejersted, F. *et al., Vekst gjennom krise. Studier i norsk teknologihistorie* (Universitetsforlaget, Oslo, 1982)
Svennilson, I., *Growth and Stagnation in the European Economy* (Geneva 1954)
Wedervang, F., *Development of a Population of Industrial Firms* (Universitetsforlaget, Oslo, 1965)
Wicken, O., *Krisen i 1930-årene*, report, Department of History (University of Oslo, 1977)

8

Andenaes, J.B., Riste, O. & Skodvin, M., *Norway and the Second World War* (Tanum, Oslo, 1966)
——*Det vanskelige oppgjøret* (Tanum-Norli, Oslo, 1980)
Askelund, B., 'Nortraships hemmelige fond', in Paulsen H., ed., *Mellom nøytrale og allierte. Studier i norsk samtidshistorie* (Universitetsforlaget, Oslo, 1968)
Aukrust, O. & Bjerve, P.J., *Hva krigen kostet Norge* (Dreyer, Oslo, 1945)
Bull, E. jr., *Klassekamp og fellesskap 1920-1945* (Cappelen, Oslo, 1979)
Christensen, C.A.R., *Okkupasjonsår og etterkrigstid* (Aschehoug, Oslo, 1961)
Derry, T.K., *The Campaign in Norway* (London, 1952)
——*A History of Modern Norway* (Oxford UP, 1973)
Egeland, J.O., *Gjennom brott og brann* (Aschehoug, Oslo, 1968)
——*Vi skal videre. Norsk skipsfart etter Den annen verdenskrig. Perioden 1945-1970* (Aschehoug, Oslo, 1971)
Grimnes, O.K., *Hjemmefrontens ledelse* (Universitetsforlaget, Oslo, Bergen, 1977)
Hayes, P.M., *Quisling. The Career and Political Ideas of Vidkun Quisling 1887-1945* (David & Charles, Devon, 1971)
Hegland, J.R., *Nortraships flåte*, 2 vols. (Dreyer, Oslo, 1976)
Hewins, R., *Quisling. Prophet without Honour* (Allen, London, 1965)
Jahn, G. *et al., Norges Bank 150 år* (Oslo, 1966)
Kjeldstadli, S., *Hjemmestyrkene*, vol. 1 (Aschehoug, Oslo, 1959)
Kloster, K.U., *Den norske stormakt. Vår skipsfart gjennom tusen år* (Gyldendal, Oslo, 1945)
Loock, H.D., *Quisling, Rosenberg und Terboven. Zur Vorgeschichte und Geschichte der nazionalsozialistischen Revolution in Norwegen* (Deutsche

Verlags-Anstalt, Stuttgart, 1970)
Milward, A., *The Fascist Economy in Norway* (Oxford UP, Oxford, 1972)
—— *War, Economy and Society 1939-1945* (Allen Lane, London, 1977)
Nasjonalinntekten i Norge 1935-1943, NOS X, 102 (CBS, Oslo, 1946)
Norges Bank. Virksomheten i hvert av årene 1940-1944 (Oslo, 1945)
*Norges Bank. Beretning om den økonomiske stilling i de forskjellige landsdeler
    for årene 1940-44* (Oslo, 1945)
Petrow, R., *The Bitter Years. The Invasion and Occupation of Denmark and
    Norway April 1940-May 1945* (William Morrow & Co., New York 1974 &
    Hodder & Stoughton, London 1975)
Riste, O. & Nøkleby, B., *Norway 1940-1945: The Resistance Movement*
    (Tanum, Oslo, 1970)
Skodvin, M., *Striden om okkupasjonsstyret* (Oslo, 1956)
Statistisk-økonomisk oversikt over krigsårene (CBS, Oslo, 1945)
Steen, S., *Norges krig*, 3 vols. (Oslo, 1947-50)
St. meld. nr. 76 (1963-4) Nortraship settlement, final report.
Valen, T., *De tjente på krigen* (Oktober Forlag, Oslo, 1974)
Vogt, J., *Vår økonomiske stilling. En kritisk vurdering av gjenreisnings-
    perioden* (Aschehoug, Oslo, 1950)
Ørvik, N., *Norge i brennpunktet* (Tanum, Oslo, 1953)

9

Andenaes, J.B., *Det vanskelige oppgjøret. Rettsoppgjøret etter okkupasjonen*
    (Tanum-Norli, Oslo, 1980)
Bergh, T., 'Norsk økonomisk politikk 1945-1965', in Bergh, T., Pharo, H. *et al.*,
    Vekst og velstand (Universitetsforlaget, Oslo, 1977)
—— *Opprettelsen og utviklingen av bransjerådene*, history thesis, University of
    Oslo, Institute of History, 1973.
—— *Fra Faedrelandssag til Storbank.Norges Postsparebank 1950-1975* (Oslo,
    1975)
Bjerve, P.J., *Planning in Norway 1947-1956* (North-Holland Publ. Co,
    Amsterdam, 1959)
—— *Trends in Norwegian Planning 1945-1975* (CBS, Oslo, 1976)
Bourneuf, A., *Norway, the planned Revival* (Harvard UP., Cambridge, Mass.,
    1958)
CBS, *Economic Survey*, annual report.
Gerhardsen, E., *Fellesskap i krig og fred. Erindringer 1940-45* (Tiden, Oslo,
    1970)
—— *Samarbeid og strid. Erindringer 1945-55* (Tiden, Oslo, 1971)
Grønlie, T., 'Norsk industripolitikk', in Bergh, T., Pharo, H. *et al.*, *Vekst og
    velstand* (Universitetsforlaget, Oslo, 1977)
—— 'Kampen om Union 1946-1949', *Historisk Tidsskrift* (1978)
Lenaes, I., *Privattelefonen i Norge* (Skien, 1966)
Justis- og Politidepartementet, *Om landsvikoppgjøret. Innstilling fra utvalg av 22.
    desember 1955 om å skaffe tilveie materiale til en innberetning fra Justis-
    departementet til Stortinget* (Gjøvik, 1961)

Munthe, P., 'Tiden etter Den annen verdenskrig', in Jahn, G. *et al., Norges Bank gjennom 150 år* (Oslo, 1966)
Reikvam, Å., 'Synet på sosialisering i DNA 1945-1953', in *Etterkrigshistorie*, vol. 1 (Universitetsforlaget, Oslo, 1970)
Shonfield, A., *Modern Capitalism. The Changing Balance of Public and Private Power* (Oxford UP, New York & London, 1965)
Sejersted, F., *Historisk introduksjon til økonomien* (Cappelen, Oslo, 1973)
Statistisk-økonomisk oversikt over året 1946 (CBS, Oslo, 1947)
Svendsen, A.S., & Wasberg, G.C., *Industriens historie i Norge* (Oslo, 1969)
——— *Union 1873-1973* (Aschehoug, Oslo, 1973)
Thon, S., *Økonomisk politikk i Norge 1945-1965* (Elingaard, Oslo, 1968)
Winch, D., *Economics and Policy. A Historical Study* (Hodder & Stoughton, London 1969) (new. ed. 1972)
Yeager, L.B., *International Monetary Relations. Theory, History and Policy* (Harper & Row, New York, 1969)
Østerud, Ø., *Samfunnsplanlegging og politisk system* (Gyldendal, Oslo, 1972)
——— *Det planlagte samfunn. Om sentralplanleggingens fremvekst og grenser* (Gyldendal, Oslo, 1979)

10

Aukrust, O. & Bjerve, P.J., *Hva krigen kostet Norge* (Dreyer, Oslo, 1945)
Aukrust, O., *Norges økonomi etter krigen* (CBS, Oslo, 1965)
Bachke, L.B. & Willoch, K., *Prispolitikken i Norge* (Dreyer, Oslo, 1959)
Bjerve, P.J., *Planning in Norway 1947-1956* (North-Holland, Amsterdam, 1959)
Bourneuf, A., *Norway, the planned Revival* (Harvard UP, Cambridge, Mass., 1958)
Brofoss, E., 'The Marshall Plan and Norway's Hesitation', *Scandinavian Journal of History* (1977)
CBS, *Economic Survey*, annual report.
Egeland, J.O., *Vi skal videre. Norsk skipsfart etter Den annen verdenskrig. Periodden 1945-1970* (Aschehoug, Oslo, 1971)
Eriksen, K.E., 'Norge i det vestlige samarbeid', in Bergh T., Pharo, H. *et al., Vekst og velstand* (Universitetsforlaget, Oslo, 1977)
Fasting, K., *Aktieselskabet Sydvaranger 1906-1956* (Oslo, 1956)
Gerhardsen, E., *Samarbeid og strid. Erindringer 1945-55* (Tiden, Oslo, 1971)
Gjølberg, O., 'Høyrebølgen – et konjunkturfenomen', in Bjørklund, T. ed., *Høyrebølgen – Epokeskifte i norsk politikk?* (Aschehoug, Oslo, 1981)
Grønlie, T., *Jern og politikk 1945-1955. A/S Norsk Jernverk* (Universitetsforlaget, Oslo, 1973)
Grønlie, T., 'Norsk industripolitikk 1945-1965', in Bergh, T. & Pharo, H. *et al., Vekst og velstand* (Universitetsforlaget, Oslo, 1977)
Historical Statistics 1968, NOS XII, 245 (CBS, Oslo, 1969)
Hope, E., 'Norges energiforsyning', in Hope, E. ed., *Næringsøkonomiske oversikter*, vol. 2 (Tanum, Oslo, 1972)
Hope, E., 'Norges industri', in Hope, E., ed., *Næringsøkonomiske oversikter*,

vol. 2 (Tanum, Oslo, 1972)

Leiserson, M.W., *Wages and economic Control in Norway 1945-1957* (Harvard UP, Cambridge, Mass., 1959)

Lie, T., *Hjemover* (Tiden, Oslo, 1958)

Meinich, P., 'Sparebankene etter 1945', in Svendsen, A.S. & Sejersted, F., (eds.), *Studier i sparing og sparebankvesen i Norge 1822-1972* (Gyldendal, Oslo, 1972)

Munthe, P., 'Tiden etter Den annen verdenskrig', in Jahn, G. *et al.*, *Norges Bank gjennom 150 år* (Oslo, 1966)

National Accounts 1954-1970, NOS, A474 (CBS, Oslo, 1972)

Pharo, H., 'Bridgebuilding and Reconstruction: Norway faces the Marshall Plan', *Scandinavian Journal of History* (1977)

Postan, M.M., *An economic History of Western Europe 1945-1964* (Methuen & Co. Ltd., London, 1967)

Svendsen, A.S., *Skipsfartpolitikken i Norge etter krigen* (NSE, Bergen, 1957)

Svendsen, A.S. & Wasberg, G.C., *Industriens historie i Norge* (Oslo, 1969)

The 500 largest Companies of Norway (Oslo, 1971)

Udgaard, N.M., *Great Power Politics and Norwegian Foreign Policy* (Universitetsforlaget, Oslo, 1973)

Wold, K.G., 'Marshallhjelpen 30 år etter', *Militaert Tidsskrift* (1977)

11

Åberg, Y., *Produktion och produktivitet i Sverige 1861-1965* (Almquist & Wiksell, Stockholm, 1969)

Amundsen, A., *Konsumelastisiteter og konsumprognoser bygd på nasjonalregnskapet* (CBS, Oslo, 1963)

Aukrust, O., *Norges økonomi etter krigen* (CBS, Oslo, 1965)

Bull, E., jr., *Norge i den rike verden.* Tiden etter 1945 *(Cappelen, Oslo, 1979)*

Cappelen, Å. & Hellesøy, A., 'Strukturelle endringer i norsk økonomi etter krigen', *Vardøger*, no. 11 (1981)

CBS, *Economic Survey*, 1982, p. 148

Forskning, teknisk utvikling og industriell innovasjon, NOU 1981:30, 2 vols. (Universitetsforlaget, 1981)

Historical Statistics 1968, NOS XII, 245 (CBS, Oslo, 1969)

—— *1978*, NOS XII, 291 (CBS, Oslo, 1978)

Hope, E., 'Norges industri', in Hope, E., ed., *Naeringsøkonomiske oversikter*, vol. 2 (Tanum, Oslo, 1972)

Hope, E., 'Jordbruket i Norge', in Hope, E., ed., *Naeringsøkonomiske oversikter,* vol. 1 (Tanum, Oslo, 1972)

Labour Relations in Norway, ILO-Committee & Royal Ministry of Foreign Affairs (Oslo, 1975)

Maddison, A., 'Economic Policy and Performance in Europe 1913-1970', in Cipolla, C., ed., *Fontana Economic History of Europe*, Vol. 5.2 (Collins, Glasgow, 1976)

Munthe, P., *Sirkulasjon, inntekt og økonomisk vekst*, 2. ed. (Universitetsforlaget, Oslo, 1981)

National Accounts 1865-1960, NOS XII, 163 (CBS, Oslo, 1965)

National Accounts 1954-1970, NOS A, 474 (CBS, Oslo, 1972)

Norsk Tidende for Det industrielle rettsvern, weekly publ. of patents.

OECD, *Economic Survey. Norway* (Paris, 1963)

——*The Residual Factor and economic Growth* (Paris, 1964)

——*Scientific Research. Norway* (Paris, 1965)

——*The Growth of Output 1960-1980. Retrospect, Prospect and Problems of Policy* (Paris, 1970)

——*Public Expenditure Trends* (Paris, 1978)

——*Trends in Industrial R & D in selected OECD Member Countries 1967-1975* (Paris, 1979)

SPRU, *Government Support for Industrial Research in Norway*, in NOU 1981:30, vol. 2 (1981)

Svinndal, Aa., ed., *Styret for det industrielle rettsvern 50 år 1911-1961* (Oslo, 1961)

Thon, S., *Økonomisk politikk i Norge 1945-1965* (Elingaard, Oslo, 1968)

12

ÅSV. Annual Reports.

Abrahamsen, E., *Kreativitet, innovasjon og konkurranseevne* (Lehmkuhl Lecture, NSE, Bergen, 1980)

Akergruppen. Annual Reports

Aukrust, O., *Norges økonomi etter krigen* (CBS, Oslo, 1965)

Balassa, B., *Industrial Development in an Open Economy: The Case of Norway* (CBS, Art. nr. 30, Oslo, 1969)

——'Accounting for Economic Growth: the Case of Norway', *Oxford Economic Papers*, vol. 31 (1979)

CBS, *Economic Survey*, annual report.

——*National Accounts*, annual publ.

Cornwall, J., *Modern Capitalism. Its Growth and Transformation* (Martin Robertson, London, 1977)

Cripps, T.F. & Tarling, R.J., *Growth in advanced capitalist Economies 1950-1970* (Cambridge UP, London, 1973)

Eriksen, I. & Norman, V., 'Skipsfarten i norsk samfunnsøkonomi', *Statsøkonomisk Tidsskrift* (1974)

Eriksen, Ø., ed., *Industri og politikk* (Universitetsforlaget, Bergen, 1980)

Hagrup, K., *SAS og den internasjonale luftfart*, Lehmkuhl Lecture (NSE, Bergen, 1974)

Hope, E., 'Norges industri', in Hope, E., ed., *Naeringsøkonomiske Oversikter*, vol. 2 (Tanum, Oslo, 1972)

Karmly, D., *Kings Bay-saken. Den politiske krisen mellom regjering og opposisjon sommeren 1963* (Gyldendal, Oslo, 1975)

Langballe, K., *Kvaernerkonsernet. Oppbygging og egenart*, Lehmkuhl Lecture (NSE, Bergen, 1975)

Munthe, P., *Sirkulasjon, inntekt og økonomisk vekst*, 2. ed. (Universitetsforlaget, Oslo, 1981)
Norges 1000 største bedrifter (Oslo, 1975)
NVE. Vår virksomhet, annual reports 1970-81
OECD, *Economic Survey. Norway* (Paris, 1976)
——*Maritime Transports 1973* (Paris, 1973)
Onarheim, O., *Tanker omkring norsk verkstedsindustri. Perspektiv og forutsetninger for utvikling*, Lehmkuhl Lecture (NSE, Bergen, 1973)
Sejersted, F. et al., *En storbank i blandingsøkomien. Den norske Creditbank 1957-1982* (Gyldendal, Oslo, 1982)
Svendsen, A.S., 'Norges skipsfart', in Hope, E., ed., *Naeringsøkonomiske Oversikter*, vol. 3 (Tanum, Oslo, 1972)
Thon. S., *Statskrift i Norge og andre land* (Elingaard, Oslo, 1960)
——*Fra Kings Bay til Husnes* (Oslo, 1964)
Vogt, J., *Elektrisitetslandet Norge* (Universitetsforlaget, Oslo, 1971)

13

Aarrestad, J., *Om utbyttet av å investere i utdanning i Norge* (NSE, Bergen, 1969)
Aftenposten, 22 January 1982: Olje (monthly Supplement)
'Alexander L. Kielland' -ulykken, NOU 1981:11.
Allen, H., *Norway and Europe in the 1970s* (Universitetsforlaget, Oslo & Bergen, 1979)
Bakke, E., ed., *Myter i norsk politikk* (Gyldendal, Oslo, 1981)
Bergland, H. & Cappelen, Å., *Produktivitet og sysselsetting i industrien* (CBS Reports 81/23, Oslo, 1981)
Bravorapporten, NOU 1977:47.
Bull, E. jr., *Norge i den rike verden 1945-1975* (Cappelen, Oslo, 1979)
Bye, T. & Høyland, T.E., *Inntektsbegreper og inntektsfordeling* (CBS Reports 81/31, Oslo, 1981)
CBS, *Kredittmarkedsstatistikk 1975-76*, NOS A 932 (Oslo, 1978)
——*Skatter og overføringer til private* (CBS Reports 82/19, Oslo, 1982)
——*Wage Statistics 1981*, NOS 8306 (Oslo, 1982)
The Economist, 15 November 1975: Norway, Special Survey.
Erlandsen, H.C., *Olje* (Bedriftsøkonomens Forlag, Oslo, 1982)
Farmand, weekly business magazine, 1982, no 44, pp 35-8
Gleditsch, N.P. & Hellevik, O., *Kampen om EF* (PAX, Oslo, 1977)
Grund, J. et al., *Helseplan for 1980-årene* (Gyldendal, Oslo, 1982)
Historical Statistics 1978, NOS XII, 291 (Oslo, 1978)
Isachsen, A.J. & Strøm, S., 'The hidden Economy: The Labour Market and Tax Evasion', *Scandinavian Journal of Economics*, vol. 82, (1980)
Klovland, J.T., *In Search of the hidden Economy. Tax Evasion and the Demand for Currency in Norway and Sweden*, discussion Paper No. 18/80 (NSE, Bergen, 1980)
Labour Market Problems in Norway, The Directorate of Labour (Oslo, 1974)
Levek årsundersøkelsen. Sluttrapport, NOU 1976:28.
Melander, J., *Oversikt over Den norske Creditbanks organisasjon og virksomhet*, Lehmkuhl Lecture (NSE, Bergen, 1978)

Muligheter og konsekvenser ved petroleumsfunn nord for 62°N, NOU 1980:25.

National Accounts 1969-1980, NOS, B 222 (CBS, Oslo, 1981)

—— *1970-1981*, NOS, B. 313 (CBS, Oslo, 1982)

OECD, *The Residual Factor and economic Growth* (Paris, 1964)

—— *Re-Appraisal of Regional Policies in OECD Countries* (Paris, 1974)

—— *Agricultural Policy in Norway* (Paris, 1975)

—— *Restrictive Regional Policy Measures* (Paris, 1977)

—— *Public Expenditure on Health* (Paris, 1977)

—— *Public Expenditure Trends* (Paris, 1978)

—— *Regional Policies in Norway* (Paris, 1979)

—— *Financial Support to the Fishing Industry* (Paris, 1980)

Petersen, K., *Kredittpolitikken i støpeskjeen. Forretningsbankenes historie i etterkrigstiden* (A/S Hjemmet − Fagpresseforlaget, Oslo, 1982)

Rødseth, T., *Inntektsfordeling i Norge*, NOU 1977:44.

Solheim, T., *70-årenes feriereiser* (CBS Reports 82/20, Oslo, 1982)

The 1000 largest Companies in Norway 1975 (Oslo, 1975)

Valen, H., *Valg og politikk − et samfunn i endring*, Forbruker- og administrasjonsdepartementet (Gjøvik, 1982)

NAME INDEX

280

SUBJECT INDEX